PRAISE FOR *THE ROAD FROM RUIN*

"In *The Road from Ruin,* Matthew Bishop and Michael Green show why companies must respond to this crisis with long-term vision and a renewed emphasis on values. An essential read for anyone who wants to learn why a corporate focus on sustainability and building a better society is the key to the long-lasting productivity growth and job creation that are needed now more than ever."

—John Chambers, Chairman and CEO, Cisco

"*The Road from Ruin* is a masterpiece. Matthew Bishop and Michael Green combine truly luminous writing with simple, clear, unprejudiced scholarship and a keen journalistic awareness of how to extract lessons from the financial crisis to begin forming an agenda for a badly needed reform of capitalism."

—Robert A. G. Monks, shareholder activist, founder of the Corporate Library, and author of *Corpocracy*

"The title suggests a map for a new, improved capitalism to follow—and that's exactly what Matthew Bishop and Michael Green provide. A steely analysis of the structural and human frailty that led to the implosion of 2008 becomes their foundation for specific future reform. Alternative remedies are scrupulously examined; some discarded, others seized upon and improved. In its clarity of both thought and expression, this is a book that leaves you feeling cautiously better about the potential of capitalism and so cautiously better about its prospects."

—Sir Martin Sorrell, CEO, WPP

Also by Matthew Bishop and Michael Green

Philanthrocapitalism

THE ROAD FROM RUIN

HOW TO REVIVE CAPITALISM AND

PUT AMERICA BACK ON TOP

MATTHEW BISHOP AND MICHAEL GREEN

CROWN
BUSINESS
NEW YORK

Published in the United States by Crown Business, an imprint of
the Crown Publishing Group, a division of
Random House, Inc., New York.

www.crownpublishing.com

CROWN BUSINESS is a trademark and CROWN and
the Rising Sun colophon are registered trademarks of
Random House, Inc.

Library of Congress Cataloging-in-Publication Data
Bishop, Matthew.
The road from ruin / Matthew Bishop and Michael Green.—1st ed.
1. Capitalism.   2. Capitalism—Moral and ethical aspects.
3. Financial crises—Prevention.   I. Green, Michael (Michael F.)
II. Title.
HB501.B538 2010
174—dc22   2009036867

ISBN 978-0-307-46422-4

Printed in the United States of America

Design by Leonard W. Henderson

10 9 8 7 6 5 4 3 2 1

First Edition

To Alan Russell—a dedicated teacher
and fine economist—who showed
us that the dismal science need not be dull

CONTENTS

CONTENTS

PART TWO
THE ROAD FROM RUIN

THE ROAD FROM RUIN

TO RUIN AND BACK

What went wrong and what we must do to put it right

Capitalism as we knew it ended on September 15, 2008. That much is clear. What we don't know yet is what will replace it and whether that new version will be any better than what went before. The choices we make now will set us on the road either to renewed prosperity or to stagnation and even depression.

On that day, Lehman Brothers, a powerful Wall Street investment bank, declared itself bankrupt. Panic spread rapidly throughout the financial markets. What had once seemed valuable investments suddenly lost most of their value, turning into "toxic assets." The instant loss of value threatened to bring down some of the world's largest financial institutions. This sparked a chain reaction that ultimately led to the worst global economic crisis since at least the Great Depression of the 1930s.

Amid the carnage of bankruptcies, soaring unemployment, and the loss of millions of family homes lay the bloody corpse of a set of ideas that had underpinned the economics of the previous thirty years. This was a period in which it was widely believed that capitalism based on markets, especially financial markets, could be relied on to deliver unprecedented prosperity. This was the "Great Moderation," an era that began in the 1980s, when the American economy embarked on an extended run of low inflation and steady growth, a trend that went global in the 1990s. As well as creating an army of billionaires, it was believed that this system would lead to a general increase in wealth, including among some of the poorest people on the planet, hundreds of millions of whom would be lifted out of dire poverty.

Faced with the collapse of this version of capitalism, government, which the orthodoxy prior to September 15 had tended to see as the problem, suddenly became the savior. The titans of Wall Street, long accustomed to complaining about big government and its wealth-destroying red tape, threw themselves on the mercy of Uncle Sam and his seemingly bottomless pockets. (The same thing happened in the City of London and other financial centers around the world.) Government, doing what it knows best, hurled money at the problem. It probably had no alternative. Symbolizing how the world had changed, as it bailed out the financial system, the American government became the world's biggest owner of bank shares.

Dealing with the toxic financial assets bequeathed by the bankers was fiendishly difficult. In the months after Lehman collapsed, the Bush and Obama administrations wrestled with various schemes to purge the rottenness from the banks' balance sheets, but recovery was painfully slow.

Yet there is an even bigger problem than toxic assets, and that is toxic ideas. The years that preceded the crisis were dominated by a set of theories that celebrated the wisdom of markets. These ideas, which shaped government policies and underpinned banking practices, were triumphant in the boom years. They had won broad acceptance because they seemed to work in practice. Capitalism had seen off communism. Countries with more market-oriented forms of capitalism seemed more productive and prosperous than those that were more planned and heavily regulated by the state.

In the wake of the crash of September 2008, the challenge is to figure out whether some, all, or none of these theories should survive the crisis. The bust has pushed an alternative set of ideas to the forefront that call for comprehensive intervention in financial markets and bigger government. Working out which of these ideas are toxic and could poison our future prosperity is the most urgent, and difficult, challenge we face.

To find the road from ruin to renewed prosperity, we must engage in a new battle of ideas to work out which elements of the conventional wisdom of the past thirty years will be needed—perhaps in an improved form—and which ideas should be jettisoned along the way and replaced with something entirely new.

As we try to figure out what to do, we have an advantage: we can learn the lessons from the booms and crashes that have punctuated the history of capitalism with remarkable frequency, stretching back to the great tulip bubble in Holland in the early seventeenth century. Then, a mania for rare flowers drove prices to astonishing levels before they crashed, as people realized that they had spent huge sums not on productive assets but on a few tulip bulbs. Nearly four hundred years ago, as now, people were shaking their heads at the madness of crowds that had challenged the wisdom of markets. Yet the people of Holland made the right decisions after the bubble burst, and as a result Tulipmania was little more than a blip in the Dutch "Golden Age" of prosperity in the seventeenth century. Hopefully we can be as wise in the choices we make.

THE ROAD TO RUIN

Who punched Dick Fuld as he worked out in the gym at Lehman Brothers, where he was the CEO? Indeed, did the widely reported incident involving an employee enraged by the bank's failure actually take place? We may never know for certain. Yet in the weeks after Fuld led the investment bank into bankruptcy and triggered the economic collapse, many Americans wanted it to be true, and plenty would have loved to thump the man nick-named "the Gorilla." Fuld was known as the scariest man on Wall Street. He had once brawled with the father of a child playing hockey against his son, which made the punishment allegedly meted out in the gym seem all the more fitting.

Fuld made an obvious instant target for those wanting some-one to blame for the economic mess that followed the bankruptcy of his firm. At hearings on the crisis a few weeks later, a con-gressman lectured an insufficiently contrite Fuld that "if you haven't discovered your role, you're the villain." A visibly shaken Fuld, who had to run a gauntlet of protesters at the Capitol wav-ing CROOK and JAIL NOT BAIL placards, was forced to justify the hun-dreds of millions of dollars he had been paid to run a bank that had now failed. His defense rested on the fact that much of the money he had been paid was in now-worthless Lehman stock. He in turn lashed out at speculative "short sellers" of the bank's shares for driving the firm into bankruptcy and bemoaned the government's decision to rescue other financial institutions but not his.

Other names were soon added to the roster of those allegedly responsible for the mess. *Time* magazine published a list of "25 people to blame." Along with Fuld, there were people like Angelo Mozilo, the former boss of Countrywide, a lender that had pop-ularized the "subprime" mortgages for poor people, which had earned him hundreds of millions yet which cost hundreds of billions in losses when those mortgages blew up. Mozilo was indicted for insider trading and securities fraud in 2009. It was also reported that he had arranged for "VIP loans" to be granted on favorable terms from Countrywide to influential lawmakers under a scheme that became known as "Friends of Angelo." Also on the *Time* list was Jimmy Cayne, former boss of another troubled investment bank, Bear Stearns. Six months before Lehman was allowed to fall, Cayne's bank had almost gone under as it struggled to stay afloat after credit markets froze in the second half of 2007. In March 2008, the government had arranged a rescue deal for Bear Stearns by selling it off to JP Morgan. Yet even as Bear Stearns teetered on the brink, Cayne was not locked in his Manhattan office trying to save the company but was playing in a bridge tournament in Detroit (which is nearly as bad as being on the golf course, where he also spent much of his time).

Blame was not confined to presidents and chief executives alone. Joe Cassano, who had led the financial services division of the insurance giant AIG, made it onto the list as the man who had built up the company's lucrative business insuring credit default swaps that imploded as a result of the crisis, lumbering the firm with tens of billions of dollars of losses. A matter of days after Lehman was allowed to go bankrupt, AIG was saved with a $170-billion bailout from the government. The fact that earlier that year Cassano, a cop's son from Brooklyn, had left the firm with a fortune of $300 million in cash and shares, as well as a $1-million-a-month pension, added to *Time's* indignation.

In a nod to the globalization of finance, the magazine also made dishonorable mention of Sir Fred Goodwin, the former boss of Britain's Royal Bank of Scotland (RBS). Known in financial circles as "Fred the Shred" for his ruthless cost cutting, he was renamed "the worst banker in the world" after the crisis. RBS was second only to Lehman in selling subprime mortgage securities. In a ruthless and reckless pursuit of profit, Sir Fred had seriously weakened RBS's capital reserves when he pushed through a $100-billion takeover of a rival bank in 2007. As a result, RBS was in no fit state to weather the financial storm that began shortly afterward, and it was eventually partly nationalized by the British government.

The list was not limited to financiers. *Time* also turned its fire on politicians and government officials, including former president Bill Clinton, who had allegedly sown the seeds of the crisis by deregulating the financial markets with one hand while pushing them to lend more to risky subprime borrowers with the other. Alan Greenspan, the former chairman of the Federal Reserve, appeared prominently on the list. Greenspan had once seemed so important to the success of the American and indeed the global economy that in 2000, presidential hopeful John McCain said that if Greenspan ever died it would be necessary to "prop him up and put some dark glasses on him, like *Weekend at Bernie's.*" Now he stood accused of pumping too much credit into the economy through his lax monetary policy.

Time even blamed foreign communists. Wen Jiabao, the premier of China, it said, was culpable for lending America too much money.

The *Time* blame list reflected the mood of the nation; indeed, it was just one of many similar lists that all tried to pin the blame on a handful of powerful people. *Time* at least acknowledged the role of American consumers ("we enjoyed living beyond our means"). Even so, these lists helped create a popular narrative in which the public was a largely innocent victim of the folly of the powerful.

This story, which is at best a caricature, apportions the blame to four categories of rogue: bankers, speculators, regulators, and politicians.

The story begins with bank chiefs, filled with hubris, earning fortunes by taking reckless short-term bets using mountains of debt and complex financial instruments that they didn't understand. When, too late, they finally realized that collapse was inevitable, they lied to the public that their banks were still sound.

In turn, as their institutions teetered, the bankers, including Fuld and Cayne, blamed financial speculators such as hedge funds for driving down the price of their shares—conveniently forgetting that for years their banks had made a fortune by financing the same speculators.

Regulators joined in the blame game. Christopher Cox, the chairman of the Securities and Exchange Commission when things started going wrong in the autumn of 2008, banned the speculative so-called short selling of shares that he said "can allow manipulators to force prices down." For many people, it was the fault of regulators such as Cox who had been asleep at the wheel and ignored reckless practices that had contributed to the bubble, such as the lack of rigor in the lending process.

Under fire, the regulators tried to shift the blame onto politicians, for taking away their powers through deregulation, depriving them of the financial tools necessary to do the job. They claimed that politicians had been cheerleaders for the asset price bubble.

Playing the blame game has its attractions. As *Time* explained, "The venting of spleen is not a science—it's a joy." It is a game that has been played after every crash in history. When the bubble in the price of shares in the South Sea Company burst in 1720, a British parliamentarian equated the crimes of the company directors to the killing of a close relative and called on them to be punished by "being sewed into sacks, with a monkey and a snake, and drowned." By comparison, being punched in the gym, or even serving the long jail terms that American courts can mete out for financial wrongdoing, should count as a lucky escape.

There is some truth to this popular account of the crisis: some of these high-profile individuals did make mistakes and, maybe, even committed crimes. Perhaps blaming them allows the catharsis society needs to get over the crisis. Yet we know for certain that punching, fining, or even jailing a few of these "villains" is not going to repair our broken economic system.

Ultimately, playing the blame game is a distraction from what really needs to be done. So, too, is another common reaction to bubbles bursting—the retreat to old orthodoxies rather than seriously attempting to separate out the good ideas from the toxic ones. Market capitalism has always divided opinion between fundamentalists, who believe the market can do no wrong, and skeptics, nowadays a loose coalition of socialists, antiglobalization activists, labor interests, and even environmentalists. If we are to figure out what really caused the financial crisis and what needs to be done to fix things, we need to move beyond preconceived ideas and orthodoxies and take an open-minded look at the evidence.

With Lehman's collapse, however, critics of the market orthodoxy wallowed in schadenfreude. As well as the usual suspects such as radical filmmaker Michael Moore and French president Nicolas Sarkozy, there were also the "Dr. Dooms," the popular name for those who had warned that a crisis was coming and now claimed to have been vindicated. Among these were billionaire hedge-fund bosses George Soros and John Paulson (who alone made a reported $3.7 billion in 2007 short selling financial shares); former trader and author of the best-selling *The Black Swan*, Nassim Nicholas Taleb; and the apocalyptic economist Nouriel Roubini. Some cheered the return of big government, and a few even dusted off their copy of Karl Marx and Friedrich Engels's *Communist Manifesto*. For these critics, despite all the wealth and jobs created and the millions of people around the world lifted out of poverty over the preceding decades, the kind of market-based capitalism that had dominated the previous thirty years had finally been revealed as toxic. The financial system at the heart of capitalism had turned out to be nothing more than a giant Ponzi scheme, and the bankers who presided over it at best incompetent and at worst criminal. Government now had to cut out the cancer, reverse deregulation, slash how much bankers are paid, and stringently control how they do business.

At the opposite end of the political spectrum, the champions of the old orthodoxy were not downcast for long—though the crisis showed why their characterization of private markets as good and government as bad had always been overly simplistic. Dusting off their own holy book, Ayn Rand's classic libertarian novel *Atlas Shrugged,* they bellowed that whatever the government offered as a cure would necessarily be worse than whatever sickness had afflicted capitalism. Arthur Laffer, Ronald Reagan's favorite economist, warned that the government's meddling would lead to "the end of prosperity," and economist and CNBC pundit Larry Kudlow accused the Obama administration—within weeks of its taking office—of declaring war on business and enterprise.

To escape from the current crisis, it is essential to move on from such comfortable but inadequate old orthodoxies. Blame and denial will not help us figure out what went wrong, or how to fix it. Fresh thinking is required.

FIVE WRONG TURNS

In the history of capitalism, crises have happened again and again, although they have not always had terrible consequences;

often crises have been followed by a quick return to prosperity. Yet sometimes prosperity has been slow to return, and things have gotten far worse before they got better, usually as a result of taking one or more of the five common wrong turns on the road from ruin.

The first wrong turn is to assume that bubbles are a wholly negative product of random outbreaks of madness, rather than a consequence of the innovation process that can add to our prosperity in the long term. Perhaps the most influential book on bubbles of the past was Charles Mackay's Victorian classic *Extraordinary Popular Delusions and the Madness of Crowds*. Most accounts of the current crisis draw, usually unconsciously, on Mackay's interpretation of bubbles as events where supposedly smart people lose their senses.

Capitalism is fundamentally an optimistic system that taps into the deep human desire to strive for a better life. Innovation and entrepreneurship are usually at the forefront of fulfilling that desire. That is why, ironically, capitalism so often experiences bubbles—for it is the hope that gets you in the end.

Throughout history, bubbles have often started with a common hope—that a rise in prices reflects a significant advance that means the old valuation rules no longer apply. Since the original seventeenth-century bubble in tulip bulbs, the world has seen manias for, among other things, trade with the New World, railways, radio, Internet companies, emerging-market debt, and, several times over, real-estate finance. What is most remarkable about these bubbles is that these "technologies," with the possible exception of tulips, each represent an economic breakthrough that did indeed generate great benefits. Yet each time, there came a point when rational hope mutated into an irrational exuberance that sucked more cash into the market until investors realized that this could not go on forever and the bubble burst.

Bubbles seem to be a frequent reaction to new ideas, as we figure out the true value of an innovation and how to put it to best use. It should perhaps be no surprise that the markets struggled to work out the true value and true risks of the Internet or financial innovations such as securitized assets. Crashes are part of the learning process.

Mackay exaggerated the disastrous consequences of bubbles. In fact, many bubbles have burst without doing significant economic harm and may even have helped accelerate the process of figuring out how to use innovations. When bubbles burst and are followed by a wider economic crisis, as happened in 2008, the danger is that we overreact and try to banish the innovations that sparked the boom, rather than learning how to use them wisely.

The second wrong turn is to believe that government must avoid bailing out the financial sector in the middle of a crisis. Governments often come to the rescue after bubbles burst, using taxpayers' money to save the financial institutions whose own risk taking caused the problem. This can provoke understandable outrage at the time. It can also cause a problem of "moral hazard": that by providing a publicly funded safety net, government actually encourages the markets to be more reckless in the future. Yet in this crisis, then U.S. treasury secretary Hank Paulson's biggest blunder was to let Lehman Brothers go under in a mistaken attempt to discourage moral hazard. There is nothing wrong with making shareholders and creditors pay for their errors; indeed, it is right that they do. By allowing Lehman to collapse in such a disorderly manner, however, Paulson unleashed panic in the already-spooked financial markets. Lehman had deals right across the banking sector and also within the so-called shadow banking sector (which did many of the same things as banks but were free of the heavy regulations imposed on banks) made up of hedge funds and other financial services companies that together keep credit flowing around the economy. Almost every financial institution of any significance in the world was thrown into shock by the decision to let Lehman go, and the already frigid credit markets froze solid as everyone asked, "Who is next?" The possibility of government support does distort the behavior of financial markets. Governments do need to find ways to ensure that when people knowingly take excessive financial risks, they suffer the consequences of their actions. The middle of a crisis is the worst time to do that, however.

In the first great crisis of Anglo-Saxon capitalism, the South Sea Bubble of 1720, investors poured in money to the point that the company became "too big to fail" and were rescued from their folly by the British government. Market purists might rail at the decision by the politicians of Georgian Britain to spend taxpayers' money rescuing foolish investors, yet the dire consequences for everyone of leaving the financial system to melt down were evident after the Wall Street Crash of 1929, when inaction by the government led to the failure of the American banking system. The Great Depression that followed was an unnecessary economic cataclysm.

Like it or not, the financial system is the lifeblood of the capitalism on which our prosperity depends. When the ability of the financial system to lend money, keep savings safe, and make payments is threatened, government needs to step in. In the aftermath of Treasury Secretary Paulson's decision to let Lehman go, the foundations of the economy were shaken in ways that threatened everybody. Letters of credit for business dried up, and even the ability of consumers to borrow to buy a car or go to college threatened to disappear. The lesson was clear: in the middle of a crisis, the risks of getting tough on moral hazard far outweigh the benefits.

The third wrong turn is to focus on addressing the financial symptoms of a crisis without tackling the underlying economic causes. While some have tried to blame the current crisis on financial innovation alone, huge imbalances in the global economy drove the boom as American borrowers took on massive, unsustainable amounts of debt, funded largely by emerging economies such as China. This has made the bust much worse.

Some crises are purely financial, but some of the most damaging crashes throughout history were caused by fundamental imbalances in the world monetary system. The gold standard had a major part to play in the prolonged depression at the end of the nineteenth century and was a factor in the Wall Street Crash of 1929 and the Great Depression that followed.

Since World War II, the world has operated on what has been effectively a dollar standard. In the 1990s, the emerging economies of Asia, Latin America, and the former Soviet Union were buffeted by financial crises as they tried to maintain the credibility of their economies with dollar investors. While their own policy errors were part of the problem, the volatility of the dollar and failure of the rich countries to help them out persuaded many of these countries that international capital was too hot to handle.

For the past decade, as a result, emerging economies, led by China, have stopped borrowing from America and have become creditors instead. The dollar standard may have made sense when America's economy was truly dominant. Now, as other economies rise in importance, the dollar's preeminence has become more of a liability than an asset for the United States, and the world. Finding a better system for managing how money flows around the world is essential to creating a stabler financial system.

The fourth wrong turn is to think that the economy will always naturally recover on its own from a financial crisis. "You're right, we did it. We're very sorry. But thanks to you, we won't do it again." This was how the now chairman of the Federal Reserve, Ben Bernanke, honored the ninetieth birthday of the great monetarist economist Milton Friedman in 2002, in recognition of Friedman's work to explain how the Fed's failure to rescue the banks, not the Wall Street Crash of 1929, had caused the Great Depression.

Although this seemed obvious to Bernanke—whose support for throwing money around to stop the economic meltdown, if necessary (as Friedman had suggested) dropping cash out of helicopters to get people spending again, earned him the nickname "Helicopter Ben"—it did not seem that way to many of his critics. Nor was it obvious to the Japanese government in 1990, when a crash in real-estate prices spread to the financial sector and, through a failure of government to face up to the problem and act decisively, resulted in a lost decade of economic stagnation.

The economy can often bounce back remarkably quickly, even after spectacular financial crashes such as Black Monday in 1987 and the bursting of the dot-com bubble in 2000—with a bit of official encouragement in the form of interest-rate cuts. Sometimes, however, when a crisis is big enough and when the banking system fails, a financial crash can turn into a prolonged economic slump, as it did in the Great Depression and during Japan's "lost decade."

In this latest crisis, governments everywhere, from America to Vietnam, have leaped in with large, and expensive, economic stimulus packages, saying that they have learned from past crises. This has drawn a lot of criticism from fiscal conservatives, who warn about the long-term consequences of such profligacy. Certainly it seems paradoxical that borrowing more is a solution to an economic crash brought on by excessive debt, though solution it is. A particularly thorny challenge is how to restore the banking system to health as quickly as possible and get credit flowing again. It is relatively easy for governments to give banks money; it is much harder to get the banks to lend it out again, especially to the parts of the economy that need it most, at a price they can afford. Governments are prone to duck the difficult questions for financial reasons to keep the cost down, as well as political ones (solutions such as public ownership are controversial).

Getting this right is certainly a tough challenge. Government may be tempted to keep its foot on the gas for too long, starting another bubble and an inflationary spiral. The greater threat, however, is denial, which could lead to prolonged economic misery.

The fifth wrong turn is to rush into more regulation of the financial markets without proper analysis of what went wrong and what can really be done to fix it. The demand for tougher regulation is the automatic response to every crisis, and this one is no exception. Some commentators want to reverse the financial deregulation of the last thirty years; others would go even further and redesign the entire financial system, with a much greater emphasis on government control.

Governments know that the public believes that "something must be done" after a crisis, but all too often throughout history governments have done the wrong thing. In the same year as Britain's South Sea Bubble, France had its own financial crisis, following the newfangled financial innovation of paper money. France responded to the Law Panic of 1720—named after the Scotsman John Law, who was behind the new economic plan—by abandoning paper money entirely, which stalled its economic development. Similarly, strict regulation of the financial sector was a central plank of President Roosevelt's New Deal reforms to tackle the Great Depression, yet many of these regulations proved to be wide of the mark. Some reforms, such as trying to stabilize the banks by forcing them to hold much more capital, made the Depression worse; others, such as splitting up the banking sector into separate investment and retail banks, imposing arbitrary caps on interest rates, and tightly regulating the stock market, hobbled the U.S. economy for nearly half a century.

Fixing what has really gone wrong rather than lashing out at all things financial is a key challenge for governments after the crisis. The events of the autumn of 2008 show that the system of regulation needs to be fixed. Working out how, without doing collateral damage to our economic dynamism, is a tougher task. Imposing inevitably arbitrary limits on how big banks can get and how much bankers are paid has a certain populist appeal, but there is no reason to think that either of these measures would have prevented the current crisis or would stop a future one. Rushed regulatory reform is likely to be light on rigorous analysis and heavy on poorly designed solutions, which will make the road from ruin longer and harder.

Learning these five lessons from history will help us avoid the mistakes of the past. Yet the challenge we face is about more than avoiding the wrong turns on the road from ruin. We should also be guided by four road signs that point the way to renewed prosperity.

THE ROAD FROM RUIN

The current crisis is an opportunity to build a capitalism that is better than the version that failed on September 15. If the biggest mistake we could make after the crisis would be to abandon capitalism, the second-biggest mistake would be to assume that capitalism does not need to change.

There are four big ideas that must shape our decisions as we create this new, improved capitalism. These are the signs that will guide us on the road to renewed prosperity: rethink economics; redesign global governance; put values back into business; and promote financial literacy.

The current crisis of capitalism is the result, first, of a tragedy of economics, a dismal failure at the heart of what the nineteenth-century writer Thomas Carlyle famously called the "dismal science." If we are to get rid of toxic ideas, economics is the place to start, because the ideas coming out of university economics departments play a powerful role in shaping the actions of many bankers and policymakers. The dominant policies of the era of capitalism that ended when Lehman Brothers collapsed, ranging from how interest rates were set to how financial markets were regulated, were underpinned by a set of economic ideas based on a view of people as essentially rational—*Homo economicus* rather than *Homo sapiens.*

At the heart of this orthodoxy was the efficient market hypothesis: the view that financial markets work so well at sharing information that it is impossible for markets to be wrong. Put simply, according to the efficient market hypothesis, bubbles cannot occur. Or—in terms of that rare thing, an economics joke—a believer in efficient markets would not pick up a $20 bill left on the sidewalk because if it really was $20, someone else would have picked it up already.

Yet the markets have been proved to have catastrophically mispriced such assets as mortgage-backed securities in a way that directly contradicts the efficient market hypothesis. Some economists had already spotted the flaws. One of them, Robert Shiller, had been talking to policymakers for more than a decade about how insights from psychology suggested that markets could behave irrationally. As far back as 1996, the then Fed chairman,

Alan Greenspan, coined the phrase "irrational exuberance" to describe the booming stock market after a presentation by Shiller. Another, Daniel Kahneman, was even awarded the Nobel Prize in 2002 for his work showing that humans are prone to miscalculate probabilities, which will distort market behavior. Yet these insights, and other new ideas in economics, did not shake the widespread faith in the omniscient market. In practice, even Greenspan continued to believe that markets were essentially right.

Abandoning the efficient-market orthodoxy does not mean abandoning markets, or abandoning financial innovation. Markets are still an excellent tool for allocating resources efficiently. But they are not perfect. Policymakers and financiers need an improved version of economics that more accurately reflects the complexity and even irrationality of the human beings who make up the economy. If the insights of this new economics can be harnessed to financial innovation, we may be able to develop new financial products to help us manage the risk of bubbles better.

After the Great Depression, the Bretton Woods Conference of 1944 created a system of global economic governance that still exists today, largely unreformed. This architecture, with the International Monetary Fund (IMF) and World Bank at its heart, was designed for a global economy that was dominated by America, and in which the dollar was unchallenged as the world's reserve currency. Today a new global architecture is needed that reflects the new balance of strength in the global economy—including institutions that give a voice in economic decision making to rising powers such as China and India.

The most pressing financial challenge is for the dollar to relinquish its role as the world's reserve currency. For much of the past sixty years, the dollar's dominance was only a problem for the rest of the world. In the last decade, it has become a problem for

America, too. The dollar's supremacy made it the safe haven for the reserves of developing countries such as China, which led to the flow of capital into America that stoked the credit boom. For any other country, the spiraling indebtedness would have led to a weakening of the currency that would have triggered measures to stop the boom. Instead, the dollar's status as the global reserve currency meant that China simply bought more dollars to lend back to America, and the cycle continued.

A global reserve currency would free the rest of the world from tying their finances to decisions made by Washington to meet the needs of the U.S. economy, and it would free the U.S. economy from the distorting effects of being the world's savings bank. This is not going to be easy, but the sooner we start to move in this direction, the better.

A new Bretton Woods should be only the first step in building a system of global governance able to deal with the challenges of the twenty-first century. Our prosperity is also threatened by a rise in protectionist sentiment, which could result in a costly pause or even reversal in the trend toward freer trade. Lowering and removing trade barriers, many of which were erected during the Great Depression, which they helped to make worse, has brought huge economic benefits in the past half century. However, these gains have not been shared equally across the world. America needs to lead the way in freeing up agricultural trade so that poor countries can share in the benefits of globalization. Failure to do so would risk a breakdown in global trade that would harm us all.

In the same way, the world needs new institutions to keep capital flowing freely across borders in times of financial stress. The global fallout of the storm that ravaged Wall Street in the autumn of 2008, as capital fled emerging markets, throwing their economies into deep recession, was graphic evidence of the consequences of the globalization of finance. The IMF, as it stands, has failed as the world's emergency "lender of last resort" and needs to be remade so that vulnerable countries have confidence that they will get the support they need in times of crisis.

If we fail to tackle these global economic challenges, we will feel the consequences through rising illegal migration and greater global instability and wars. That would be even more true of failing to tackle the most pressing global economic challenge of all: climate change. This is a problem caused by how we run our economies and can be resolved only by fundamental changes to our economic structures. There is no greater threat to our prosperity. Although this is not a problem directly related to the financial crisis, a root-and-branch reform of the institutions of global economic governance may give us our best opportunity to create the framework to solve this potentially devastating problem.

Solutions to big global-governance issues will have to come from our political leaders, but bigger government cannot be the answer to everything (indeed, the reforms we need require better government rather than bigger government). The crisis was also the result of a general failure of leadership in the business world. Too often corporate executives excused themselves from asking deeper questions about where things were going by focusing on rising quarterly profits as the only yardstick of good capitalism. This failure of values at the heart of capitalism needs to be addressed by the capitalists themselves.

Capitalism has been a victim of its own success. The defenders of the free market, as part of the ideological battle with communism, built up capitalism into more than just an effective economic tool. Like the promoters of the efficient market hypothesis, capitalism's advocates trumpeted it as perfection and in doing so lost touch with reality. Free marketeers loved to quote the words of their founding father, the eighteenth-century Scottish thinker and author of *The Wealth of Nations,* Adam Smith, that "it is not from the benevolence of the butcher, the brewer, or the baker that we expect our dinner, but from their regard to their own interest." This was bastardized into a mentality that "greed is good," or that just about anything that is profitable is necessarily morally right. Smith would have been appalled—his *Theory of Moral Sentiments* specifically attacks this idea. For Smith, moral values must be an integral part of successful capitalism.

The defenders of unrestrained capitalism have also conflated short-term profitability with long-term success. As the financial crisis showed, this is not good capitalism. Yet too many banking executives have defended their actions on the grounds that they could not go against the conventional wisdom of the industry. Even those with a professional duty to consider the longer term, such as accountants and credit-ratings agencies, too often got caught up in the excitement of short-term triumphs and failed to question what executives were doing.

Thinking long term also requires a broader vision about what makes a successful company. While the primary responsibility of business is to create value for its shareholders, business does not exist in a vacuum. Business cannot shuffle off responsibility for the environment or for the wider good of society as a whole onto government. Though it is often possible for firms to increase their profits in the short run by doing things that hurt society, long-term profit maximization for business as a whole requires that companies operate sustainably and give back to society, to discover the secrets of "doing well by doing good."

The idea that long-term success requires a broader vision than short-term profitability was already permeating parts of the business world before the crisis. We have called this movement philanthrocapitalism, which encompasses a values-driven approach through corporate and individual giving, responsible commercial practices, and even socially oriented business models that trade off

profitability for social benefits. For too long, capitalism's supporters have been content to agree with its opponents that it is a system
built solely on greed. Business needs to rediscover the long term,
including its responsibility to build a better society, which will ultimately allow well-run firms to enjoy greater financial success.

Company bosses may protest that their shareholders do not
want them to pursue long-term value and that what really interests
them is higher short-term profits, which are rewarded by higher
share prices. They have a point. Perhaps the most striking absence
of long-termism—and arguably the weakest link in the entire economic system—is in the leadership of the institutional shareholders who manage the retirement savings of all of us. Yet they
more than most shareholders should be focused on what the
value of companies will be in ten, twenty, or thirty years' time and
how the businesses they invest in can shape the society in which
their customers will retire.

We live in a world of massively increased financial complexity
in which the great majority of people seem to be incapable of
making sensible, prudent decisions about what to do with their
money. The poorer customers, with subprime mortgages that they
could not afford, were not the only ones who took on too much
debt in the false belief that the good times would roll on forever.
Once-affluent retirees who thought that they would never have
to work again and that they could live on the profits from their
investments have been severely hit by the collapse in the stock
market, which they thought would keep going up in value. Some
have even had to go out and find a job again.

The mass failure of prudence, or financial literacy, by most of
us is not just a problem for our personal finances. Society faces
complex economic choices and tradeoffs. Since the crisis of
autumn 2008 it has emerged that members of the Bush administration, such as Treasury Secretary Paulson, at times did not pursue

policies that they thought would work best because they believed that the public would not have understood and supported them.

Looking ahead, our governments have added hugely to the public debt. This will take decades to pay off, presenting voters with hard decisions to make about the balance between higher taxes and lower expenditure. The danger is that the public will choose the options that look least painful in the short term yet would have the most damaging long-term consequences, such as letting inflation get out of control as a way of reducing the real value of public debt. The same is true of the debate about the future of the financial sector. Populist regulation of the banks, particularly of bankers' salaries, risks hobbling our economies with unnecessary bureaucracy.

If we are to resist the temptation of easy populism, we need a mature, reflective debate about the choices that will make or break our future prosperity. Part of the answer rests with the media, which swung during the crisis from cheerleaders of boom to prophets of doom. Thoughtful journalism from the new and old media alike has been in short supply. The media, along with politicians and businesses, need to raise the level of debate to match the gravity of the decisions we face.

Part of the answer also rests with all of us. Constitutional theorists have long recognized that in the field of politics, a well-informed and well-educated citizenry is an essential bulwark against tyranny and is a mainstay of our democratic system. We teach civics in our schools to prepare children for the responsibility of being citizens. Yet we have done little to make people competent economic citizens. This needs to change.

This is the moment that will shape the twenty-first century, and we stand at a crossroads. Behind us lie the ruins of the discredited old capitalism. In one direction is the path of denial: to do nothing to revitalize the financial system or to stimulate the economy, to just let the crisis run its course in the hope that we come out stronger. This was the road taken in 1929 and again in Japan in the 1990s. Hopefully the lessons of those disasters have been learned, for it is the road to depression. The more crowded route of blame heads in the opposite direction: to hand control of the economy back to government, with higher taxes, lots of regulation, and maybe a dose of inflation. This was the road taken by France in the eighteenth century and again in New Deal America. It is the road to stagnation. Straight ahead lies perhaps the more difficult choice, because it is one without a road map of old orthodoxies. It will involve preserving the much that is good in capitalism while finding ways to make it work better. This is the road from ruin to renewed prosperity.

PART ONE

THE ROAD TO RUIN
How Things Go Wrong

1

NOBEL LAUREATES
AND SHOESHINE BOYS

How innovation leads to bubbles

In April 2006, Goldman Sachs, the world's leading investment bank, raised $494 million by selling securities linked to the performance of some 8,274 mortgages taken out on American homes. Although these were risky "subprime" mortgages, on which the average loan amounted to over 99 percent of the stated value of the property, innovative new financial engineering had transformed them into apparently safe securities. Investors, believing they offered high returns at low risk, snapped them up—inside and outside America.

Three years later, most of the value of these securities had been wiped out as falling house prices led borrowers to default en masse on their mortgage payments. The Goldman Sachs Alternative Mortgage Product Trust 2006-S3, or GSAMP as it was called, was probably the bubbliest, and subsequently the worst-performing, of a multitrillion-dollar bubble in subprime mortgage securities.

This was just the latest, and one of the biggest, in a long series of bubbles in financial markets. It was no coincidence that this bubble was linked to an innovation, the creation of the mortgage-backed security, since this connection has been a feature of bubbles throughout history. Bubbles are not merely a result of the madness of crowds; rather, they are typically about people overreacting as they try to figure out the true value of a genuinely useful innovation. They are an inevitable part of economic progress, although that does not make them any less painful when they burst—as the mortgage-market meltdown made all too clear.

The year 2006 was the peak of the boom in mortgage-backed securities. The Goldman issue was one of 916 that year that together raised $592 billion—a lending binge that had in turn led to an unprecedented bubble in house prices. This was the moment when, as in every bubble, so many people are enjoying the benefits of the innovation that the downsides are forgotten and overconfidence sets in.

As long as house prices kept going up, as high as 100 percent mortgages seemed a safe bet. After all, even if a borrower could not make his or her payments on the mortgage, the property could be sold to repay the debt and perhaps even turn a profit in the process. Borrowers and lenders took reassurance from the fact that, while there had been localized housing crashes, average house prices in America as a whole had risen relentlessly since the 1930s.

Yet house prices could not defy gravity forever. So when, toward the end of 2006, prices started to fall, defaults and losses began to rise, and what had seemed like low-risk investments suddenly turned out to be very risky indeed.

What explains the popularity of securitization, the particular form of financial innovation behind this bubble? For investors, including many pension funds and university endowments, it seemed to offer an efficient way to put money into America's huge housing market without having to get involved in the expensive and time-consuming business of finding and vetting mort-gage clients.

For mortgage lenders, it offered the chance to do far more business, by shifting some or even all of the risk off their own bal-ance sheets to other investors. Among other things, this meant that banks, in particular, could lend more without having to increase the reserves of capital that regulators required them to hold as a cushion against borrowers defaulting.

For mortgage borrowers, especially those at the subprime end of the market, it offered access to credit at affordable prices. Indeed, before the subprime market boomed, many people who later became borrowers had little chance of qualifying for a mort-gage and thus of owning their home.

Politicians and central bankers also liked securitization because it increased the spread of homeownership, and because it seemed to allow society to manage risk better, by spreading it around rather than concentrating it in the banking sector. In the past, the concentration of mortgage risk in banks meant that when borrowers started to default, banks had to cut back on their lending throughout the economy, which had often resulted in recession. Securitization, most people believed, diluted that risk and made a credit crunch less likely.

The clever part of this innovation was the idea of bundling together thousands of mortgages and then slicing them up into portions with different levels of risk. An investor willing to accept lower returns from a relatively safe bet would take one of the top slices, which would lose money only if a large proportion of bor-rowers defaulted on their mortgages. Investors with an appetite for greater returns, and a willingness to take on greater risk, could buy the bottom slice, which paid a higher yield but would be the first to suffer losses in the event of borrowers starting to default.

In the case of GSAMP, the top slices, accounting for 68 percent of the money raised, were given a super-low-risk initial rating of triple-A by Moody's and by Standard & Poor's, the world's leading credit-ratings agencies. Slices accounting for a further 25 percent were given an almost-as-safe "investment-grade" rating. That left only 7 percent in the highly risky category known in the markets as "junk." Three years later, it was not just the junk slices that were in default. The investment-grade middle slices had also defaulted. Even the top slices, which were supposedly as safe as U.S. Treasury bonds, had been downgraded to junk.

Not only were the losses on GSAMP and other mortgage-backed securities far larger than expected, they were also far less spread around the financial system than policymakers had believed. Securitization did not provide the hoped-for buffer between mortgage losses and the banking system, in part because banks had become major lenders to investors in subprime securities and, believing their own hype, had even invested heavily in these securities themselves.

Looking back, it seems hard to believe that so many supposedly smart people were fooled into thinking that financial alchemy could turn so much subprime lead into investment-grade gold. True, there was some mis-selling and fraud. Chasing deals, salespeople had encouraged borrowers to take on mortgages that they could not afford, disguised by artificially low initial "teaser" interest rates and, sometimes, falsely high property valuations. The mortgage companies had also failed to carry out basic checks on some borrowers' creditworthiness. (This was the era of so-called NINJA loans, whereby people with No Income, No Job or Assets, took out "liar mortgages" by falsely exaggerating their financial health.) Yet this does not explain why highly skilled bankers and analysts were so inaccurate in their judgments on the probability of borrowers defaulting on their mortgages if house prices started to fall.

They simply put too much faith in a financial innovation that was new and untested. Securitization had boomed since the 1990s as a way of raising money while spreading the risk of the underlying asset defaulting. Basing securities on subprime mortgage assets, however, was a new application of the innovation, which took off as house prices soared in the first years of the new millennium. Initially banks were nervous that the clients for this type of product were just too risky. A few pioneers tested the waters and reported surprisingly low default rates. In a booming housing market, even if borrowers could not make the repayments, there seemed little risk of outright default since the proceeds of the sale of the property would more than cover the value of the mortgage.

The only risk that could hurt the supposedly supersafe middle and upper tranches of these securities was a countrywide fall in house prices. Analysts at the banks and the ratings agencies took comfort that this was highly unlikely, with no prospect of a surge in interest rates or recession in sight. As a result, they extrapolated too readily from the very low default rates of the early waves of subprime mortgage securities and thought this trend would go on for the foreseeable future. Investors trusted that the financial engineering worked, and went on a spending spree, no questions asked.

The bursting of the U.S. housing bubble and the financial crisis that followed caused a revival of interest in the work of the economist Hyman Minsky, who had died in 1996. Minsky saw bubbles as endemic to capitalism, as a product of overconfidence. He described three stages of a bubble. First come what he called the "hedge" investors, with enough cash to pay the interest and the principal on what they borrow. As the bubble inflates, "speculative" investors who can meet the cost of the interest on their borrowings but not the principal move into the market (speculative investors therefore need to keep taking out new loans to refinance their borrowing). Finally, "Ponzi" investors come in. In 1920 a penniless ex-con called Charles Ponzi (born Charles Bianchi) suckered investors with a supposedly lucrative scheme to buy international postal-reply coupons. Money poured in, until an investigation by the *Boston Post* revealed that his business was a fake, and the company collapsed owing $4 million.* The Ponzi investors in Minsky's theory cannot even pay the interest on their borrowings, so, in the same way that Ponzi's scam needed new investors to provide cash to pay returns to existing investors, Ponzi investors need the price of assets to keep rising, so that they can sell at a profit and pay off the interest and the principal (many subprime mortgage borrowers would count as Ponzi investors). When the market stops rising or does not rise fast enough, said Minsky, then the Ponzi investors are forced to default and the bubble bursts.

After the crisis began in 2008, Minsky's supporters pointed out that he had warned that deregulation of financial markets would lead to more bubbles. They were among those swift to · denounce securitization, accusing it of being an innovation with no merit other than its ability to (temporarily) swell the wallets of the bankers who designed it. Blaming the innovation in this way is a standard response to most bubbles and, judging from the experience of history, is likely to be proved wrong. A better expla-

---

* Ponzi was jailed but on release went straight back into swindling, this time selling swampland in Florida. After another jail term, he was deported to his native Italy and ended up working for the government of Fascist leader Benito Mussolini. Having mismanaged Il Duce's finances, he fled to Brazil, where he died in 1949, finally confessing to his crimes on his deathbed.

nation, on past form, is that people simply got carried away by the potential of an innovation that, in years to come, will prove to be both uncontroversial and extremely useful—provided, that is, we learn the right lessons from the bubble.

Every bubble is different, but each contains lessons for us as we figure out how to respond to this latest bubble. The common theme is that most bubbles start with an innovation. Sometimes that innovation is useful but has been overvalued, such as the Internet technology that sparked the dot-com bubble of the 1990s, or the railway boom of the nineteenth century. Sometimes an otherwise valuable innovation has been mismanaged by firms; Long-Term Capital Management and Enron are two examples. Where bubbles differ is in their consequences—although that in turn may reflect the different ways we have responded to them over the centuries. The bursting of the current bubble has been followed by a massive economic crisis, comparable to the one that followed the Wall Street Crash of 1929. In contrast, the massive stock market crash of 1987 had little effect on economic growth, like the first great bubble of modern capitalism, Tulipmania.

We need to understand why bubbles form and why some have far worse consequences than others.

THE FIRST BUBBLE

Today, Holland is the center of the global flower industry, exporting blooms and bulbs worth $8 billion in 2008 alone. A mere plant may seem the unlikely basis for a financial bubble, yet in the early years of this industry, in the seventeenth century, there occurred one of history's most famous speculative frenzies: in tulip bulbs.

In February 1637, just before the bubble burst, the price of a pound of tulip bulbs for delivery that summer soared to 1,500 guilders (more than $20,000 today), from 125 guilders less than two months earlier at the end of 1636. According to Charles Mackay's Victorian best seller *Extraordinary Popular Delusions and the Madness of Crowds*, published in 1841, a single bulb of the rare Viceroy variety even changed hands for 2,500 guilders, and a hapless sailor was imprisoned for eating a valuable bulb owned by a rich merchant, having mistaken it for an onion.

In part, the bubble was the result of a broader mania for gambling among the Dutch at that time. Plague had gripped the country, killing a third of the population of Leiden in 1635 and more than one in ten people in Amsterdam and Haarlem in 1636. Survivors seem to have adopted a "live for the day" mentality, and were flush with inherited money from plague victims. This attitude combined with the legalization of a new form of financial innovation to send tulip prices sky-high.

The Dutch Republic had emerged as the world's leading financial center in the decades after it was formed in 1581, when seven Protestant states declared their independence from Catholic Spain. Under prolonged threat of reoccupation (its independence was not recognized by Spain until more than half a century later), the fledgling republic had to build up its economic strength to pay for constant wars. This had unleashed a period of frenetic financial innovation. In 1602 the government sponsored the creation of the Dutch East India Company, which had a monopoly on the lucrative trade with Asia. For the first time anywhere, the law gave investors in the company protection from part of the risk by granting them what we now call limited liability: they stood to lose only the money they had invested and were not liable for the entire debt of the company if it went bankrupt. By limiting investors' downside risk if the venture failed, this new legal structure made it more attractive to put up risk capital in hope of return. Without limited liability, the most popular legal form for corporations today, there would probably be no capitalism as we know it.

Out of this innovation came the world's first stock market and the creation of a series of financial products that made it easier for investors to speculate. The Dutch East India Company needed cash largely to invest in the infrastructure of trade, such as the forts that were an essential part of the business in that, literally, buccaneering age. Yet the company's need to make big capital investments up front meant that shareholders were required to lock up their money for ten years. Any investors wanting to liquidate their investment within that time were not allowed to reclaim their cash from the company. Instead, they had to sell their shares to other investors, in what became the stock market.

Investors looking to manage their risks in what had quickly become a liquid and volatile secondary market in shares entered into contracts to buy and sell shares at pre-agreed prices in the future. As today, these "futures contracts" soon became a means of speculation and source of controversy. In 1609, Isaac Le Maire, a former director of the Dutch East India Company, used futures contracts to bet that the company's share price would fall—akin to what we today call "short selling." His attempt to manipulate the market to win control of the company failed, and the Dutch government responded by banning futures trading, which it called *windhandel:* trading in the wind. It was the lifting of this ban in 1636 that triggered Tulipmania. This would not be the last time that attempts to stifle innovation by trying to put the genie back in the bottle had unintended consequences.

Tulips had been prized in the wealthiest homes of Europe since they were first imported from the Ottoman Empire (now Turkey) in the fifteenth century. The flowers were valued not just for their brightness and elegance but for their many varieties. Rare bulbs could attract particularly high prices. (We now know that this diversity is due to the mosaic virus, which causes tulip bulbs to "break" into new and unique patterns.) The Dutch Republic became the center of the tulip trade in Europe when experts at the University of Leiden figured out how to cultivate the bulbs in the late sixteenth century.

The tulip's brief flowering season in April and May was followed by the formation of another bulb as well as secondary buds, which could be uprooted and transferred between June and September. Thus for most of the year, outside those summer months, buying and selling bulbs involved a contract for future delivery that had to take into account the risk that the bulb would not survive.

Without legal protection, these futures contracts were risky and unreliable. However, at the end of 1636, futures trading was legalized again and formalized through "colleges" of buyers and sellers held in local taverns. No payment was required up front, except a 2.5 percent commission known as "wine money," paid by the buyer. With the legalization of futures trading, money flowed into the market and the price of bulbs for delivery the following summer soared.

No one quite knows why the speculative fever broke in the middle of February 1637, causing prices to plunge. But it did, and in April the government stepped in, suspending all tulip contracts. The messy process of disentangling these futures deals took several years, with sellers typically getting back only a small percentage of the initial contract price.

People often refer to Tulipmania as the ultimate crazy bubble. After all, what besides the madness of crowds could have caused the price of flower bulbs to rise tenfold in two months? Actually, it made sense for the price of bulbs in futures contracts to rise after those contracts were legalized. When contracts were informal and did not enjoy legal protection, there was a risk that they would not be honored, which was reflected in a lower price. In trying to establish the correct price after this legal change, the market certainly overshot—but that is often a part of the price-discovery process that follows a valuable innovation.

So how did madness become the accepted explanation of the tulip bubble? That was largely the work of propagandists, backed mostly by the church and the aristocracy, who were opposed to the newly prosperous trading classes and saw the bubble as a stick with which to beat them. One of their tactics—which has been deployed after many subsequent bubbles—was to exaggerate the extent of the mania. "Nobles, citizens, farmers, mechanics, seamen, footmen, maidservants, even chimney-sweeps and old clotheswomen, dabbled in tulips," wrote Mackay. However, it is now believed that most of these stories, including that of the tulip-eating sailor, were invented by the propagandists, whose pamphlets were the main source of Mackay's account.

It is this exaggeration of the crisis that has led people to believe that the tulip bubble was a catastrophe for the Dutch economy. In reality, the bubble was a blip, and the Dutch economy was barely affected, in large part because no serious effort was made to stifle financial innovation. And rightly so—the bubble may have followed the legalization of futures contracts, but to blame financial innovation would be like blaming the tulip. Markets do not always adjust smoothly. When new information enters a market, as it did following the deregulation of futures trading, there can be booms and busts as participants try to work out how much the change has affected the value of the product.

Thanks chiefly to its dynamic financial sector, the Dutch Republic remained the world's leading economic power throughout the rest of the seventeenth century. Nearly three centuries later, the United States, which had recently inherited the position of global economic superpower, experienced its own bubble driven by financial innovation. This time, at the dawning of the era of popular capitalism centered on Wall Street, it did result in mass panic.

CAPITALISM FOR THE MASSES

"When the time comes that a shoeshine boy knows as much as I do about what is going on in the stock market, it's time for me to get out." There was probably some poetic license in Joseph Kennedy's explanation for his prescient decision to sell his shares a matter of months before the great Wall Street Crash of 1929. Yet the founder of the Irish-American political dynasty was a shrewd (some say unscrupulous) investor, and his comment captured an important truth about the causes of the Great Crash. In the 1920s, for the first time, investing in shares became a mass-market activity. Professional intermediaries took financial products that had been the preserve of the sophisticated investor and turned them into a genuine innovation in finance: a popular capitalism, which by 1929 had drawn nearly 3 million American households into the stock market. It was these new investors, above all, who ended up getting carried away.

As its nickname suggests, the "Roaring Twenties" was a time of unprecedented prosperity, as the frugality of wartime was forgotten and a middle-class consumer society started to emerge. The booming stock market became the symbol of this new age. Thanks to a doubling of corporate profits in the twelve years after 1913, in what became known as the (President) "Coolidge bull market," share prices roared ahead as never before.

Ordinary households were encouraged to share in this success. Buy shares, argued John J. Raskob, a former treasurer of General Motors, in an article entitled "Everyone Ought to Be Rich." An investor who put just $15 each month into the market and reinvested the dividends would, he asserted, be sitting on $80,000 in twenty years' time.

A whole industry grew up to facilitate the new craze for investing. New York was the epicenter of the stock mania, but brokerage houses spread the enthusiasm across the country, more than doubling in number from 700 in 1925 to 1,600 in 1929. As they spread, they also changed, from a service for sophisticated high-end investors into more down-market shops. This was when Merrill Lynch's aggressive team of salesmen earned their nickname "the thundering herd." These new brokerage outlets gave everyone with some spare dollars a chance to put their money into the market. Better still, the new army of speculators could watch their wealth increase in real time on the broker's stock-price ticker-tape machine. (This may seem painfully familiar to those who were glued to the CNBC business channel during the past decade or so.)

In this already febrile atmosphere, bullish investors were given the chance to take even bigger bets trading "on margin." There was nothing new per se in allowing an investor to borrow from a broker to buy shares, later (all going to plan) settling the loan out of the profits he or she earned when the shares increased in price. But in the late 1920s, the market for brokers' loans to finance margin trading in New York grew as never before, soaring from $2.5 billion in 1926 to $6 billion by the end of 1928. (The same thing happened in the years before the crash of 2008, when the "prime brokerage" arms of investment banks lent huge sums to hedge funds.)

Much like the institutional investors who bought mortgage-backed securities during the recent housing bubble, believing them to be a relatively low-risk investment, in the 1920s wealthy Americans, corporations, and foreigners saw an opportunity to make a profit by financing (for a generous fee) these brokers' loans. They believed that the inevitably rising stock market made this a risk-free way of making money—though when the market crashed, it proved otherwise. Even an energy utility, Cities Service Corporation, entered into this market by issuing bonds to raise money to lend to brokers.

With money flowing rapidly into the market, financial companies responded with new products that were eagerly snapped up. The leading banks launched investment vehicles modeled on the holding companies that had earlier come to dominate the industrial sector, such as U.S. Steel and Standard Oil. These "investment trusts" were a great moneymaker for the sponsoring banks, among them Goldman Sachs. By 1929, one-third of new shares were sold using this mechanism. Investors seemed untroubled by the fact that the value of these trusts was by then typically almost double that of the securities they held.

The *New York Times* Industrial Average surged from 181 at the end of 1926 to 331 by the end of 1928. It peaked on September 3, 1929, at 542—nearly two-thirds higher than it had started the year. It drifted lower for a few weeks, then deteriorated alarmingly on Thursday, October 24. It actually ended that tumultuous day only 12 points lower—but that was due to an organized buying effort by the leading banks led by Richard Whitney, the president of the New York Stock Exchange.

The panic soon returned as the market fell by more than 40 points the following Monday. Tuesday, October 29, "Black Tuesday," is the date most history books pinpoint, when the market fell another 43 points on the back of massive, frenzied trading. On those frantic days, in a prequel to the current crisis, the panic was made worse by a lack of transparency in prices as the heavy selling volume caused the much-watched ticker-tape machines to fall hopelessly behind. By November 13, the Industrial Average stood at 224, down by almost 60 percent from its September high.

The stock market was sped on its way down by the unwinding of the brokers' loans that had helped to inflate share prices on the way up. There was a liquidity crisis as the investors who had financed brokers' loans realized that they were at greater risk than they had previously thought: their money flowed out of the market as quickly as it had flowed in. In turn, as speculative bets turned sour, brokers called in more assets from the investors as collateral against the loans, forcing those investors who did not have large cash reserves to dump whatever good shares they did own on the market, depressing prices further. Much the same process of "deleveraging" was experienced by speculators such as hedge funds that had borrowed heavily before the credit crunch that began in 2007.

Why did the bubble burst? Throughout 1929, talk was rife that the market was in the grip of a speculative fever. In March, the venerable banker Paul Warburg predicted a crash. (Not every expert agreed, however: shortly before they tumbled, eminent economist Irving Fisher wrote that "stock prices have reached what looks like a permanently high plateau.")

As early as 1926, some of the governors of the Federal Reserve had started to worry that share prices were rising unsustainably due to what they might have called irrational exuberance. However, fearing that the market might overreact and throw the economy into recession (as an effort to deflate a speculative bubble in Germany in 1927 had done), they moved cautiously. The Fed slowly pushed up interest rates, starting in 1927, and waited until 1929 to try to restrain trading on margin by limiting how much banks could lend to brokers to fund their clients' speculation.

These moves had, at most, a modest effect. Instead, it was the

Fed's data that pricked the bubble: in early October, its quarterly index of industrial production showed that the economy was already in recession. Realizing that the good times were over, at least temporarily, investors raced to take their profits out of the market while they could, setting off the downward spiral in share prices.

In the years following the crash, much of the financial innovation that had underpinned the popular capitalism of the 1920s was suppressed by regulations from Congress. These included the 1934 act that created a new markets regulator, the Securities and Exchange Commission, whose first head was the poacher-turned-gamekeeper Joseph Kennedy. This heavy regulation was introduced because, unlike after Tulipmania, the bursting of the bubble was followed by a sharp decline in the economy that politicians blamed (mostly unfairly) on Wall Street.

Certainly, there was some wrongdoing on Wall Street, as there always is during bubbles. Perhaps the most notable example was the attempt by Goldman Sachs Trading Corporation, an investment trust launched by the bank in December 1928, to support its share price by buying its own shares. However, such examples then, and in general, are usually tangential to what caused the bubble. In this case, although Congress held extensive inquiries, seeking out bankers, speculators, and other ne'er-do-wells to blame, these were largely inconclusive.

Moreover, there is little reason to think that the bursting of the bubble, and the innovations that had helped to inflate it, were to blame for the Great Depression of the 1930s. The depth and longevity of that economic decline owed far more to mistakes in government policy in America and abroad, as we will discuss later. The crash of 1929 only took share prices back to around what they were at the start of 1928; it was what followed the bursting of the bubble, mostly a series of inept economic policy decisions, that returned the Industrial Average to what it had been in 1921, when in June 1932 it bottomed out at 58.

Indeed, there are strong reasons to think that the suppression of financial innovation during the 1930s slowed the pace of wealth creation in America for several decades—until deregulation, in response to economic sluggishness, allowed financial innovation to resume nearly half a century later. The deregulation of the 1980s was quickly followed by an asset price bubble. This time, unlike the aftermath of the crash of 1929, it was just a blip.

THE CRASH THAT NEVER WAS

The year 1929 had its Black Tuesday. Similarly, 1987 had Black Monday, when on October 19, the stock market lost 20 percent of its value, which dwarfed any previous fall in a single day. This sent shock waves around the world, prompting many foreign stock markets to fall too. This was the most significant crash since 1929.

The unease was all the greater because there was no obvious reason for the stock market to crash in 1987 (to this day economists argue about what might have triggered it) and because many of the smartest minds then investing in the market believed that recent financial innovations meant that crashes were no longer possible.

Starting in the 1950s, academics had developed a new branch of economics now known as "modern finance." This tried to understand financial risk, and how to manage it better, by using complex mathematical models to describe and predict how markets behave. One of the big ideas that came out of this was the efficient market hypothesis. This asserted that in an efficient market, prices correctly reflect all available information. In such a market, the sort of mispricing that is the essence of a bubble was logically impossible. Prices could plunge dramatically, but only as a result of new, seriously bad information—of which there was none on or around October 19, 1987.

Deregulation of finance, which began in the 1970s, had provided the opportunity to take these ideas out of the university classroom and onto the trading floor. A golden age of financial innovation dawned as economists and mathematicians turned theory into financial products. Such was the complexity of this new business that soon Wall Street was hiring physicists to turn them into financial "rocket scientists."

One of the reasons that, by 1987, many investors had come to believe that the stock market was crash-proof was a financial innovation called portfolio insurance. In 1981, three academics—two economists and an engineer—Hayne Leland, Mark Rubinstein, and John O'Brien started a company to profit from their theories about how to manage risk.

They believed that investors could insure their portfolio of shares against falling prices by using derivatives such as futures contracts. A key element of this portfolio insurance was that as prices fell, the investor would sell some shares to build up a cash reserve. This money would then be used to buy back into the market once it had recovered, at advantageous prices that had already been secured by the insurer through futures contracts.

This had been working fine during the normal ups and downs of the market. The problem on Black Monday was that the initial sharp fall—cause unknown—was large enough to set off a mass dumping of shares by investors with portfolio insurance. This resulted in a further fall in prices, causing computerized insurance programs to trigger yet another round of dumping. And so, disastrously, on.

Despite the predictions of doom at the time, and the folk memory that survives today that it was a great calamity, the crash of 1987 was a case of "small earthquake, no one hurt." Once investors understood that out-of-control computers had been driving down prices, the stock market quickly stabilized at around the level it had started the year. Modest interest-rate cuts helped restore confidence. The economy barely noticed, and grew steadily throughout 1988.

Nicholas Brady, who was later appointed U.S. treasury secretary, chaired a much-hyped presidential task force to look into the causes of the crash. As a result of this inquiry, stock market regulations were later tweaked, nothing more, with the introduction of "circuit breakers" that paused trading after significant price declines to give investors time to think.

As for the investors, they concluded that the fault lay not with modern finance theory itself but with the particular application of it in portfolio insurance, which they consigned to the dustbin of history. But they had already seen enough benefit from new risk-management tools such as derivatives that the pace of financial innovation continued faster than ever.

The multitrillion-dollar industry in derivatives and other financial innovations eventually contributed mightily to the meltdown that began in 2007. Once again, financiers had forgotten that, for all their advantages, these innovations had limitations. This was a lesson they should have learned from the 1987 crash, and from two subsequent mini-meltdowns: of Long-Term Capital Management and of Enron.

WHEN CONFIDENCE OVERSHOOTS

Ten years almost to the day after the 1987 crash, modern finance received the strongest possible endorsement from the economics mainstream when the Nobel Prize for economics was awarded to Myron Scholes and Robert Merton. They were two of the three authors of the Black-Scholes option pricing formula, which was the big new idea in modern finance theory and had quickly become the keystone of the booming mathematically based finance industry. The third author, Fischer Black, who had left academia to work for Goldman Sachs, had died in 1995 but would certainly have shared the Nobel Prize had he lived.

Like Black, Scholes and Merton had by then decided to use their theories to make money. In 1993 they had cofounded, along with legendary Wall Street trader John Meriwether and others, a hedge fund called Long-Term Capital Management (LTCM). They based LTCM in Greenwich, Connecticut, a leafy suburb an hour from New York City that in the 1990s became the center of the fast-growing hedge-fund industry.

The term "hedge fund" covers a wide variety of investment vehicles. Their only common factor is that they are lightly regulated, because they cater to supposedly sophisticated investors rather than to the mass retail market. (One regulatory response to the 1929 crash was to introduce protections for retail investors; sophisticated investors were exempt from these because they were thought to be able to handle risk.) Hedge funds pay their managers handsomely if they succeed (and generously even if they do not): a typical pay structure is for the managers to charge 2 percent a year of the assets invested in the fund plus 20 percent of any profits.

Some hedge funds are very simple, merely buying shares the managers expect to rise. Some short-sell those shares they think will fall in price. Some take bets on macroeconomic trends, such as that the dollar or the price of oil will rise or fall. Like the "margin traders" of the 1920s, many hedge funds add juice to their bets by borrowing to double up (sometimes several times over).

LTCM's founders set out to take the hedge-fund model to the next level, by deploying cutting-edge quantitative models to find investment opportunities and using new risk-management models to increase their bets (and profits) with unprecedented amounts of debt relative to their equity.

These advocates of the efficient market hypothesis were not so blinkered by their ivory-tower existence to deny that there are many unsophisticated or foolish investors betting in financial markets. But they believed that the temporary mispricing of assets caused by these so-called noise traders would be overcome by the smart investors who accurately valued the assets.

One way in which investors drive out mispricing is known as arbitrage. In the purest form of arbitrage, smart investors would find two identical securities that were differently priced, then buy the cheap one and sell the overpriced one. This would raise the price of the former and lower the price of the latter, bringing both closer to the true price.

LTCM used its complex mathematical models to scour financial markets all over the world to find securities that had similar risks but different prices. It then bet that their prices would move closer together as the markets began to price the risk more consistently. Often the mispricing was very small, which meant that arbitrage needed to be beefed up with a lot of borrowed money to be worth doing.

To see the effect of borrowing, consider this example. If an investor buys a bond for $100 and it increases to $101, he makes a 1 percent profit, which is not very exciting (especially if there was some risk that it would not rise that much or might even fall). What if instead the investor used $1 of his own money and borrowed the rest to buy the bond? If its price then rose to $101, as before, after the debt had been repaid (let's ignore borrowing fees here) he would be left with a profit of $1 on an investment of $1—which is a rate of return of 100 percent, more than enough to excite any investor.

In its first few years, LTCM's strategy achieved spectacular success, generating annual returns of over 40 percent for its investors. But less than a year after the award of the Nobel Prize to its cofounders, LTCM imploded, threatening the entire financial system as it did so.

In a way, LTCM became a victim of its own success. With the supply of big arbitrage opportunities drying up, the fund had even handed billions of dollars back to its investors because its managers could not find profitable ways to use the money. The deals they could find offered ever smaller profit margins, and thus needed ever greater leverage with debt to achieve the returns on capital it required. By the start of 1998, LTCM was managing nearly $5 billion of funds and leveraging $125 billion in debt to finance its trading positions, which included a portfolio of derivatives with a face value of $1.25 trillion.

As its leverage grew, LTCM became increasingly reliant on the ability of its risk-management systems to withstand a nasty shock—which duly arrived in August 1998 when the erratic Russian government of Boris Yeltsin defaulted on its debt. Although this had little direct impact on LTCM, the panic that spread through the markets after the default sent many other asset prices in the opposite direction to that predicted by LTCM's mathematical models. As the market value of its portfolio plunged, eating into its equity capital, its leverage soared. In September, its capital was barely one-tenth of what it had been at the start of the year, and its debt-to-equity ratio was now an eye-watering 200 to 1.

At first, LTCM's owners hoped that this would be a short-lived liquidity crisis that would pass when the markets understood that the fundamental value of their portfolio was strong. But with the fund's capital base eroding, insolvency seemed increasingly inevitable. The managers tried to find a buyer for LTCM, approaching both Goldman Sachs and Warren Buffett, one of America's richest men, but to no avail.

Meanwhile, the Fed became convinced it faced a crisis that could potentially bring down the entire financial system because so many banks had lent large sums to LTCM. The Federal Reserve Bank of New York, led by Bill McDonough, decided to stop the chain reaction by summoning the heads of the major Wall Street banks and urging them to put together a rescue plan to bail out LTCM and thereby save themselves. Although the Fed was credited with arranging the $3.5 billion rescue, no public funds were involved.

The one bank that refused to participate in the rescue of LTCM was the investment bank Bear Stearns, led by the bridge-playing golf fanatic Jimmy Cayne. A decade later, in a moment of poetic justice, in March 2008, McDonough's successor at the New York Fed and later treasury secretary, Tim Geithner, also found himself calling the heads of Wall Street firms, this time trying to save Cayne's bank. Bear had built up massive exposure to mortgage-backed securities and relied heavily on short-term loans from the money markets to operate. As a result, when the credit crunch hit in 2007, it was more exposed than other banks. As it headed toward bankruptcy, Geithner arranged for Bear to be sold to JPMorgan Chase bank for $2 a share, a fraction of what the shares had been worth before the credit crunch. (Protests from Bear shareholders later got the price raised to $10.) Unlike the LTCM rescue, however, the deal had to be sweetened by government guarantees to JPMorgan Chase against toxic assets lurking on Bear's balance sheet.

Under its rescue deal, LTCM's portfolio was gradually liquidated, a process that even generated a small profit for its rescuers. Finally, in 2000, LTCM was wound up, by which time its cofounders had moved on, either back to academia or to other parts of the investment industry.

The conclusion implicitly drawn by regulators, and Wall Street, was that there had been nothing fundamentally wrong with LTCM's business model. Its collapse had been a combination of bad luck—the Russian default had triggered a "once-in-a-thousand-years storm" in the markets, they said—and personal hubris. Perhaps only Nobel Prize–winning economists could believe that their risk-management models could withstand gambling with such huge amounts of debt (even if LTCM's traders ignored some red lights from the models). Even the name Long-Term reflected their belief that they had engineered a way to survive short-term volatility in the market. What Wall Street should have concluded is that it needed to be more careful with models.

From today's perspective, supposedly one-in-a-thousand-years storms seem to occur every few years in the financial markets. The former trader and best-selling author Nassim Nicholas Taleb has led the criticism of the financial models used by the banks, which have failed to factor in the frequency of what he calls "black swan" events such as this. It appears that LTCM's mathematical models had missed this point, by relying too heavily on the past performance of different financial assets and the past correlations between them to predict how they would behave in the future.

In reality, past performance and correlations can be a lousy guide to future risk, particularly in turbulent markets. For example, in a world of strict controls on global capital flows, the prices of bonds in two different countries may have been unrelated, but in a world rapidly globalizing due to deregulation, they might start to move together, becoming highly correlated in a way that a model based on historical data could not predict. It is also worth remembering that Russia had shuffled off communism and emerged from the wreckage of the Soviet Union only six years earlier, so the market had very little information about the way its bonds would perform. The same problem would later occur with mortgage-backed securities. Although these were newfangled financial products with little track record, banks and ratings agencies took their initial success as a sign that they were supersafe. When historically uncorrelated local housing markets suddenly started to fall together, like LTCM in 1997, they found that this was a scenario that their risk models had not planned for. Indeed, as the financial crisis worsened in 2008, all sorts of financial assets became more correlated, in ways not predicted by financial models. Investors who had relied on low correlation to diversify their risk found themselves suddenly highly exposed to it.

LTCM was also naive about the all-too-human way that market participants behave in times of stress. Lenders who had promised to keep lending to LTCM, come what may, suddenly found reasons to deny it the credit it needed as it plunged toward bankruptcy. LTCM's founders remain convinced that if the debt had continued to flow they would eventually have emerged successfully and profitably from the crisis—but their financial counterparties denied them the chance. Lehman Brothers and Bear Stearns said the same about their collapse in 2008. In the future, perhaps the models will take into account that at times of panic, credit markets have a tendency to freeze.

CRIMES OF HUBRIS

No one seriously accused LTCM of fraud. The same cannot be said of Enron, which offered a toxic combination of flawed mathematical models, hubris, and criminality. Jeff Skilling, who had been Enron's chief executive, was sentenced to twenty-four years in jail for his part in the downfall of the firm in 2001—at the time, America's largest corporate bankruptcy ever. Its chairman, Ken Lay, was found guilty but died before he could be sentenced. Andrew Fastow, who as Enron's chief financial officer was widely regarded as the mastermind behind the fraud that destroyed the firm, was jailed for only six years, thanks to a plea bargain in which he agreed to testify against his former bosses.

These sentences look light in comparison to the 150 years handed out to the man who had taken on Charles Ponzi's mantle in 2008, Bernie Madoff. Madoff had lured rich and powerful investors by boasting that his "split-strike conversion strategy" would earn spectacular returns on their investments. This, of course, was nonsense. Part of the secret to his (con artist) success was his credibility as a former chairman of the NASDAQ exchange. Madoff confessed in December 2008 because he did not have money to pay back investors who had been forced to ask for their cash back because of the financial crisis.

Madoff was believed to have run off with $65 billion of other people's money, which is about the same as what Enron was worth before it went bankrupt in 2001. Just as the victims of Madoff cried out that "something must be done," so politicians reacted to the collapse of Enron. The Sarbanes-Oxley Act, which was rushed through Congress without proper reflection in 2002 to reduce the risk of corporate fraud, manifested the widely held view that it was criminality that had caused the collapse of Enron. The new rules on auditing and the responsibilities of chief executives for accurate financial reporting were all backed up by Section 404 of the act, which set out draconian new criminal penalties for transgressors. This may have obscured some more-important lessons about the dangers of mishandling financial innovation.

Until shortly before its collapse, Enron was lionized for its pioneering use of the new financial techniques and products that had transformed what started out as a boring, low-risk natural-gas utility in Houston, Texas, into a high-risk financial trading firm that many people likened to a hedge fund. As its share price soared, *Fortune* magazine hailed Enron as "America's most innovative company" for six years in a row, from 1996 to 2001. In the summer of 2001, Enron's headquarters sported a banner declaring, "The World's Leading Company."

Enron was indeed an innovative company—ultimately, too innovative for its own good. Its transformation began with the deregulation of America's electricity markets in the 1990s. Enron saw the chance to use tools such as derivatives that had become established in finance to build a market in short- and long-term energy contracts. This proved hugely profitable. Enron's ambitious managers pressed ahead into other markets. It started to trade energy overseas and established itself in the telecoms market, trading bandwidth—the digital pipelines of the Internet age.

In order to establish a dominant position in these new markets, Enron needed to raise lots of cash—and to help it do so, it used every legal trick in the book to push up its reported profits. Working with its auditor, the global giant Arthur Andersen, Enron tested the limits of America's legalistic accounting rules. The first was to book all the expected profits from its deals as soon as they were signed, rather than as they accrued over the lifetime of the deals. This could be seen as counting chickens before they hatch, given that the risks inherent in many of these investments meant that the future revenues were by no means certain. In particular, the profits it booked on bandwidth deals seemed to be the product of an especially optimistic imagination.

Enron was also skilled at using "mark-to-market accounting," a way of measuring the value of a company's assets in terms of what they are worth now, rather than the price they were bought at. Mark-to-market, also known as "fair value" accounting, was conceived in the 1970s when high inflation was rapidly making nonsense of the valuation of assets that were recorded on company balance sheets in terms of the price paid for them. This gave a distorted picture of the true value of a company. Adjusting asset values to reflect their current market value makes a lot of sense but is open to abuse, since it can give companies discretion in how they report the value of their assets. Mark-to-market valuations are particularly vulnerable to manipulation when the market price of assets bounces around a lot (so there are plenty of different market prices to choose from) or when an asset is thinly traded (so the company has to estimate what the market price would be). Enron was not alone in choosing favorable prices and in using mark-to-market accounting to book gains in the market value of the assets it owned as profits. It was far less assiduous in recognizing falls in market value of its assets as losses.

Enron's pursuit of immediate profits, and its desire to make its balance sheet look as strong as possible, also made it a pioneer in the use of securitization. Working closely with some leading Wall Street investment banks and law firms, it started to off-load various assets by shifting them into "special purpose entities" (SPEs), many of which, bizarrely, it named after characters in the *Star Wars* movies (Jedi, Raptor, and so forth). By doing this, it was able to both shift risk off its balance sheet and book a steady stream of income in return.

Enron's demise began when legal technicalities forced it to reabsorb some of these SPEs. As a result, it had to restate its profits and balance sheet, which now looked far weaker. Investors, lenders, and ratings agencies, alert at last to its extremely aggressive interpretation of the accounting rules, were spooked. Since Enron had turned itself in effect into an investment bank, this loss of confidence was fatal. As with LTCM, when the market started to lose faith in its highly indebted financial operations, liquidity evaporated in an instant, making bankruptcy inevitable. Enron went bust in December 2001.

Enron drove financial innovation too hard, too fast—and ultimately fraudulently. Yet Wall Street firms regarded many of its innovations as valuable and, upon its demise, rushed to take over its lucrative energy-trading business or build similar businesses of their own. Securitization went from strength to strength as banks enthusiastically booked profits for creating securities while shifting the risk off their balance sheets—in accounting terms, at least, though, as it often turned out, not in reality.

Enron's auditor, Arthur Andersen, took most of the rap for the company's inflated profits. Following outcry over its shredding of Enron-related documents, the firm was driven out of business by government prosecutors in early 2002 (although the Supreme Court later—too late!—threw out its conviction on charges related to the shredding). A new watchdog for audit firms was created. Yet the accounting rules that Enron exploited were largely unchanged.

It was only in 2007–08 that another weakness in mark-to-market accounting was exposed. Just as the value of assets is marked up as prices rise, so it crashes along with market. As financial institutions deleveraged, they had to unload assets onto the market at prices that they believed, often justifiably, were way below their true market value. Mark-to-market accounting then transmitted these "distressed asset" prices to similar assets that the banks had not sold, further weakening bank balance sheets, forcing a further round of distressed selling to raise capital, and leading to further falls in market prices. This downward spiral was halted only by the controversial suspension of America's mark-to-market accounting rules in April 2009. Figuring out a way to account for asset values that is better than historic cost but that does not add to the instability of the financial system is a high priority, though it will not be easy.

Enron's problems were part of a trend that stretched back to Tulipmania in which worthwhile financial innovations have been pushed too far. The result has been spectacular booms and busts. But this failing has not been unique to financial innovations. Breakthroughs in industrial technology have often led to financial bubbles, too.

TECHNOLOGY BUGS AND BUBBLES

The dot-com bubble began to inflate on August 9, 1995, when Silicon Valley entrepreneur Jim Clark, backed by leading venture capitalists, launched an initial public offering (IPO) of shares in Netscape, which owned the leading Web browser at the time. With the Internet growing rapidly, investors saw huge potential, and the firm's share price almost trebled on the first day, reaching $75. This set a pattern for a sequence of "hot IPOs" of dot-com companies that was to continue for nearly five years. Many of these companies ultimately proved worthless, especially when they could no longer get the fresh capital they needed after the bubble burst in March 2000.

The Internet mania was driven by new information entering the market, in the form of widespread optimism that this new technology would transform the business world, generating huge profits in the process. This was not the first time that investors would be ruined by mistaking a valuable technological advance for a valuable investment. The promise of automobiles and radio had played a part in the market fever of the 1920s, yet the performance of the shares of most companies in these industries was disappointing.

The technology that had the bubbly consequences most similar to the dot-coms was the railway in the nineteenth century, which held out the prospect of huge benefits to individuals and companies from fast, reliable transport across long distances. Britain was bitten by the railway bug first, in the 1820s. Despite warnings from the prime minister, Lord Liverpool, investing in railway companies turned into a bubble of speculation in the 1830s, as shares were touted not just to professional investors but to "ladies and clergymen" keen to jump on the ever accelerating bandwagon. Building railways was a risky business that involved huge up-front costs, which were prone to overrun, and future revenues were highly uncertain. When investors realized railways were not the license to print money they had expected, the bubble burst, as did another in the 1860s.

The U.S. railroad bubble came later, in the 1870s, and was inflated in part by inexperienced investors from Continental Europe who, for the first time, were sending their money abroad in search of opportunities. (British investors, who led the world in foreign speculation, were less enthusiastic, perhaps because of their bad experience with railways at home.) The benefits of railroads in such a huge country were obvious, including opening up the West. But these foreign investors had little information about the relative risk of companies in this highly leveraged business, in what was, after all, then still an emerging market.

All was fine between 1868 and 1870, when only one American railroad company defaulted on its debt. But as defaults rose from three in 1871 to twelve in 1872, European investors (already made jittery by their weakening domestic economies) started to panic. With little way of knowing which companies were toxic, they abruptly halted investment in U.S. railroad stocks and bonds. This credit drought caused a further wave of defaults in 1873 and a collapse in stock prices across the sector.

The implosion of railroad stock prices infected the entire

financial system, because many of the banks had large holdings of railroad bonds. When one of the largest banks, Jay Cooke and Co., was forced to close in September 1873 after a default by Northern Pacific Railway, one of thirty-five railroad companies to fail so far that year, there was a run on the banks. After a 25 percent fall in share prices, the New York Stock Exchange announced an indefinite closure, which eventually lasted ten days.

The riskiness of investing in railroads prompted a new financial innovation in 1909, when the stock analyst John Moody published his *Analyses of Railroad Investments,* which for the first time assigned grades to securities. These easy-to-understand measures of risk quickly caught on, and the credit-ratings industry boomed, led by Moody's, Standard & Poor's, and Fitch. In the 1970s, government regulators singled out these three firms as "nationally recognized," which helped them attract business from bond issuers who would pay for a rating.

The rating agencies' credibility took a blow when they failed to spot Enron's accounting shenanigans and was blown out of the water by the 2008 crisis, when they so clearly failed in their analysis of mortgage-backed securities. The rating-agency business is dogged by worrying conflicts of interest—ratings are paid for by the sellers of bonds, and since the dawn of time, he who pays the piper has tended to call the tune—but investors must also take the blame for relying too heavily on ratings (although, to be fair, this was sometimes at the behest of regulators). As in the railway bubbles of the nineteenth century, and the broader stock market bubble of the 1920s, this investor naïveté played a big part in the dot-com craze of the late 1990s.

In the 1990s the new technology of the Internet inspired another financial innovation: online share trading. Through their home computers, individuals could now buy and sell shares directly, rather than through an expensive middleman, and many found that dot-coms were a great way to make money: just buy at the IPO and cash in when, Netscape-like, the price had soared. With the NASDAQ Stock Market's tech-company-based index rising faster than a homesick angel, more and more investors were drawn in to this apparently effortless way of making money. Some became day traders, addictively watching CNBC and hunched over their computers, trying to profit by betting minute-by-minute on movements in share prices.

From 1997 to 2000 the NASDAQ soared from 1,200 points to over 5,000 as a stream of entrepreneurs and venture capitalists with change-the-world business ideas—some good, many absurd—met a ready pool of investors, egged on by analysts making bold predictions about the companies' future profits.

It was not just the dot-coms and the technology sector that were booming at this time. So too were many "old" economy stocks traded on the New York Stock Exchange. It was when the Dow Jones Industrial Average broke 6,000 at the end of 1996 that Alan Greenspan, the chairman of the Federal Reserve, had famously asked whether "irrational exuberance" was leading to an asset price bubble. The markets listened, paused, then surged again.

In 1999, Greenspan suggested that there might be a rational explanation for the seemingly implausibly high price of dot-com shares. If people have a strong preference for big wins over small wins, he speculated, they may be willing to pay over the odds for a punt at the big prize. Pointing to the popularity of buying lottery tickets, which offer a poor risk-return ratio, as the odds of winning are so low, Greenspan suggested that there was a "lottery premium" in the price of a dot-com share: the small number of dot-com companies that would eventually succeed would probably do so spectacularly, delivering handsome returns to their lottery-winner shareholders. Although the majority of dot-com shares would probably turn out to be worthless, the possibility that one of them might be one of the few that succeed made it worth a punt.

Well, it was a theory. Greenspan concluded that there was nothing the Fed could do to stop the buying frenzy anyway— though he said it would at least stand ready to clean up the mess if and when the bubble burst, as was his habit.

On March 20, 2000, *Barron's* magazine published an article that analyzed 207 dot-coms that had held an IPO. It showed that 74 percent of those supposed gold mines had negative cash flow and that many of them would soon run out of money unless they could raise more capital. Meanwhile, venture capitalists, who knew the true state of these firms, were starting to cash out by selling their shares. (Netscape's Clark had already bailed out of the market in 1998, a couple of billion dollars richer, just as his Web browser was being overtaken by its Microsoft rival, Explorer.)

Despite predictions by some bubble-headed commentators that the Dow would soon soar to 36,000, the stock index had already peaked at just below 12,000 in January 2000—a level it did not reach again until 2007. Following the article in *Barron's*, confidence rapidly ebbed away from the dot-com sector. The NASDAQ index, which had peaked at 5,048 on March 10, 2000, was one-third lower a month later. It bottomed out in October 2002 at less than one-quarter of its peak.

This collapse certainly hurt the Silicon Valley economy, and sharply reduced the amount of money invested in the venture capital that funded innovative start-ups. However, the American economy suffered only a mild recession, which may have owed far more to the impact of the terrorist attacks of September 11, 2001, and the failure of Enron and several other scandal-hit big companies, such as WorldCom, soon after.

THE CASE FOR INNOVATION

Financial bubbles tend to be seen as catastrophes fueled by the madness of crowds, almost like giant Ponzi schemes. Yet they often begin with potentially valuable innovations. Indeed, some people have argued that bubbles can actually be a good thing. For instance, the dot-com bubble, they argue, allowed America to explore the potential of e-commerce, to find out what works and what does not, faster and more thoroughly than if there had been no bubble—a sort of "fast-forwarding of experimentation," as one commentator put it. Well, maybe.

What is certainly true, as we have seen, is a strong correlation between bubbles and genuinely exciting advances, whether in technology or finance. The link with financial innovation is particularly strong. According to a 1999 study of a hundred financial crises from the 1970s to the 1990s by Graciela Kaminsky and Carmen Reinhart, the frequency of banking crises quadrupled with deregulation of the financial sector in the 1980s and 1990s. It seems that, freed of regulatory constraints, banks start to innovate and, in doing so, often begin to inflate a bubble.

The other factor present in bubbles is overconfidence, as investors come to believe that an innovation will generate huge benefits. The bubble forms when expectations exceed reality. Yet no matter how much we think that "this time it's different," busts have inevitably followed booms, as former IMF chief economist Kenneth Rogoff (with Carmen Reinhart) has demonstrated conclusively in his analysis of two centuries of financial crises.

Even if the consequences of bubbles are not always as severe as those that followed the one that finally burst in 2008, there is certainly much to be gained by finding ways to prevent bubbles from forming, or at least from getting too big. To Hyman Minsky

the answer was strict regulation by government. Rather than trying to stop the innovation around which bubbles form, a better
answer may be to recognize the psychological factors that allow a
rational appreciation of an innovation to tip over into irrational
exuberance. That said, we may have to accept some occasional
bubbles as a fact of life, human nature being what it is.

Yet that may not be so bad. As we shall see, the really nasty
economic consequences tend to result not from bubbles per se
but from the wrong reaction when bubbles burst, or when government actions, rather than restraining a bubble, have the effect
of blowing extra air into it. Alas, both of these are common errors.

2

THE MORAL MAZE

How governments people the world with fools

What on earth was Hank Paulson thinking when he let Lehman Brothers collapse on Monday, September 15, 2008? Looking back it seems to have been a ludicrous decision. Even at the time people were shocked.

Panic spread through the financial markets on the news, with the frenzy focused on credit default swaps (CDSs), derivative financial instruments that were supposed to insure lenders against borrowers' inability to pay. If Lehman could fall, the market wondered, who would be next? Fear of further bankruptcies and defaults spread like wildfire. American International Group (AIG), the world's biggest insurer, had massive exposure to CDSs, the value of which plummeted as Lehman failed, propelling it toward bankruptcy. This time the Federal Reserve rode to the rescue and provided an $85 billion loan to bail out AIG the following day.

The action now switched to the money markets as investors pulled cash out of funds that held securities issued or guaranteed by Lehman. This was the moment when the severity of the crisis became clear to the millions of Americans who held savings in money market accounts, which they believed were as safe as bank accounts protected by federal deposit insurance. In the panic after Lehman failed, the value of money market accounts fell below a hundred cents on the dollar, something that was previously unimaginable. On Thursday the government stepped in to guarantee the money markets. Finally, on Friday, September 19, Paulson outlined a $700 billion rescue plan for the entire financial system. Within a week the treasury secretary had switched from being a stern judge forcing Lehman Brothers to take responsibility for its mistakes to being an indulgent parent splashing much larger sums of money around the financial system than it would have taken to save Lehman, lest anyone come to harm. In doing so, he was reverting to the role that most people on Wall Street had expected him to play.

By 2008, most participants in the markets had come to believe that a government rescue when the system faced a crisis was one of the rules of the game. Only one week before Lehman had filed for bankruptcy, Paulson had bailed out the government-backed mortgage finance companies Fannie Mae and Freddie Mac. Previously, in March, the Fed had even engineered the rescue of one of Lehman's rivals, the investment bank Bear Stearns.

As early as 1999, Wall Street had started to use the phrase "Greenspan put" as shorthand for the view that the government would not let prices in financial markets fall too low.* As the chairman of the Federal Reserve, Alan Greenspan had supported the rescue of failed institutions such as Long-Term Capital Management (albeit through a private bailout) and had frequently used

---

* The buyer of a "put option" is entitled to sell the underlying asset (e.g., a share) in the future at an agreed price, minimizing the buyer's losses if the asset price falls. By cutting interest rates to support the market whenever it fell, Greenspan was seen to be guaranteeing that prices would not fall too far, therefore providing the equivalent of a put option.

interest rates to give the financial markets a boost whenever the going got tough, from the 1987 market crash and the bursting of the dot-com bubble in 2000 to the aftermath of the 9/11 terrorist attacks of 2001.

Paulson's decision to throw Lehman to the wolves—a decision that was supported by Federal Reserve chairman Ben Bernanke and New York Fed boss Tim Geithner—amounted to a dramatic reversal of policy from the Greenspan era. It was also one that ignored all the lessons of history. Nearly three centuries before, at the dawn of Anglo-Saxon capitalism, when the South Sea Bubble burst, the British government had realized that it needed to step in to rescue the fledgling financial system. By contrast, after the Wall Street Crash of 1929, Andrew Mellon, like Paulson a wealthy investment banker turned treasury secretary, chose to get tough with the banks. As a result, the whole financial system broke down, tipping America into the Great Depression. No American government had been as negligent since—until now.

Paulson's justification was that he and the Fed had tried and failed to organize a private rescue of Lehman and that he drew the line at pumping in taxpayers' money. He was worried that banks might continue to be reckless if they thought that the government would always ride to the rescue and wanted to send a message that troubled banks should not presume that there would be someone to catch them if they fell. "I don't take moral hazard lightly" was how he explained his decision on September 15.

Paulson was not suggesting ethical lapses by the management of Lehman. Moral hazard is an idea that goes back to the early days of the insurance industry in the sixteenth century and refers to the problem that once persons are insured against a risk they may, consciously or unconsciously, change their behavior and act in a more reckless way, in the knowledge that they are now protected against that risk: high-wire artists will try more-daring stunts if they know there is a safety net. The problem of moral hazard, as Herbert Spencer, the nineteenth-century British philosopher who invented the term "survival of the fittest," put it, is: "The ultimate result of shielding man from the effects of folly is to people the world with fools."

Governments worry particularly about this problem in the financial sector because moral hazard might encourage banks to try risky strategies that promise huge profits for managers and shareholders if they work, and an enormous bill for the taxpayer if they go wrong. The moral hazard argument makes intuitive sense: the belief that the government will bail them out probably does make financial institutions more reckless with risk. Moreover, moral hazard does not apply just to financial institutions that take on too much risk for themselves; it also applies to others who lend their money to, or deposit their money in, those institutions. Moral hazard therefore distorts the behavior of all market participants, not least by causing them to rely on government when they should be keeping an eye on each other's behavior.

The challenge for government is to know when to provide a safety net, without allowing bankers to believe that they will always be saved from their mistakes. Governments have tried to solve this dilemma by talking tough before a crisis to suggest that there is no safety net, to discourage recklessness, while being willing in practice to splash the cash around when a crisis occurs, to protect society from the consequences. But participants in the financial markets know that in a crisis the government's bite seldom matches its bark. As a result, they typically base their strategies on what they expect government to do rather than what treasury secretaries and Fed chairmen say they will do.

Paulson's decision to draw a line in the sand and refuse to bail out Lehman was not what Wall Street was expecting. This worsened the panic in the financial markets. As a result, Paulson spent far more taxpayers' money to save the system than it would have cost to save Lehman. What started as an attempt to crack down on moral hazard and limit taxpayers' exposure to mistakes made on Wall Street probably had the opposite effect. The financial sector is likely to conclude that future treasury secretaries will be less likely to act tough in the way that Paulson did with Lehman Brothers. If anything, Paulson's attempt to reduce moral hazard has succeeded only in making it greater.

As the crisis developed during 2008, Paulson's actions seemed so erratic—bailing out some institutions and not others—that they, at least, provided some stimulus to the conspiracy-theory business. Paulson had come to government from the top job at Goldman Sachs, Lehman's main competitor in the investment banking business. The rumormongers speculated that the chance to knock over this great rival had been just too tempting. The conspiracy theorists heaped coals on Paulson's head by pointing to the other Goldman alumni in government, such as President George W. Bush's chief of staff Joshua Bolten, speculating that they could have formed an anti-Lehman cabal and noting that Goldman itself had benefited from public help at the height of the crisis. When Paulson appointed former Goldman executives to run the bailed-out AIG and administer the financial-sector rescue package, the *New York Times* quipped that the firm was so entwined with the public sector that it could more accurately be called Government Sachs.

Rather than a conspiracy, Phillip Swagel (a Treasury official at the time and now an academic) pointed to economic, legal, and political reasons for Paulson's actions. Swagel argued that, unlike in the case of Bear Stearns, Lehman and the markets had been given fair warning that the government was not going to provide a safety net. "It was almost as if Lehman management was in a game of chicken and determined not to swerve," he explained. Government action, particularly when trying to clean up the banks, was also severely constrained, he said, by a lack of legal authority. He argued, specifically, that Paulson lacked the legal power to save Lehman.

Of course, the government could have tried to change the laws, but that was not an easy answer. Swagel painted a vivid picture of the political furor that had followed the rescue of Fannie and Freddie. As a result, he said, Paulson concluded that he would only be able to bring legislation to rescue the financial system to Congress once "the crisis was at the doorstep, even though by then it could be too late to head it off." So much for the idea that the job of the executive branch is to lead rather than to avoid tough decisions.

It is clearly right that banks should not always be rescued when they fail, but it should have been clear that the government needed to act in the middle of the crisis. Some say that Paulson's timidity may have been a product of his hope to stay on as treasury secretary if John McCain won the presidential election that November. If so, this would not have been the first time that moral hazard and politics had become entwined to produce a financial crisis.

THE BIRTH OF "TOO BIG TO FAIL"

Politics and moral hazard, albeit unspoken, underpinned one of the earliest and most dramatic crises in modern capitalism: the

South Sea Bubble in Britain in 1720. Most people think of this episode of spiraling stock prices, fueled by frenzied speculation and followed by a catastrophic crash, as simply a giant Ponzi scheme. In reality, the South Sea Company was yet another example of a financial innovation that ran out of control, in this case a new sort of public-private partnership to manage the public debt. But with government involved from the start, moral hazard inevitably followed and ultimately led to a financial crisis that nearly destroyed Britain's nascent capitalism.

By the end of the seventeenth century England's public finances, like those of most other European powers, were in a mess. Lavish living by the monarch did not help—Charles II had called a "stop of exchequer" and defaulted on his debts in 1672—but the real problem was wars, which were costly affairs that were hard to finance. In 1693, to restore confidence, Parliament took over responsibility for the public finances from the Crown. The following year, Parliament gladly signed up to a deal with a Scotsman, William Paterson, for a scheme to reduce the cost of servicing these debts. Paterson and a group of investors set up the Bank of England, a private company that would later become Britain's central bank, to lend the government £1.2 million. In return, the bank charged a very profitable 8 percent rate of interest and received a monopoly on the issue of the newfangled monetary instruments known as banknotes.

Spotting a great business opportunity, another group of investors led by one John Blunt tried to muscle into the market by setting up the Sword Blade Bank (bolted on to a company they had set up to make actual sword blades), but were quickly squashed by the Bank of England through its connections to the government of the day. The party politics of this time was fluid and complex, and by 1711 Blunt's allies were now in power and granted him a monopoly by royal charter on British trade with Latin America. This monopoly was exercised through the South Sea Company. Commerce with the New World promised great riches, but, as with many of the modern dot-coms, the prospect of a financial return was highly uncertain—in this case, because Spain still controlled the South Atlantic and the peace that held between the two nations was fragile.

At first the company dabbled in slave trading with the Caribbean. This ended when hostilities with Spain were renewed. It was then that the South Sea Company returned to the idea of a public-private financial partnership. With the political winds still in its favor, the company offered to convert part of the government's expanding debt into shares in the company in exchange for an annual payment from the Treasury.

This deal was supposed to be a win-win-win. Government got to lower its debt-service payments. Debt holders avoided the risk of government default (the government paper that was circulating at the time was trading at 60–70 percent of face value because of the uncertainty about the government's ability to pay) and also got a chance to profit from the potentially lucrative trade with Latin America. The directors of the company were allowed to sell some of the stock for cash, in addition to swapping shares in the company for government debt, and thus likewise stood to make a fortune if the deal worked and the stock price rose.

Despite the backing of its allies in government, the company struggled to win the approval it needed in Parliament. Political friends of the rival Bank of England tried to undo what they saw as a lucrative stitch up for the South Sea Company, and in January 1720, Parliament forced the Treasury to run a competitive tender between the company and the Bank of England for this new business opportunity. The company only beat the rival bidder by offering a £4 million lump-sum payment to the Treasury and a

promise of a further £3.5 million in the future. These new obligations threatened the profitability of the new company, and it
needed to raise capital quickly. It had to sell its shares at a price
of at least £140 if it was to make money.

Nepotism and intrigue were part and parcel of commercial
life in Georgian Britain. The best way to build confidence in the
share issue was to demonstrate political backing for the scheme, so
the company sold shares to Members of Parliament at discounted
rates. This evidence of political support sent the share price soaring to £335 at the start of April 1720. A wave of profit taking soon
followed, including by the physicist Sir Isaac Newton, who made a
tidy £7,000, and the financier Thomas Guy, whose profit of nearly
£200,000 later paid for the eponymous hospital that still exists in
London today. With the share price falling back as early investors
cashed out, the company used its political connections to borrow
£1 million from the Treasury to lend to investors to finance
another share issue. The price steadied at £300 by the end of April.

To pump the market up further, the company recycled the
cash it received from share sales to provide more loans to investors
to buy yet more of its shares. As a result, the company's stock price
surged again. This strong performance raised confidence across
the market, benefiting other shares. (Royal African Company
shares were four times the value they had been at the start of the
year. Even the Bank of England's stock value rose by a third.)

Just like the dot-com bubble, the success of the company's IPO
attracted lots of others wanting to get in on the act. New ventures
sprang up offering investors the chance to back a range of
schemes, from the practical to the absurd. It is unclear whether
there ever really was a stock issue for a company whose purpose
was "carrying out an undertaking of great advantage, but nobody
to know what it is," but the rumor itself was a sign of the times.

The company feared that it would lose out as money moved

into hotter new shares and decided to crush the competition. Again thanks to political connections, Parliament was persuaded to pass what became known as the Bubble Act in June, which stopped these new share issues. (This is as if, after its flotation, Netscape had gotten the government to ban any new IPOs.)

As bubbles often do, soaring share prices led to distortions in other asset prices as people acted as if the money they had made on paper from speculating in the company was real wealth. House prices rocketed and land outside London sold for an unprecedented forty-seven times the annual rent. The character of investors started to change, too, as the fashionable London set started to jump on the bandwagon. The rush of investors lifted the share price above £1,000 by the end of June.

The bubble finally burst when the South Sea Company announced its dividend as scheduled at the end of August, giving a rude awakening to investors. The company's decision to pay a 30 percent dividend to shareholders in the current year and a guaranteed 50 percent dividend for the following ten years appears generous. Yet even a 50 percent dividend meant only a 5 percent return for the later investors who had paid ten times the face value of the shares. Faltering peace negotiations with Spain that jeopardized potential trade with Latin America also dented confidence in the company's ability to meet even these existing dividend commitments.

The share price collapsed back to £180. Everyone who had bought in after the price began to surge had lost money. One unsuccessful investor was Sir Isaac Newton, who had bought back into the market and had now lost more than he had earned when he had taken his profits in April. "I can calculate the motions of heavenly bodies, but not the madness of people," he observed afterward. With confidence in the company and the whole financial market gone and many people overextended because of credit raised on their now deflated land assets, England was hit by a credit crunch during the winter of 1720. A financial scandal was turning into an economic crisis.

The company made a desperate bid for a bailout by the very organization it had tried to supplant, the Bank of England, and was unsurprisingly rebuffed. Having failed to be rescued privately, it was forced to turn to government, although this was now controlled by its political opponents.

The final deal reflected a careful political balance, with the Treasury relinquishing its claim on some of the company's cash in exchange for liquidation of a proportion of the shares, the sale of a portion of the company's debt to the Bank of England, the forgiveness of 90 percent of the value of loans made by the company to enable investors to buy shares (138 Members of Parliament stood to benefit from this provision), and the redistribution of the remaining shares to compensate those who had bought in at the top of the market.

Why is the popular description of the South Sea Company as a Ponzi scheme wrong? The restructured government-debt obligations were real assets, as was its monopoly on trade with Latin America (albeit a risky asset). Some estimates suggest that a share price of £300–400 would not have been unreasonable. How then did the conspirators think they were going to get away with driving the share price up to two or three times that value? The answer is moral hazard.

"Their illusion was that multiplication of their shares among the propertied public would give that public such an interest in the new monopoly's survival that it would at last dominate the whole scene and put its promoters beyond the reach of any reprisal," explains John Carswell in his definitive history of the bubble. Even though the government never guaranteed the company, in a world where finance and government were so intertwined it seems that the plan was to become "too big to fail," forcing the government to ease the terms of the deal with the Treasury. The government was in no position to refuse. This was not simply the failure of a private institution: since the scheme was about converting government debt, the collapse of the company into insolvency would have been equivalent to a public default, and the credit crisis would only have worsened.

Investors were gambling on politics, too. Seeing so many politicians putting their money in, perhaps unaware that a lot of this was financed by bribes from the company, they presumed that this was a safe bet. This strategy worked for shareholders who bought in early. Even the investors who bought at the peak had their losses reduced by the bailout. The directors of the company were in some ways unlucky that the political pendulum swung against them at a crucial time, which meant that they were not allowed to profit from the inevitable bailout.

The rescue was a masterful display of British pragmatism. By saving the company and protecting shareholders, the government prevented a systemic collapse in the emerging financial sector. Despite public and parliamentary calls for violent retribution, most of the perpetrators simply had their property confiscated to compensate the victims of the scheme. As to the company's management, John Blunt was treated leniently for testifying against his colleagues. The other ringleader, Robert Knight, had already fled the country. Since not all the directors of the company had been in on the scam, they were treated on a case-by-case basis, depending largely on their political connections. The government officials who had colluded with the company were given the stiffest sentences: the chancellor of the exchequer, John Aislabie, was imprisoned in the Tower of London.

The British government's willingness to bail out the South Sea

Company may have owed a lot to the fact that politicians were up to their elbows in the conspiracy, yet it was also the right thing to do. It took America nearly two centuries to learn the lesson that massive intervention to stop a systemic failure of the financial system is better than letting the crisis run its course. Ironically, this first systemic bailout was led not by the government but by the private sector itself, in the form of legendary banker J.P. Morgan.

WHEN BAILOUTS WERE PRIVATE

A chill breeze flows through the study in what was the Madison Avenue home of the banker J.P. Morgan and is now a museum showcasing his collection of fine art. Maybe it is just a draft created by the draw from the enormous fireplace, but some say it is the ghost of the titan of banking who so dominated Wall Street in the early twentieth century that he was known as "Jupiter." Here he sat on the evening of November 2, 1907, playing solitaire while across the hall in his library, where he had locked them in, the bankers of Wall Street thrashed out a deal to save the financial system. No government officials were in attendance; this was a private-sector bailout.

The financial innovation that was exposed in the crash of 1907 was the banking trust. At the time, America's banks were severely restricted in what they could do, due to tough federal and state rules. The result was a sedate, rather inefficient banking system that offered poor returns to savers. Banking trusts grew up outside these rules, enjoying lighter regulation, such as lower reserve requirements, and by 1907 they had started to move into riskier investments, such as speculating in shares. Depositors flocked to these new institutions, attracted by the better savings rates, although lighter regulation meant that there was a greater risk that a banking trust could collapse.

The banking trusts illustrate one of the main dilemmas for regulators that contributed to the crisis of 2008: strict regulation that squeezes bank profits creates incentives to find ways around the rules that offer better returns to investors and depositors and better returns to shareholders. The modern equivalent of the banking trusts of a hundred years ago was the "shadow banking" system. This included investment banks like Lehman, but also private-equity and hedge funds. They did not finance their lending by taking money from depositors—avoiding the requirements of federal regulation to keep large sums of capital to insure against losses and runs; instead they used bonds and securitized assets to raise and lend money. The trusts were the shadow banking system of their day.

Crashes are often triggered by smaller events that of themselves do not pose a risk to the whole financial system yet start a domino effect that does. The crisis of 2008 started with the collapse of the American Home Mortgage company on August 6, 2007, following big losses on its subprime-mortgage lending. This was followed on August 9 by a decision by French bank BNP Paribas to suspend three investment funds that were exposed to the subprime market. This triggered a widespread freeze in global credit markets that was to prove the undoing of the financial system.

A century before, the trigger for the crash of 1907 was a decline in the share price of the United Copper Company (UCC). The U.S. economy was already wobbling in 1907. After growing at more than 7 percent for the previous ten years, the San Francisco earthquake of 1906 had dented confidence, and the New York Stock Exchange was in a bearish mood, though not a wild panic. UCC was the central pillar of a highly leveraged financial edifice constructed by a German immigrant named Augustus Heinze, who worked with American speculator Charles W. Morse. The slide in UCC's share price had hit the value of Heinze's collateral against his mountain of debt. With his creditors getting jittery, he needed to prop up the share value of UCC to save himself.

Heinze's plan was to corner the market in UCC shares in order to stop short selling and drive the price back up. Though initially successful, the scheme failed when he ran out of money to finance share purchases and the price began to fall back. Panicked investors dumped UCC stock and Heinze's business empire collapsed, owing $1 million to the Mercantile National Bank. This in turn triggered a run on other New York banks. However, the banks operated a system of mutual support called the "clearinghouse system," of which the Mercantile National was a member. So the clearinghouse system acted to stop the run. Yet the panic did not stop. Instead it shifted over to the banking trusts, which were outside the clearinghouse system and had no agreed mechanism to support each other. The run centered on the Knickerbocker Trust, which was known to have lent money to Heinze.

J.P. Morgan had made his name building great industrial conglomerates in the railroad and steel sectors. A gift to caricaturists with his enormous nose, he had already bailed out the federal government in 1895, when, during a previous financial panic, he had arranged a syndicate to lend the Treasury $65 million worth of gold. Twelve years later, with the markets in turmoil again, Morgan realized that the whole financial system was at risk. He began by bullying the trusts to support each other, promising to put in his own money as well (the Treasury and fellow tycoon John D. Rockefeller were later persuaded to chip in, too).

As they scrambled to save themselves, in an echo of the credit crunch in 2008, the banking trusts of 1907 started pulling cash out of the New York Stock Exchange by withdrawing loans to brokerage firms and selling shares. This caused a liquidity squeeze that threatened many of the brokers, who had borrowed heavily from the trusts to finance their trading. Again Morgan leaped to the rescue with a cash injection, this time to support the brokers. With impeccably bad timing in such a weakened market, New York City had to make an urgent $25 million bond issue or become insolvent. There was little chance of a successful auction in a market then starved of liquidity. Yet a failure would have paralyzed City Hall. Morgan again intervened to underwrite and save the bond issue.

Financial fires were springing up faster than Morgan could put them out, and the conflagration was growing in intensity. Rescue attempts were hampered throughout by the lack of transparency across the banking sector. In a precursor to the credit crisis of 2008, no one really knew the real value of each other's balance sheet, leading to sudden withdrawals of cash that increased the panic.

Over the weekend of November 2, Morgan organized the defense. After their temporary imprisonment in his library, the heads of the banking trusts agreed to continue to support each other. Next, he had to rescue the brokerage firm Moore & Schley, which was $30 million in debt and about to dump its holdings of the Tennessee Coal, Iron and Railroad Company (TC&I) onto an already jittery market. To prevent a stock-price meltdown that would affect the asset value of more brokerages and trusts, TC&I needed to be acquired. The only company with the resources to do this was U.S. Steel, the near monopoly whose creation Morgan had financed in 1901. After fevered haggling over the price

U.S. Steel would pay for TC&I, on Sunday, November 3, the deal was done. Now the focus of the rescue moved from the financial to the political arena.

Even in this case of a private bailout, government had a crucial role to play. Theodore Roosevelt, a Progressive who had earlier that year denounced big corporations like U.S. Steel as "malefactors of great wealth," was still president. Would he agree to further consolidation of power in the steel sector? Morgan's staff dashed to Washington for an urgent meeting with the president on Monday morning, and, following Roosevelt's reluctant consent, the market rallied, the panic subsided, and the financial sector survived.

In the aftermath of the crisis, following a sharp recession in 1908, the U.S. economy recovered quickly. But no good deed went unpunished: the popular clamor for retribution against the finance bosses was exploited by Roosevelt's successors. Perhaps to put his former patron and predecessor in a bad light, President Taft launched an antitrust action against U.S. Steel in 1911 over the acquisition of TC&I, which Roosevelt had personally approved. Worse was to follow for Morgan, who was the center of a congressional inquiry into "money trusts." The rigors of the hearings are widely believed to have hastened his death in 1913. Flags were flown at half-mast on Wall Street to mark J.P. Morgan's passing—a fitting mark of respect for the man who had saved the financial system.

At the end of the twentieth century, bankers were again corralled in a room when they saved the hedge fund Long-Term Capital Management in order to prevent a systemic collapse. Yet this time the key was held by the government, in the form of the Federal Reserve. Morgan had so dominated Wall Street that he was able to rally the banks in 1907, but it had been too close for the comfort of Wall Street's leaders, who decided that they needed a central bank to be their "lender of last resort."

LEARNING HOW TO BE THE

"LENDER OF LAST RESORT"

The Federal Reserve System that emerged from the crisis of 1907 was put to the test for the first time in the aftermath of the Wall Street Crash of 1929. It was found wanting. In the year after the crash, the banking sector had seemed pretty stable, despite an economic slump, as savers were content to sit on their cash deposits. Nearly 1,000 banks failed during this period, but this was not so unusual in America's fragmented banking system, where it was common for 500 small banks to fail even in a good year.

The real trouble started late in 1930 when the Bank of United States in New York was found to be insolvent as a result of fraud and imprudence. When a run on this bank started on December 10, the New York Fed took on the J.P. Morgan role, trying to strong-arm the banks to finance a private rescue plan. However, this time the bankers were reluctant, fearing that bailing out a recalcitrant, insolvent bank would create moral hazard (although as the Bank of United States was Jewish-led, anti-Semitism was probably a motivation as well). The New York Fed could not force a deal and was left to close the bank down.

No cataclysm followed the collapse of the Bank of United States, but a steady drain on bank reserves began as nervous depositors withdrew money. The cumulative effect of these withdrawals was a 10 percent slump in bank credit by the middle of 1931, when a run on the banks that started in Chicago spread across the country. Treasury Secretary Andrew Mellon failed to grasp the seriousness of the problem and did nothing. The Federal Reserve was as powerless as it was clueless. Bank after bank failed, and the financial system went into meltdown as the lender of last resort failed to lend. It had tied itself in knots over the problem of moral hazard that had plagued the debate about the role of a central bank since one was first mooted by Treasury Secretary Alexander Hamilton in the early days of the republic.

A central bank was to be one of three financial pillars of the new nation, along with a mint and an excise tax. Hamilton believed that the new bank would sort out the monetary chaos in the country and build up its ability to borrow. There were more than fifty different currencies in circulation, and banknotes were issued by private corporations. (In the early days of the nation, a fraudster by the name of Andrew Dexter had taken advantage of this freedom by buying controlling stakes in small, remote banks and printing huge quantities of money. When his chicanery was discovered in 1809, his Farmers Exchange Bank in Rhode Island was found to have issued more than $600,000 of banknotes backed by just $86.48 worth of gold and silver. America had suffered its first bank failure.)

Hamilton's plan had enthusiastic backing from northern merchants but was greeted with suspicion by southern farmers. After much wrangling, the First Bank of the United States (no relation to the later Bank of United States that collapsed in 1930) was established in 1791, after a deal was struck to move the federal capital from Philadelphia to the Potomac. The First Bank operated successfully for twenty years as banker to the federal government, but it was always resented as an infringement of basic liberties by the advocates of states' rights. When the bank's charter expired in 1811, it was not renewed.

The 1812 war with Britain unleashed inflation in the United

States that hampered the financing of the military effort. To restore monetary order, Congress in 1816 agreed to charter a Second Bank of the United States, a copy of the First Bank, again for twenty years. Southern Democrats, in particular, remained hostile to the idea, and when one of their number, Andrew Jackson, took control of the White House in 1833, he quickly removed all federal deposits from the bank, which slid into bankruptcy eight years later.

With the demise of the Second Bank, monetary policy became a state responsibility. Throughout this period, starting with the Panic of 1837, American banking was prone to runs and failures. This was caused in part by weaknesses in the banks themselves but worsened by the absence of a central bank to provide temporary liquidity to stop otherwise solvent banks being brought down by a run. Bank regulation was also entirely a state matter. Another banking panic in 1863 finally drove Congress to act. Legislators toyed with the idea of creating a central bank but opted instead to impose tight regulations on the banks, supported by the clearinghouse system of mutual aid to protect against volatility, which bent but did not break in 1907.

For most of the nineteenth century, American banks were something of a backwater in the global financial system dominated by London. Of course, British depositors, for all their imperial phlegm, were just as prone to the jitters as their American cousins. Yet over time, the Bank of England had taken up a backstopping role in the system to provide cash to other banks during occasional panics. This role of "lender of last resort" was described by one of the early editors of *The Economist* magazine, Walter Bagehot, in his classic 1873 exposition on banking, *Lombard Street*.

Bagehot was writing in response to the collapse of what he called "the most trusted private firm in England," the London bank of Overend, Gurney and Company, which had speculated recklessly in railway stocks and failed to hold sufficient cash reserves. When the bank's investments went wrong, it suffered huge losses; those investments, Bagehot says, "were made in a manner so reckless and so foolish, that one would think a child who had lent money in the City of London would have lent it better."

In 1866 the bank's headquarters in Lombard Street in the City of London became the focus of a bank run (which, until the run on Northern Rock in 2007, had been the last run on a British bank). The Bank of England had refused to bail out Overend, Gurney and Company and then had been hesitant in lending to other banks that were sucked in by a spreading panic that caused several to fail. Bagehot argued that in a liquidity crisis such as this, the lender of last resort should be unequivocal in its support for the banks. In 1907, J.P. Morgan played this role, following to the letter Bagehot's dictum to "lend freely, boldly, and so that the public may feel you mean to go on."

It is ironic that the Federal Reserve System that was signed into law by President Woodrow Wilson in 1913 and promoted as an antidote to the money trust of northern financiers was substantially shaped by Wall Street bankers. Congress had established a National Monetary Commission, chaired by Senator Nelson Aldrich, in 1908 to look at setting up a central bank. By 1912 the concept seemed to be going nowhere. To revive the idea, a senior partner at the J.P. Morgan bank, Henry Davison, convened a small meeting of the banking elite in secret on Jekyll Island, off the coast of Georgia. The one politician at the meeting was Senator Aldrich, who became the frontman for their plan for a National Reserve Association.

The Federal Reserve System that finally emerged from Congress in 1913 was the product of the usual political horse trading.

The new system gave banks access to an emergency facility, known as the Discount Window, which would be their lender of last resort in times of crisis. But, contrary to the plan devised on Jekyll Island, it was constructed as a system of twelve regional Federal Reserve Banks, overseen by a board of presidential appointees, rather than as a single entity. The problem with this compromise structure was, of course, that the Federal Reserve struggled to provide real leadership when it was put to the test before and after the Wall Street Crash of 1929.

In the immediate crisis after the crash, the Fed did take the bold move to provide reserve funds to the banking system, forestalling a banking crisis. But as the economic crisis set in, it failed to grasp or respond to the growing banking crisis, in part because of Walter Bagehot. To address the problem of moral hazard created by a lender of last resort, Bagehot had made clear that the central bank was there to solve temporary problems of liquidity, not problems of insolvency. It was this argument that the bankers used when declining to save the Bank of United States at the end of 1930, and it was this argument that the Fed clung to as banks fell like dominoes.

But what did this distinction mean in a situation where consumer and asset prices were spiraling downward, withdrawals by panicked depositors were causing bank reserves to shrink, and capital-starved banks were being forced to contract lending or sell off assets cheaply? The distinction between illiquidity and insolvency had lost all meaning. In 1931, as in September 2008, this was no time to be worrying about moral hazard.

In the face of inaction by the Fed, in the fall of 1931 President Herbert Hoover made a last desperate attempt to save the smaller banks by getting the Wall Street giants to put up $500 million for a support fund. But the age of J.P. Morgan had passed (due in part to the creation of the Fed). The bankers' response was less than halfhearted.

The consequences of this failure were disastrous. The closure of 4,000 banks caused credit to shrink by 20 percent across the whole country by 1932. From September 1931 to June 1932, industrial production fell 25 percent and investment 50 percent; unemployment soared past 20 percent. Fear of moral hazard had put the Great in the Great Depression.

One of the major reforms to the financial system that came as part of President Franklin D. Roosevelt's "New Deal" that followed his victory in the 1932 presidential election was deposit insurance. By offering federal government protection of depositors' money, it was hoped that banks would be protected from runs. Deposit insurance appears to be an elegant solution to the moral hazard problem: it is not a promise to save a failing bank, so recklessness by its managers will still be punished, yet it should stop panic-driven bank runs that threaten otherwise healthy banks. Roosevelt was never completely comfortable with the idea. In his opinion, creating the Federal Deposit Insurance Corporation could encourage imprudence, creating moral hazard in other ways. The savings and loan crisis of the 1980s proved that he was right to worry.

FROM BORING TO RECKLESS

Mortgage banking was once an easy, if dull, life run according to the 3:6:3 formula: pay savers 3 percent on deposits, lend to homebuyers at 6 percent, play golf at 3 in the afternoon. This was the basic business model of savings and loan (S&L) institutions, otherwise known as "thrifts." The risk in this model was that the banker had to lend for a period of many years, while depositors could withdraw their money at any time. This did not present a problem as long as interest rates remained stable, which they did, until the 1970s.

As inflation rose during the 1970s and interest rates soared, the business model of more than 3,000 S&Ls broke down. Unable to increase interest rates to borrowers and hemorrhaging deposits because their savings rates were capped by a piece of unreformed 1933 legislation called Regulation Q, the S&Ls were hit by a double whammy and started losing money.

The trouble caused by Regulation Q should have been foreseen, if any of the legislators had read up on their Roman history. Nearly 2,000 years previously, the Roman emperor Tiberius had imposed a ceiling on interest rates, which had led to a credit crunch. Like modern banks, the Roman finance houses thought they had sensibly diversified their risks across different ventures throughout the empire. This diversification proved illusory when apparently uncorrelated events started to move in sync. In A.D. 33 a fall in the prices of ivory and ostrich feathers that hit companies trading with Ethiopia, a strike in Phoenicia, and an uprising in what is now Belgium caused two banks in Rome to fail, triggering a run on the banking system. Lacking liquidity because of the cap on interest rates, banks were forced to dump assets in a falling market, accelerating a downward spiral. Tiberius was at his retreat on the Mediterranean island of Capri, so the people of Rome had to wait in dread for four days as messengers hurried to get his decision and bring it back to the city. We do not know whether Tiberius worried about moral hazard. Crowds thronged the Forum to hear his proclamation that the imperial treasury would lend 100,000,000 sesterces to bail out the banks. The financial system was saved.

In an effort to shore up depositors' confidence in the S&Ls before a crisis hit, the administration of Jimmy Carter expanded the protection of savings under the Federal Deposit Insurance scheme, so that the full value of deposits up to $100,000 was safe. This was followed, in 1982, by a deregulation of the S&L sector by the Ronald Reagan administration, which aimed to give the thrifts the freedom to work themselves back to financial health.

The S&Ls were now free not only to do simple things such as increase their savings rates to attract depositors but also to issue credit cards and invest in real estate. To help them to do this, they were further given the reassurance of the right to access funds when needed, at the Federal Reserve's Discount Window. The S&Ls abandoned their simple, boring business model and rushed to take on much more risk, supported by the new guarantees of government support if things went wrong.

Free and emboldened, many of the S&Ls charged into the real-estate market. In search of high returns, they also dabbled in risky investments such as "junk bonds," an expanding part of the securities market, the riskiness of which the S&Ls were poorly equipped to judge. When, in the mid-1980s, house prices slumped and, soon after, the junk bond market collapsed, their already fragile balance sheets were wrecked. In some cases things were made even worse by fraud.

From 1986 to 1989 nearly 300 S&Ls failed and had to throw themselves on the mercy of the federal government. Faced with a costly mess of assets to clear up, much of it real estate such as half-built shopping malls and offices, in 1989 the government created the Resolution Trust Corporation (RTC) to minimize the cost to the taxpayer by squeezing what value it could from the portfolio. After quickly selling off the prime assets, the RTC offloaded most of the portfolio in billion-dollar chunks to what Alan

Greenspan described as "vulture funds and speculators whose reputations could have used a face-lift." The RTC had little choice because these were the only people who were willing to buy at this point.

The final bill for the taxpayer to sort out the S&L debacle was $125 billion. Political recriminations followed. The shadow of the S&L crisis even stretched over the 2008 presidential election when it was recalled that the Republican candidate, Senator John McCain, had been an enthusiastic supporter of the early 1980s deregulation. Worse, he had been implicated in an attempt in 1987 to lean on regulators to allow the Lincoln Savings and Loan, owned by a business associate of McCain's, to take on even more risky investment. McCain was rebuked by the Senate Ethics Committee for "poor judgment" in 1991.

Poor management played a part in the extinction of half of America's S&Ls between 1986 and 1996. Yet government has to take a large part of the blame. After deregulation, savers faced moral hazard because they did not have to ask how the S&Ls were able to finance such generous savings rates, since they knew that their deposits were guaranteed. And maybe S&L managers saw the deregulation as permission to take risks with an implicit assumption that the government would bail them out.

At least in the S&L crisis the government acted swiftly to resolve the problem and prevent a threat to the rest of the financial system. The RTC mechanism also worked well as a way of maximizing the return to taxpayers from a mountain of assets of uncertain value. Vulture funds may have profited initially, but by making a market for future sell-offs, the RTC achieved as good an outcome as possible within the time allowed. The RTC model has been used widely since then as a way to clear up banking crises around the world.

Did the S&L bailout create an expectation of future bailouts and therefore more moral hazard? Almost certainly. Was there a better alternative? Almost certainly not. As long as there is a government that can step in when there is the threat of systemic collapse, there will be moral hazard.

THE CASE FOR BAILING OUT

Monday, September 15, 2008, should be celebrated as "Free Market Day," said Congressman Barney Frank, Democratic chairman of the powerful House Banking Committee, soon afterward. That was because on that day, Lehman Brothers was allowed to slide into bankruptcy and the free market to work. Letting wealthy bankers fail has obvious populist appeal. But that does not excuse Paulson's reckless decision on Lehman Brothers, or his lack of any consistency or strategy in dealing with moral hazard before and after Lehman's collapse. As for his claim that the administration was not allowed by law to rescue Lehman, according to Richard Posner, one of America's leading judges, "although the Federal Reserve claims that it lacked the legal authority to save Lehman by lending it the money it would have needed to stave off bankruptcy, the claim is unpersuasive."

America had learned the lesson once before, in the 1930s: that, whatever the followers of free-market dogma say, moral hazard is no excuse for letting the financial system collapse. Our prosperity depends on the ability to lend, borrow, and save. Like it or not, government has a duty to protect the public from a meltdown of the financial system. Moral hazard does matter, but it should be addressed before the system is on the brink of a collapse, not in the middle of a crisis.

If we are to avoid a repeat of this crisis in the future, we need to find ways to deter financial institutions from taking on excessive risks that could bring down the whole system and be ready, if they do fail, to have ways of clearing up the mess that protect the interests of taxpayers, not bankers. Managers and shareholders should not be relieved of responsibility for the risks that their banks have taken, and the financial system as a whole needs to bear the cost of the de facto insurance policy it receives from the government.

Meeting these challenges is not simple. Sadly, the government had clearly failed to think through these issues before the crisis of 2008, which is why the response was so haphazard and inadequate. Figuring out answers to these questions is an urgent priority so that we will be ready the next time.

3

MONEY MAKES THE WORLD GO WRONG

A brief history of global imbalances

A week before he abandoned Lehman Brothers to its fate, Hank Paulson had thrown $200 billion at the mortgage finance companies Fannie Mae and Freddie Mac to save them from collapse. Why did Paulson treat Fannie and Freddie so differently from Lehman Brothers? Maybe it was the sheer size of these companies. But could it also have been the fact that one of the biggest investors in Fannie's and Freddie's securities was the People's Republic of China?

Paulson knew that the American economy was floating on a sea of credit from China and the rest of the world. His nightmare was that the collapse of Fannie and Freddie would scare away these investors. If that happened, America would find it much harder to borrow the enormous sums needed to finance its public debt and the value of the dollar could collapse, turning a financial crisis into an economic meltdown.

America's dependence on foreign credit highlights a worrying fault line in the world economy. There's nothing wrong per se with borrowing from China, or anywhere else, but the imbalance in global capital flows as capital poured into the American economy from the rest of the world fueled the boom and is now one of the toughest problems to deal with after the bust.

For centuries, financial bubbles and crashes have been caused or amplified by foreign money rushing in or out of a market. This is often thought of as a problem exclusively for poor economies, such as Mexico, or woefully mismanaged ones, such as Iceland in recent years. Yet unstable flows of money around the world, in and then out of countries, contributed to America's first Great Depression in the 1870s, the near-catastrophic crash of 1907, and the Great Depression of the 1930s. This is a problem again today for America, as well as for the rest of the world.

These crises have typically provoked a nationalistic reaction, with calls by politicians in the country affected to reduce the ability of capital to flow in and out and sometimes policies that try to put such barriers in place. This is a hugely costly strategy, as money from abroad can be an important source of finance for economic growth that no country can easily do without. The challenge, instead, which the latest crisis has made more pressing than ever, is to rewrite the rules of international finance in a way that keeps investment flowing around the world in search of the best returns, while protecting against volatility that can cause financial crises.

This has been attempted before, with the gold standard and then the Bretton Woods system after World War II, but these approaches were flawed in ways that at times made bubbles and crashes worse. We can do better in the twenty-first century. However, this will require our leaders to rise above their traditional nationalistic agendas—especially the leaders of America. One of the lessons of history is that the international rules of finance tend to be designed by the dominant economic power of the day and that, too often, the leaders of those powers have not delivered the rules that in the long run are best for the global economy, or their own.

AMERICA IN HOCK TO THE WORLD

America was the world's financier for most of the twentieth century. World Wars I and II could not have been won by the Allies without U.S. financial as well as military power. The dollar was the linchpin of the post-1945 economic system, and American capital flowed around the world to fund investments by governments and private companies. Poor countries took out massive loans, denominated in dollars, to fund their development.

Since the start of the twenty-first century, this flow of capital has reversed. From the late 1990s until the credit crunch of 2007, funds from China, South Korea, and other developing countries were used by U.S. consumers, corporations, and banks to build up a mountain of debt, which was spent inflating the bubble in the housing and stock markets. As America spent more and more, it saved less and less. Higher spending sucked in imports, and the trade deficit widened. But capital kept flowing into the American economy to finance this spending binge. Without an apparently infinite supply of credit from countries such as China, interest rates in America would have risen, slowing economic growth but, perhaps, preventing such a catastrophic crisis.

In the past, developing countries borrowed from overseas to fund investments to grow their economies—savings from rich countries funded the development of poor countries. Those capital flows were always a mixed blessing for developing economies—international capital is easily spooked, and developing economies, most notably in Latin America, suffered regular crises when the funding from America and other industrialized countries was suddenly cut off, as happened with surprising frequency. When that occurred, the value of their currencies would usually plummet, making their dollar-denominated debts even more burdensome.

Sometimes the fault lay with the government of the developing country that had not used the money wisely and had built up debts that it could not service, leading to default, as Mexico did in the 1980s. At other times, policy decisions by the U.S. government, such as an increase in interest rates to slow the American economy or boost the value of the dollar, have led to an outflow of capital from the borrowing countries to America. Either way, the benefits of access to foreign capital have always come at the cost of exposure to volatility. Developing countries used to believe that this risk was a price worth paying—until the 1990s.

In the 1980s, a number of countries, many of them in Southeast Asia, were growing so quickly that the term "developing country," which had acquired a connotation of stagnation, no longer seemed appropriate. A new term, "emerging markets," stuck as these dynamic export-led economies became of growing interest to international investors rather than to aid agencies. However, in 1997 the emerging markets were rocked by a financial crisis as investors from the rich world who had poured in capital for years suddenly decided to pull it out again. As the value of their currencies fell, they sought help from the International Monetary Fund (IMF), which was supposed to be the lender of last resort in the global financial system that could provide them with the precious dollars they needed. But the IMF did little to help. From Thailand to Argentina, currencies crashed and economies were thrown into painful recessions. Policymakers in emerging markets concluded that international capital is just too hot to handle and switched to financing their development increasingly from domestic capital.

As a result, developing countries have cut their dependence on foreign capital by building up their currency reserves, hoarding dollars to protect against a repeat of the events of 1997. This buffer would serve two functions: its mere existence was intended to discourage speculative attacks on these nations' currencies, and, if worse came to worst and there was an attack, they could spend these reserves to support their exchange rate.

To build up these reserves, they adopted aggressive policies to promote exports and restrict imports. In the past, developing countries had tried to prop up the value of their currencies to keep down the cost of servicing their dollar-denominated debts. Now many countries, including China, keep the value of their currency artificially low (in some cases, formally fixing their exchange rate with the dollar) to make exports competitive and imports expensive, using the money earned from trade, rather than foreign borrowing, to finance their development. This paid off spectacularly with massive trade surpluses, which they squirreled away as massive dollar reserves.

America's huge trade deficits were a direct consequence of these policies. Textbook macroeconomics predicted that as America spent more overseas and dollars flowed into nations running trade surpluses, such as China, so the wealth of those nations would increase. Theory suggested that that should have led to an increase in their prices and wages and a strengthening of their currencies against the dollar that would have made America's exports more competitive, leading to a reduction in the U.S. trade deficit that would rebalance the system. But the countries running trade surpluses insulated themselves from this effect by holding on to the dollars and lending the money back to America rather than spending it.

U.S. treasury secretaries did little to stop this, except to make futile requests to the Chinese government to revalue their currency. China declined to do so. In 2007, *Newsweek* columnist Robert Samuelson described China's policy as "mercantilist." This idea, which was once the orthodoxy in economic thought, treats trade as a game of winners and losers, where countries that export more are the most successful. Adam Smith's classic exposition of free-market economics, *The Wealth of Nations*, was largely a rebuttal of mercantilist ideas. Smith explained how trade expands the total amount of goods, benefiting exporters and importers alike. Countries that pursue mercantilist policies to build up their foreign currency reserves are hurting themselves as well as others.

China's economic strategy has certainly had perverse consequences. While American consumers enjoyed easy credit and cheap goods, Chinese consumers, including 800 million people still living in poverty, have had to go without, at least relative to the spending boom they might have enjoyed if their government had pursued less mercantilist policies. By 2005, America was saving a mere 14 percent of its national income, most of this by the corporate sector, as personal saving turned negative. China, by contrast, was saving an astonishing 59 percent. The result was what Fed chairman Ben Bernanke described as a "glut" of savings from China and other reserve-accumulating countries. This glut propped up the value of the dollar, financed cheap credit in America, and helped to inflate the asset bubble to unprecedented levels.

This process could not go on forever. In the end, the mountain of debt that America had built up collapsed under its own weight in the financial crisis of September 2008. A rapid deleveraging by private-sector borrowers in America and other rich countries began. Perversely, the value of the dollar rose in response to the market panic—even though the U.S. economy was teetering on the brink, investors still thought that the dollar was the safest port in the global financial storm.

China's booming economy of the past couple of decades had caused some commentators to argue that it had "decoupled" from America. After the crisis, some, briefly, speculated that this was the moment the emerging markets would finally come into their own and maybe even ditch the dollar as the currency of choice for their reserves. But the creditor countries have found that they are as much at risk from this crisis as the borrowers.

Through their "sovereign wealth funds," many of the surplus countries had bought stakes in some of the world's leading banks, a move that was intended to make money by helping these institutions survive the credit crunch. The model was supposed to be the investment made in 1990 by Saudi prince Al-Waleed in Citibank, which at the time seemed in danger of going bust. The success of this investment, which made Al-Waleed one of the richest men in the world, was not repeated this time. As the financial crisis got worse, the value of the shares bought by the sovereign funds fell. As a result, when an increasingly desperate Lehman Brothers sought a sovereign savior in the spring and summer of 2008 (South Korea was the likeliest candidate), it found no takers (at least, at a price it was willing to accept). Although these bank stakes were small compared with the vast amounts of American debt held by countries such as China, their falling value highlighted the vulnerability of these emerging countries to problems in the American economy, and to the risk that a sharp fall in the dollar would dramatically reduce the real value of their dollar reserves. China (and other developing countries) needed America to keep consuming as much as America needed China to keep lending, it turned out, because China's growth depends on continued exports to the United States.

Rather than decoupling, it's clear that the world's economies have become more entwined than ever, due to the globalization of business and finance. At the center of this web of finance is the dollar, the world's reserve currency. Yet now that the United States is no longer the world's financial hegemon but the first among equals, the American economy has been destabilized by global money flows in a way that was once the preserve of the developing world.

This is just the latest chapter in the turbulent history of flows of money between countries. If this chapter is to have a happy ending, we need to learn the lessons from past attempts to build a global financial architecture, starting with the first modern global exchange-rate system, the gold standard.

GOLD FEVER

As the New York Stock Exchange began to melt down on Thursday, October 24, 1929, one not entirely detached observer in the visitors' gallery was the British politician Winston Churchill. Not only was he watching his speculative investments evaporate, Churchill was also witness to the consequences of his decision four years previously, as chancellor of the exchequer, to take the pound back onto the international monetary system known as the gold standard.

Returning to the gold standard, membership of which Britain had suspended because of the financial pressures of World War I, had been disastrous. To fix the value of the pound to a specific quantity of gold, Britain had to prove it was creditworthy by reducing the massive debts it had built up during World War I. But the postwar economy was crying out for more spending to get industry going again. As policymakers tried to navigate a course between these two contradictory objectives, the British economy had staggered from crisis to crisis. Now, following an earlier interest-rate cut by the U.S. Federal Reserve to try to ease pressure on the beleaguered pound, the already overheated U.S. economy had boiled over.

As Churchill was never much of a fan of economics—he complained that his civil servants at the Treasury "all talk

Persian"—returning to the gold standard was a decision that he had resisted. But, in the end, even Churchill had given in to the prevailing economic orthodoxy that gold was the only reliable basis of "sound money."

Money does not grow on trees. Nor is there any intrinsic reason why, for centuries, money was made out of metal dug from the ground. Civilizations had used seashells, pieces of wood, and even paper as money, but the rarity and durability of metals such as gold and silver gave them the advantage that they would hold their value and could pass from hand to hand without wearing out. (Sweden experimented with copper money in the seventeenth century, but the metal was worth only one-hundredth of the value of silver, so the coins were large and unwieldy—the largest weighing some forty-three pounds.)

As populations grew and societies became wealthier, this rarity value of gold and silver posed problems because there was only a limited amount of metal in circulation, which meant less money per person to go around. The only way to produce more money was to mine it, but this was a slow process. As a result, when Europe finally started to recover from the Dark Ages, states ran up against a shortage of precious metals, particularly silver.

One obvious solution to the money shortage was to steal it from someone else. The Crusades of the Middle Ages were not just about eternal salvation; Arab silver also offered economic salvation. Alternatively, governments faced with shortages of precious metals could steal from the public by reducing the amount of silver or gold in coins, bulking them out with cheaper alternatives. The public was not fooled by government attempts to "debase" the coinage: prices were quick to rise to reflect the lower value of the money in circulation, which we now call inflation.

Reducing the amount of metal in coins was a game that the public could play too. By shaving off a bit from a gold coin here and a silver coin there and passing it off to someone else while keeping the fragments of bullion was literally an easy way to make money. Governments did not like to be robbed from and, worried about the consequences of a loss of confidence in their coinage, developed such techniques as milling the edge of coins to frustrate the "coin clippers," who faced gruesome punishments such as blinding, amputation, or the death penalty if caught.

From the sixteenth century onward, the expanding population of Europe found an abundance of silver in the New World. Spain, which controlled this resource, benefited the most. But the supply of goods could not increase as quickly as the supply of silver and, with a surplus of silver, prices rose, first in Spain and then across Europe. Spain's ready supply of money also led to reckless spending by the Crown, which was followed by reckless borrowing, and then by default that ruined many of Spain's Italian creditors in the seventeenth century.

Spain's mishandling of its monetary windfall and the ruination of Italian finance proved to be a boon to the rising maritime powers of England and Holland. Financial innovation was starting to take off in these countries, with accidents such as Tulipmania along the way, and where they really excelled was in management of the public finances by creating national banks.

In 1694 the English Parliament chartered the Bank of England, then a private institution, to lend money to the government and started to build the country's reputation for monetary prudence. The gold standard emerged from the next step in Britain's progress to global financial dominance. This came in 1717 through a unilateral decision by the man in charge of the nation's coinage, the great physicist (and unsuccessful speculator in the South Sea Company) Sir Isaac Newton. Newton had grown concerned at the erosion of the value of silver through inflation and the persistent problem of coin clipping. To put the pound on a sounder footing, he therefore switched to using a gold-based system of money.

Britain began to build a reputation for sound finance that drew money to London. From the middle of the eighteenth century, British government debt became the most trusted and internationally traded financial asset in the world. Foreign investors were happy to pay high prices for British bonds, secure in the knowledge that Britain would honor its debts, denominated in gold-backed pounds that would not lose their value. Even at times of financial stress such as war, the British government enjoyed unequaled access to foreign credit. The City of London flourished as the financial center of the world.

The Bank of England kept the value of the pound firmly locked to gold and jealously guarded its stores of the precious metal, raising interest rates when necessary to keep capital in London and maintain reserves. Other countries had to dance to the tune of the pound. As the nineteenth century wore on, as they aspired to the same credibility for their currencies, they too joined the gold club.

Under this gold standard of international finance, countries that ran a trade deficit, importing more than they exported, would have to transfer gold to countries that ran a trade surplus. This decline in the money stock—that is, holdings of gold—would push down prices in the deficit country and therefore make its exports more competitive relative to the surplus country, whose prices would rise as money came in. All of this was based on the value of currencies being irrevocably fixed against an amount of gold, so that the holders of dollars or pounds or francs had the right to demand that their banknotes be converted into gold.

The system was believed to be self-stabilizing, with movements of gold leading to movements in prices that would restore balance and harmony to global finance. That was the theory, at least.

But by the end of the nineteenth century, America was running a huge, persistent trade surplus because of its agricultural abundance and its emerging manufacturing industry. Gold flowed steadily westward across the Atlantic, much the same way as dollars have flowed eastward to China in the past decade.

London was still the center of the gold standard. But Britain's gold reserves were dwindling and its power was waning. The only way to keep gold in London was to increase interest rates to attract gold deposits from other countries, which in turn caused the British economy to slow.

The growing global imbalance in gold contributed directly to the American financial crisis of 1907. With gold reserves falling, the Bank of England had already pushed up interest rates that year. When this move failed to stem the outflow of bullion from the country, the bank followed up with new regulations to make it harder for American companies to raise money in London that would be invested on the gold-rich other side of the Atlantic. This interruption in the flow of gold to New York caused the liquidity crunch that underlay the Wall Street panic of 1907, although American restrictions on interstate banking must also take some of the blame. (Money would flow out of New York to the western agricultural states at harvest time, then only trickle back as farmers made purchases, rather than being recycled by the banking system. This resulted in seasonal shortages of money in New York.)

Britain's grip on the global monetary system may have been weakening, but its financial credibility had still been a major asset during World War I, allowing the Allies to borrow freely from the United States to fund their military effort. By the war's end, however, Britain was deeply in hock to America and could no longer pretend to be the "conductor of the global financial orchestra."

All the European powers had suspended their membership

in the gold standard during the war years, and none of them had the economic strength to return when peace came in 1918. The dollar alone had remained on gold. Nonetheless, European financiers thought there was no choice but to return to the gold standard in due course. Britain had been in a similar situation after the Napoleonic Wars a hundred years before and had clawed its way back onto a gold monetary base through austerity measures to cut spending and drive down prices. Now, again, returning to "sound money" became the overriding policy goal for the Bank of England and the British government.

A young Cambridge economist by the name of John Maynard Keynes came to prominence in this period as an eloquent opponent of the return to the gold standard. He argued that restoring the pound to its prewar exchange rate with gold would be too demanding for the fragile British economy. According to his biographer, Robert Skidelsky, Keynes thought that the financiers' obsession with gold was so irrational that it must be psychological: "'a furtive Freudian cloak' for repressed infantile anality."

Such was the force of Keynes's (economic) arguments that Winston Churchill, then the chancellor of the exchequer, hesitated when the bankers told him in 1925 that the time was right to restore the convertibility of pounds into gold. Keynes was invited to challenge the Bank of England in a mealtime discussion at the chancellor's residence at Number 11 Downing Street. Whether it was the occasion or the generous amounts of drink that surely flowed at Churchill's table, Keynes's persuasive powers deserted him that evening and the decision was made to return to the gold standard, in what Churchill would later call his "biggest blunder."

The roaring American economy of the 1920s continued to suck in gold from Europe, where fear of social unrest meant policymakers were reluctant to impose the austerity measures needed to stem this flow. In 1927, in a rare act of international solidarity, the Federal Reserve agreed to cut U.S. interest rates to try to slow the inflow of gold into America. This cheaper credit pushed the already booming U.S. economy into speculative overdrive. The rate cut was quickly reversed, but that move could not stop the stock market frenzy that finally ended on Black Tuesday in 1929.

As the global economy slid into recession after the crash, Britain was still clinging to the golden anchor of sound money, but not for long. More surprisingly, the dollar quickly followed suit.

THE CROSS OF GOLD

"Follow, follow, follow, follow, follow the yellow brick road," the Munchkins sing to Dorothy in *The Wizard of Oz*. For some, this is not fantastical nonsense but one of the allegorical references to monetary policy in L. Frank Baum's classic children's story. The novel was published in 1900, just as America was emerging from a generation-long debate about whether to build its currency on gold alone or on a more flexible mixture of gold and silver. The road is yellow, like gold; Oz is the shorthand for ounce, the standard unit of measurement for gold; Dorothy puts on silver slippers (changed to ruby slippers in the 1939 film version); and so on. Whether or not this was Baum's intention (his family says not), the monetary interpretation highlights the controversy about Congress's decision in 1875 to move the dollar onto gold.

The financial muscle of Victorian Britain was the envy of the world. If rising powers such as the United States and Germany were to rival Britain's ability to borrow and lend, it was argued, they too needed sound currencies based on gold. Germany had secured its position as a European military superpower when it humiliated the French in the Franco-Prussian War of 1870–71. With big ambitions, the new German state used this victory to start the process of moving to a gold-backed currency, dumping its supplies of silver on France.

The United States started to move in the same direction. America was in a monetary mess after the Civil War. The federal government had printed "greenback" dollars, which were widely accepted across the country but could not be exchanged for gold. In order to end the chaos and rebuild financial credibility, Congress passed the Resumption Act in 1875 to shift to a gold-backed currency.

This switch to gold as the monetary base of the world's main trading powers meant that demand for gold rose, while demand for the no-longer-needed silver fell, pushing down its price. This weakened the currencies of countries such as France that still used money based on both metals. Moreover, with a pretty much fixed amount of gold to go around, the world's supply of money shrank as silver was demonetized in America and Germany. Combined with the rising global population and growing industrial production, this meant that a greater quantity of goods was being traded using a smaller amount of money. So the price of those goods had to fall.

The result of the rush to gold was a long period of deflation. Even Britain, which was using gold already, was affected: over the six years after 1873 the British price level fell 18 percent. As prices and wages fell, the cost of servicing debts rose and consumers and businesses cut back, leading to a collapse in production and trade. The long downswing in the economic cycle in the 1870s, which in America became known as the first Great Depression, was caused not by the stock market crash and bank failures of 1873 but by the contraction in the supply of money due to the new, self-imposed "golden fetters."

The gold standard provided sound money but at a huge economic cost. To be off the gold standard diminished a country's ability to borrow. To be on the gold standard imposed a rigid monetary straitjacket that did not expand to accommodate rising global production.

The deflationary bias in the gold standard was recognized at the time. Alfred Marshall, the "father of modern economics," had warned about the danger of linking prices to the "hazards of mining" since the ability to increase the world's stock of money depended on how fast gold could be extracted from the ground. Some statesmen recognized the problem. In 1878 France, which was still using silver as well as gold, and America, which was on the way to a fully gold-backed currency but experiencing economic and political difficulties with that decision, convened an international monetary conference of the "Great Powers" in Paris to try to agree on a switch from the gold standard to one based on a mixture of gold and silver. But Britain had no intention of surrendering its hard-won financial hegemony based on gold. Nor was Germany going to give up its newfound advantage over the French. The Paris conference ended without an agreement.

In America, popular unrest about the abandonment of silver simmered throughout the rest of the nineteenth century, centered on small farmers in the South, who suffered most from falling prices and the economic contraction. In the 1890s the campaign to restore silver's place as part of the monetary base alongside gold (known as bimetallism) was led by William Jennings Bryan. He ran as the Democratic candidate in the 1896 presidential election, famously warning that "you shall not crucify mankind on a cross of gold."

Bryan lost the election to sound-money Republican William

McKinley, in part because the bimetallic argument was losing its economic rationale. In the 1890s massive gold deposits had been discovered in South Africa, and a new chemical process had been developed to extract the precious metal from the ore more efficiently. The hazards of mining were now working in the right direction, pumping much-needed money into the expanding world economy. The American economy grew at a thumping 7 percent a year for the decade that followed Bryan's defeat. Even he had ditched the bimetallic cause by the time he unsuccessfully challenged for the presidency again in 1900. (According to the monetary reading of *The Wizard of Oz,* Bryan is the Cowardly Lion because of his abandonment of silver.)

America followed the yellow brick road for more than thirty years after the publication of *The Wizard of Oz,* until imbalances in the global economy made this impossible to sustain during the Great Depression of the 1930s. Ironically, it was Britain that broke the gold standard that it had created.

It had been hard enough to maintain the pound's value against gold when the economy was growing in the 1920s. By 1931, as the British economy slumped into recession, the task proved impossible. The British government was facing social and political unrest as unemployment soared and the clamor for government action grew. But sound money dictated further cuts in public expenditure that would have hit the poor and required further wage cuts.

In the end, there was no alternative but to exchange the restrictions of sound money for the flexibility to set economic policies that would revive the economy. In September 1931, a naval mutiny over pay cuts was the final straw, causing a run on the pound that could not be stopped. On September 20 the government removed the pound from the gold standard. Its value plunged.

Britain's unilateral act threatened monetary anarchy. Countries that remained on the gold standard, among them France and America, suffered from a loss of competitiveness, since British goods were now significantly cheaper. "England has played us for a bunch of suckers," protested Henry Wallace in 1933, shortly before he became President Roosevelt's secretary of agriculture. He was echoing a popular view that Britain had cheated by dropping off gold. The anti-gold populism of William Jennings Bryan also enjoyed a comeback. The creator of right-wing shock-jock talk radio, Father Charles Coughlin, preached against the bankers in 1932, who he claimed had "shackled the lives of men and of nations with the ponderous links of their golden chain."

America still enjoyed the lion's share of the world's gold supply, but, fearing a loss of trade and willing to try anything to get the U.S. economy going again, Roosevelt made the radical decision early in 1933 to take America off the gold standard.

By then the British economy was just starting to recover. Yet the fall in the value of the dollar after it left the gold standard wiped out all the benefits to Britain's competitiveness of its earlier devaluation of the pound. The American decision to abandon gold threatened to throw Britain back into the economic hole it was just starting to climb out of.

The Great Powers met in London in 1933 to try to reach a settlement that would stabilize the global economic system. The roles were reversed from the 1878 Paris conference—this time Britain was the disadvantaged supplicant and America the intransigent hegemon—but the result was the same: nothing.

Abandoning gold ultimately did help Britain and America to recover from the Depression of the 1930s. In contrast, France, which saw gold as a defense against German aggression, clung to the gold standard until 1936 and suffered accordingly. Its economy was the slowest to come out of recession.

The gold standard collapsed under the tension between the two rival functions of an international monetary system: stability in the value of money, to provide certainty in transactions that cross the borders of countries with different currencies; and flexibility in the value of money, allowing countries to adjust to changes in economic fundamentals. This tension is always there but becomes particularly hard to manage during financial crises, as became all too painfully clear in 2008.

SIZE DOES MATTER

On September 28, 2006, the 200,000 citizens of Reykjavik, Iceland, stood and stared at the night sky as all the lights in the city went out. The eco-conscious Icelanders had organized the event to connect with their simpler past. Two years later, almost to the day, Iceland's booming financial sector was wiped out by the crisis in global capital markets, and the lights of the economy went out for real. They are expected to stay off for a long time. Iceland is a small country, but it was the biggest loser from the financial crisis.

This sorry saga began in 2003 when Iceland privatized two large banks, Landsbanki and Kaupthing Bank. The banks went on a huge borrowing spree, raising billions from overseas lenders and then sucking in savings from other countries, by offering tempting interest rates, to shore up their capital base. Iceland has a population of only 300,000 people—about the same as the American city of Macon, Georgia—so its stock of savings is pretty small. By the time the crisis hit, an equivalent number of Britons alone, tempted by attractive interest rates, had opened savings accounts at Icelandic banks, many of them through Landsbanki's Internet-based savings account, "Icesave."

With foreign savings providing the capital they needed to back their borrowing in the international capital markets, by 2007 the Icelandic banks had built up loan portfolios worth more than eight times the national income of the country (the massive finance sector of the City of London had managed to lend only 450 percent of Britain's national income). Flush with liquidity, the economy boomed. Icelanders borrowed freely to spend, spend, spend. On average, each Icelandic household took on debts amounting to 213 percent of their disposable income; even credit-junkie American households managed only 140 percent.

When global credit markets froze in 2007, Iceland's banks began to wobble as they struggled to refinance their debts. When the financial markets collapsed in September 2008, so did Iceland's banks and its currency, the kronur. The government nationalized the banks, making the Icelandic people responsible for the banks' debts. These included $8.2 billion owed to foreign Internet depositors—an amount almost half the size of Iceland's entire economy.

Worse, during the good times, when the kronur was rising, many Icelanders had borrowed in foreign currencies to get lower interest rates. Now, as the value of the currency plummeted, the cost of servicing these debts soared. To stem the torrent of foreign currency leaving the country, the Icelandic government introduced restrictions on international capital movements, which meant that foreign savers, already worried about the safety of their deposits, could not get at their money.

The rescue of the financial sector took a brief, farcical turn when the Icelandic government announced that it would not guarantee the deposits of the foreign customers of its banks. This breached the deal it had made with the European Union that had allowed its banks to take money from foreigners in the first place.

The British government responded by threatening to use antiter-rorism legislation passed in the aftermath of the September 11, 2001, attacks in America to seize Icelandic assets—not at all what the legislation was intended for. In the end, thanks to a $2 billion credit from the International Monetary Fund and loans from some of its neighbors (the British government lent Iceland the money to compensate British savers), the situation stabilized.

One Icelandic newspaper, *Morgunbladid,* claimed that relative to the country's size, the debt to Icesave depositors alone is bigger than the reparations demanded of Germany after World War I. The IMF's best guess was that clearing up the mess in the banks would cost 80 percent of Iceland's national income. "If I met a banker, I'd kick his ass so hard, my shoes would be stuck inside," said one participant at an antigovernment rally in Reykjavik. Really, you could not blame her if she did.

Icelanders have had to learn to be tough over the centuries. One of their national dishes is made from a shark that has to be left to rot for up to three months to drive toxins out of the flesh (you have to wonder how anyone discovered this trick). No longer poisonous, *hákarl* still reeks of ammonia and is unpalatable to most foreigners. In other words, it is not unlike the Icelandic financial sector today. Unable to borrow from abroad and facing many years of austerity to clean up the mess, it is going to be a long, dark night for the Icelandic economy.

Iceland was vulnerable because its economy was small and its banks had been particularly reckless. But some wondered how different it was from other smallish, open economies with big financial sectors that had borrowed a lot of cash from overseas. For a while, a joke made the rounds: "What's the difference between Iceland and Ireland? One letter and about three months."

In the end, Ireland survived because it was a member of the

European Monetary Union (EMU), whose single currency, the euro, was highly unlikely to collapse like the Icelandic kronur. This reassured foreign investors in Ireland that they would get their money back. But it also came at a price. As the currency of the biggest neighboring economy, the British pound, fell against the euro, the Irish economy lost competitiveness, worsening the country's economic crisis.

This was the same dilemma that smaller countries on the gold standard, such as Poland, faced in the 1930s. Lacking the resources and the financial credibility of the Great Powers, they could not easily abandon the straitjacket of gold. Fearing that their currencies would plummet in value and capital would fly out of the country, the Poles chose adherence to the gold standard as the lesser of two evils, despite the economic cost of lost competitiveness as other countries, including Germany, Britain, and America, devalued.

In 2008 a westward glance across to the complete meltdown of the Icelandic economy quickly reassured the Irish that they had made the right choice by joining the euro. Iceland seemed to share this conclusion and quickly began negotiations to join the eurozone. Willem Buiter, an economist at the London School of Economics, wondered if even the British pound had become vulnerable, musing whether London could become "Reykjavik-on-Thames." The best protection would be for Britain to follow Ireland's lead and adopt the euro, he argued.

We will never know how close the British economy came to Icelandic-style collapse in 2008. Maybe past glories gave the pound some additional credibility in the markets. Maybe the British economy is still big enough to withstand even such a major storm in the global financial markets. In the end, as in the 1930s, Britain was able to manage an organized retreat; the pound fell enough to boost competitiveness without a rout and complete collapse of the currency. Whether it could do so again and whether British adoption of the euro is simply a matter of time are still hotly debated.

The strength and weakness of the euro, like the gold standard, is its rigidity. By signing an irrevocable treaty to adopt the euro, a small country such as Ireland was able to convince investors that there was no risk of an Icelandic-style currency collapse, so their money was safe. Doing so, however, meant that Ireland could not use devaluation to boost its recovery and had to live with interest rates set by the European Central Bank to meet the needs of the eurozone as a whole, rather than what the former "Celtic tiger" economy needed.

The success of the euro in the aftermath of the crisis of 2008 does not mean that the tension between rigidity and flexibility in international monetary rules has been resolved. The euro worked because it covers a group of relatively similar economies with the will and the resources to help each other out in times of need (though exactly how willing richer eurozone countries are, or should be, to transfer resources to poorer ones again became a source of political controversy in the aftermath of the crisis). Some economists think the European Union is too diverse to share a single currency, complaining that it is not an "optimal currency zone," but, then again, neither are the fifty states that share the U.S. dollar.

A single currency could not work for the global economy, where countries are at different stages of economic development. To create one, not that there is any appetite to do so, would be simply to repeat the mistakes of the gold standard. The need for flexibility as well as stability in the global monetary system was recognized in the new rules for the global economy written by the

Great Powers at the end of World War II. Yet this system also failed. To figure out what we need to do now, we need to understand why.

THE GOLDEN DOLLAR

With victory inevitable, in July 1944 experts from the triumphant Allied Powers gathered for a financial conference at the Mount Washington Hotel in the New Hampshire resort of Bretton Woods. Their goal was to map out a new monetary world order. (Mount Washington was not the most elegant resort, but, unlike swankier venues, it did admit Jews, which meant that U.S. Treasury Secretary Henry Morgenthau was allowed to attend.) No one proposed a hasty return to the gold standard. Exchange rates needed to be anchored to something, they agreed, but not to an arbitrary supply of metal.

In the end it was decided that the de facto reserve currency of the new system would be the dollar, reflecting America's position as the world's biggest creditor and biggest exporter. All other countries would fix the value of their currencies to the dollar, and the dollar would be the only currency convertible into gold. However, the role of lender of last resort to the global financial system would not rest with the United States. Instead there would be a global central bank, the International Monetary Fund, which would provide loans to support embattled currencies and, hopefully, prevent the monetary anarchy of the 1930s, when countries competed with one another by devaluing their currencies.

When the Bretton Woods system came into force at the end of the war, the pound, the sick man of the gold standard, was devalued by about 17 percent from its prewar exchange rate, to $4.03.

By then, Britain was much more indebted than it had been in the 1920s. It was understood that it was going to take time for Britain and other European countries to rebuild their finances and thus to maintain their exchange-rate pegs under the new system. So, rather than rushing into full convertibility with the dollar, the European currencies were protected from sudden outflows of cash through restrictions, known as capital controls, that limited investors' ability to move money across borders. As a result, for many years after the war, everyone, even British tourists, had to get permission to take anything but a small sum of money overseas. The United States also supported the efforts to rebuild the European economies with massive aid through the Marshall Plan, which provided a flow of precious dollars into Britain and Europe. Even with this support, the pound could not maintain its value against the dollar and, in 1949, had to be repriced at $2.80.

It was only in the 1960s that most countries in Europe were able to defend their new exchange rates without the protection of capital controls. As these controls were lifted, capital was able to flow more freely between countries. Yet with the cost of war debts still holding its economy back, Britain remained economically weak and struggled to cling to the agreed exchange rate with the dollar. As in the 1920s, it was politically impossible to impose the austerity measures that would have been necessary to strengthen the pound. As a result, there were frequent currency crises as Britain ran perilously short of dollars. In 1967 the government accepted the inevitable and allowed the pound's peg against the dollar to slide again, to $2.40. This prompted one of the most barefaced lies in the history of economic policy, when British prime minister Harold Wilson told the nation that "it does not mean, of course, that the pound here in Britain, in your pocket or purse or in your bank, has been devalued." Yes it did.

The pound was just one satellite circling around the dollar, so its erratic orbit was no threat to the Bretton Woods system. The problems really began when the dollar itself started to wobble. Whereas the weakness of the gold standard was that the amount of gold available was too rigid, the Bretton Woods system had the opposite problem—the growing tendency of the U.S. government to supply too much money. From the late 1960s, the United States was printing more and more money to fund President Lyndon Johnson's ambitious social programs at home and the ever more costly war in Vietnam. Where there had once been a dollar shortage in the world, there was now a "dollar glut." The United States was supposed to be the anchor of the global financial system, but its reserves were dwindling and the dollar's value in gold was untenable.

The link between money and gold was finally severed on August 15, 1971, when President Richard Nixon announced that the dollar would no longer represent a guarantee of a fixed amount of gold. After centuries of using gold and silver as the basis of money, the world had now entered the era of "fiat money" (the term is derived from the Latin for "let it be"), in which the value of money was based solely on the willingness of governments to print it. Nixon was simply giving in to the inevitable. As America produced more and more greenbacks, confidence in the dollar was slipping and investors were switching their money into gold because America was spending more than it earned.

After Nixon's decision to renounce dollar convertibility into gold in 1971, the leaders of the G-10 industrialized nations feared that abandoning the golden anchor of the international monetary system would lead to economically damaging volatility. This time the Great Powers met in Washington, at the Smithsonian Institution, and made a deal to revalue their currencies against the dollar. This "Smithsonian Agreement" did nothing, however, to deal with America's overspending. The system finally broke down in 1973, when the dollar was devalued again and the values of other currencies were allowed to float free.

The Bretton Woods system could, perhaps, have been saved by restricting the flow of money across borders by reimposing capital controls. But for policymakers, allowing capital to flow freely around the world was by then more important than protecting the system of fixed exchange rates. Countries were therefore able to borrow on international capital markets, usually in dollars, although they had to live with the risk that the cost of servicing their debts could rise if the value of their currencies fell against the dollar. Living with exchange-rate volatility, it was believed, was a price worth paying for access to international capital. That faith was shaken in the 1990s.

THE DANGEROUS DOLLAR

In 1997 the prime minister of Malaysia, Mahathir Mohamad, branded the American financier George Soros a "moron" and a "criminal" for what he believed was the role that Soros's Quantum hedge fund had played in the collapse of Malaysia's currency and its subsequent economic implosion. By spreading panic in global financial markets, argued Dr. Mahathir, speculators such as Soros had precipitated crisis after crisis across Asia.

The emerging-markets financial crisis of 1997 and 1998 challenged the prevailing conventional wisdom that the quickest route to prosperity lay through developing countries opening up their economies to international capital. As the dollars flooded out during the panic even faster than they had flowed in and the value of their currencies crashed, governments in the developing world, including Malaysia's, concluded that the price of relying so heavily on loans from abroad was just too high. They felt betrayed by the International Monetary Fund, the supposed global lender of last resort, which had failed to ride to their rescue. In the immediate aftermath, however, the main focus of their rage was speculators, such as Soros, who they believed had worsened the crisis to turn a quick profit.

In search of the best returns, capital has long been attracted to emerging markets. As early as 1822, British bankers raised £20 million in bonds for newly independent countries in Latin America. They soon learned that the promise of higher returns brings with it higher risk. In what has become a familiar cycle, by 1829 the Latin American debtors could not pay, and most of their bonds were in default.

Lending to emerging markets in the nineteenth century was not for the fainthearted. Indeed, at one point a group of London bondholders asked the British foreign secretary, Lord Palmerston, to bless a vigilante mission to send privately funded warships to punish Mexico for reneging on its debts. Palmerston declined and the plan was shelved. The French emperor Louis Napoléon had no such qualms in 1863 when Mexico's republican president Benito Juárez announced that his government would stop interest payments on its foreign debts. The French army was dispatched to sort out the upstart Mexicans. This did not, however, prove to be a particularly successful incursion, as America intervened on the Mexican side. France's puppet emperor of Mexico, the Austrian archduke Maximilian, was deposed in 1867 and the Juárez government restored (the unfortunate Maximilian was executed, an act captured in a famous painting by Edouard Manet).

France's failure to prevent default through force did not deter the British. By 1872 more than half the world's sovereign borrowing was taking place in the finance houses of London. British financiers had extended large loans to Egypt, which though formally part of the Ottoman Empire was largely under the autonomous rule of a khedive (viceroy), the modernizing Ismail the Magnificent. The Egyptian economy, which had thrived as a result of soaring cotton prices during the U.S. Civil War, started to run into trouble in the 1870s as the U.S. economy recovered and the price of cotton fell. Egypt's export earnings plummeted and the country could no longer service its borrowings. In desperation, Ismail was forced to sell Egypt's share in the Suez Canal to the British in 1875, but even the £1 million that this raised could not rescue the public finances. British and French administrators moved in (the British representative was a member of the Barings banking dynasty), and Ismail was replaced by his son Tawfiq. When a popular revolt broke out in 1882, the British occupied the country and took direct control of the finances. The bondholders had been protected.

In 1902, Britain, allied with Germany, intervened in Venezuela after the country's new dictator, Cipriano Castro, declared a default on more than £4 million worth of bonds. British, German, and, later, Italian, battleships blockaded the mouth of the Orinoco River, sinking Venezuelan ships and bombarding forts. The U.S. ambassador to Caracas had already warned President Castro: "You owe money, and sooner or later you will have to pay." The crisis ended with a U.S.-mediated deal in which Venezuela met its debt obligations.

Perhaps inspired by Britain's successful gunboat financial diplomacy, and determined to be the troubleshooter in its own backyard, America intervened in the Dominican Republic in 1905, seizing control of the country's customs revenues to meet its obligations to foreign creditors. U.S. troops enforced this deal when the Dominican Republic threatened another default in 1911. The following year they did the same in Nicaragua.

Political and diplomatic considerations, as much as finance, played a part in the decisions of the Great Powers to send in the troops. Military action did not follow every default. In 1890, for example, the distinguished London finance house of Barings suffered a default on a large loan to Argentina. According to the governor of the Bank of England, Barings had no one but itself to blame; it was the product, he said, of "haphazard management, certain to bring any firm to grief." No battleships were sent to save Barings, although the Bank of England did lead a private bailout to save Barings from going under, but only with help from the state banks of France and Russia. Ironically, it was emerging markets that finally did in Barings in 1995, when a rogue trader in its Singapore office, Nick Leeson, racked up losses of more than $1 billion through unauthorized trades in futures markets.

Gunboats were no longer tools of international finance by the 1970s. Yet despite the risks, the siren call of the Latin American markets once again lured in foreign investors. The dollars that had flowed out of America, particularly to the oil-producing states of the Middle East, were looking for a place where they could be invested to earn good returns. For the governments of Latin America, cheap credit from abroad was an attractive way to finance strategies to boost their economic performance. With willing lenders and eager borrowers, capital began to flow again into emerging markets. Mexico quickly became the biggest borrower, building up its stock of foreign debt from $75 billion in 1975 to over $300 billion by 1982.

Mexico's debt burden might have been sustainable if credit had stayed cheap, but weakening global demand for oil had pushed down prices, reducing the amount of petrodollars available for lending to emerging markets. In the industrialized nations, cracking down on inflation had also become a priority. Interest rates rose everywhere, led by Federal Reserve chairman

Paul Volcker in the United States, which drew money away from the emerging markets. Mexico and other countries that had borrowed heavily found it harder to attract capital, and they had to pay more for the loans that they could arrange.

Unable to service its debts, the Mexican government declared a default in 1982. Its economy was thrown into a sharp recession as the flow of foreign capital dried up completely and the government was forced to adopt austerity policies to repair its finances. Real income per head in Mexico in 1986 was 10 percent lower than it had been in 1981.

The fates of Mexico and the banks that had lent to it were now locked together. Mexico had borrowed too much when money was cheap and could not repay those debts when interest rates rose. But by defaulting on its debts, Mexico had become an even worse credit risk, which made it harder to refinance or earn its way out of its problems, which made it even less likely that the international bankers would get their money back. In 1989, U.S. Treasury Secretary Nicholas Brady cut a deal that allowed the international banks to convert their Mexican debt into bonds, with a reduction in the loan principal and U.S. government backing for the remaining balance. These "Brady Bonds" helped the banks by swapping a large, decaying debt on their balance sheet for a smaller but safer bond that they could sell on to someone else. Mexico got a reduction in its debt burden and a chance to rebuild its reputation in the global financial markets.

In the aftermath of the 1980s debt crisis, Mexico took the economic medicine prescribed by Washington. Prudent fiscal and monetary policy became the norm over the next decade in much of Latin America as governments sought to restore their credibility with the global capital markets in order to start borrowing again. Argentina went for the tightest economic straitjacket by introducing a "currency board" that locked the value of the country's currency, the peso, to the dollar in the same way that the value of the dollar had once been fixed against gold. Running a trade deficit would therefore lead to an outflow of dollars from Argentina and a direct reduction in the amount of money in the Argentine economy, which would force down prices and wages. Such a rigid regime obviously had costs, but to policymakers this was a price worth paying to be able to borrow cheaply from overseas and prevent future financial crises. That was the hope anyway.

Having narrowly survived yet another Mexican crisis in 1995–96, this hope was shattered in the crisis of 1997, which not only hit the newly virtuous governments of Latin America but also swept away the "tiger economies" of Southeast Asia that had long been seen as paragons of monetary virtue.

The trouble started in Thailand, which had benefited from massive inflows of foreign capital as the economy boomed. Awash with money in the 1990s, Thailand went on a spending spree. Skyscrapers shot up in Bangkok and so did real-estate prices. Unlike Mexico twenty years previously, this borrowing was being done by private companies, not the government. Thailand's public finances were in good order, so the borrowing was not a problem, argued the optimists.

As an asset price bubble inflated, so wages increased, making Thailand less competitive in the global economy and less able to earn the foreign currency it needed to pay back its debts. Cracks started to appear when this loss in competitiveness began to hit the profits of the companies and banks that had borrowed so heavily. International investors began to lose confidence in Thailand and cut back lending. As the flow of capital into the country slowed, the Thai currency, the baht, started to weaken.

The Thai government faced a dilemma. It could hike interest rates to get foreign capital flowing back into the country. But that would worsen the economic slowdown that was already under way. Alternatively, it could devalue the baht. But that would make companies' international debts, denominated in dollars, more expensive. As the government dithered, hedge funds started to bet that the baht would fall, which they did by borrowing baht to buy dollars. By selling these baht, they were eating away at Thailand's reserves of dollars, adding to the pressure on the baht to fall. The cost of paying off these loans would be much lower if the baht devalued, allowing the hedge funds to make a substantial profit.

It was exactly this tactic that George Soros had used in 1992, when he became the best known of the hedge fund managers who bet that the British pound would be forced out of the European Exchange Rate Mechanism, the precursor to the euro. With the British economy already in recession, Soros anticipated that Prime Minister John Major's government would not have the will to defend its exchange rate by pushing interest rates ever higher. Soros bet and won big on that occasion. But so did the British economy. Freed from having to keep up interest rates to defend the pound, and with British exports more competitive in world markets following its devaluation, the economy recovered quickly.

Perhaps with the British experience in mind, the Thai government finally opted for devaluation. But confidence in its economy was not restored. The hedge funds reasoned that having fallen once, the baht could fall again. Money began to pour out of the country once more, as foreign and domestic investors feared that the value of assets held in Thailand would be damaged by the depreciation of the currency.

The trouble did not end there. Capital started to flow out of countries across Southeast Asia as investors worried that others in the region might be as vulnerable as Thailand. Indonesia, Malaysia, and South Korea were each forced to devalue. Only Hong Kong, a bastion of financial rectitude with a longstanding

currency board arrangement, successfully fought off a speculative attack. The crisis then moved on from Asia, as panic spread
to all the emerging markets. Russia, which had lately started to
receive large sums of international capital, defaulted on its debts
(a shocking decision that triggered a global financial crisis that
ended with the rescue in New York of the hedge fund Long-Term
Capital Management).

Argentina eventually abandoned its currency board. The real,
which had been fixed at $1.00, lost more than two-thirds of its value,
until one real bought only $0.30. Deep recessions took place
throughout the emerging markets. Shell-shocked governments, like
Dr. Mahathir's, blamed the excesses of the speculative hedge funds.
Soros hit back, calling Mahathir a "menace to his own country."

The two men buried the hatchet in 2006 at a meeting in Kuala
Lumpur when Mahathir accepted that Soros had not been part of
the speculation after all. By then, the governments of the crisis-hit
countries had decided to blame the international capital markets
much more broadly and to take steps to ensure that they did not
fall victim to them again. Malaysia, for one, introduced capital
controls—for example, banning foreigners from repatriating
money invested in the country for a period of one year—to make
the flow of international funds in and out of the country less
volatile.

Reckless lending may have played a part, but the governments
of the emerging markets were not entirely blameless. In Thailand,
a crony capitalism based on murky political connections between
government and business had led to widespread misuse of the
money borrowed from abroad and moral hazard for lenders, who
thought that the Thai government was guaranteeing loans
extended to private companies.

More fundamentally, had the existence of an international
lender of last resort, the International Monetary Fund, and the

precedent of the Mexican debt deal in 1989 created an international moral hazard problem? Had investors undertaken risky
lending to emerging markets in the belief that they would be
bailed out by the IMF if things went wrong? Maybe, but it was
clear that the IMF had failed in its duties as the international
lender of last resort, providing too little money too late to prevent meltdown.

A 2008 paper reviewing evidence from financial crises over the
past 800 years, by former IMF chief economist Kenneth Rogoff
and Carmen Reinhart, concluded that the emerging-market crisis
of the late 1990s was typical of a "rite of passage through history for
nearly all countries as they pass through the emerging market state
of development." While Latin American countries have been
prone to repeated crises since their independence, in fact all countries have experienced difficulties adapting when opening up their
economies to foreign capital.

The problem for the emerging markets in the 1990s was not
just that they had borrowed too much in the good years and were
not ready for the lean years. They also suffered from the fact that
their international borrowing was denominated in dollars, the
value of which was determined by policy decisions in Washington
that were guided primarily by America's domestic needs. Borrowing from abroad in this way meant exposing these nations'
economies to massive exchange-rate risk. The failure of the IMF
to help when things went wrong meant that if these governments
took on this currency risk, they were doing so without an effective
safety net. It is no surprise that the lesson many governments in
developing countries took from the crisis of the late 1990s was
that relying on international capital was more trouble than it was
worth, and that if they were going to take part in the international
capital markets, it would be as investors and lenders rather than
as borrowers.

AFTER THE DOLLAR?

The Bretton Woods system tried to compensate for the failings of the gold standard by creating the IMF as a lender of last resort for the global economy but failed to equip it with the money and the authority to play that role.

The IMF's performance has often been awful. A more fundamental problem was making the dollar the global reserve currency, which made the world's monetary policy largely a slave to the domestic needs of the American economy.

This has become a problem as much for America as for the rest of the world. The constant flow of credit to the United States from abroad inflated the bubble that burst so spectacularly in the autumn of 2008. But America's creditors now face the problem that their reserves are held in dollars. If America owes you $1 billion, America has a problem; if America owes you $2 trillion, you have a problem.

One man who foresaw the problem of using the dollar as the global reserve currency was Keynes. He had predicted the chaos that resulted from Britain's return to the gold standard in 1925. In 1944 at the Bretton Woods Conference, he was the undoubted star yet found himself once again playing the role of Cassandra, the Trojan princess in Homer's *Iliad* who is cursed with an ability to foresee the future but never to be believed. Keynes argued that the new monetary order should not be based on a reserve currency controlled by a single country. Instead, he proposed a global reserve currency called "bancor." But Keynes's negotiating position was weakened by Britain's feeble finances. His proposals were defeated by the United States' lead negotiator, Harry Dexter White (who was later said to be a Soviet agent), who argued that the dollar, the currency of the world's leading creditor nation, should be at the center of the global financial system.

Keynes was proved right once before, when the gold standard collapsed. The current crisis has proved him right again, about the vulnerability of using the dollar as the global reserve currency. Are policymakers ready to follow his advice this time? Or will they choose, once again, to try to muddle through with superficial reforms to the dollar standard that will be no better at handling the problems that caused the crisis of 2008? Or, even worse, will they retreat into the economic nationalism that did so much to prolong and deepen the Great Depression?

4

THE DANGERS OF DENIAL

How inaction leads to depression

I f we don't act swiftly and boldly, most experts now believe that we could lose millions of jobs next year." The champagne had barely lost its fizz after Barack Obama's victory in the U.S. elections of November 2008 when the president-elect used his first radio address to the nation to prepare the American public for an unprecedented spending binge.

Within weeks of his inauguration the following January, President Obama had persuaded Congress to vote through an economic stimulus package that piled $800 billion onto the public debt, in addition to the $700 billion it had agreed to a few months earlier to bail out the banks. The Federal Reserve had already cut interest rates to near zero and started printing money. Other countries followed suit with massive government spending and easy monetary policy, seemingly regardless of the burden these steps would load on future generations who would have to pay the bill.

The lesson from history that guided Obama and others was that some crashes are so big that they can tip the economy into a long, deep recession that could even turn into a depression—unless government acts decisively to stop that from happening.

"For every day we wait or point our fingers or drag our feet, more Americans will lose their jobs," President Obama warned. "More families will lose their savings. More dreams will be deferred and denied. And our nation will sink deeper into a crisis that, at some point, we may not be able to reverse."

The nightmare scenario haunting political leaders in 2008 was the Great Depression of the 1930s that had followed the Wall Street Crash of 1929. An initial slowdown in 1930 got sharply worse in 1931 and 1932. By 1933, America's gross national product was nearly a third less than it had been in 1929, and a quarter of the American workforce was unemployed. Although recovery began in 1933, progress was slow and industrial production did not return to precrash levels until 1937. Moreover, the human cost scarred a generation. This was captured in literature by the rage of John Steinbeck's *The Grapes of Wrath* and in Studs Terkel's seminal collection of oral histories, *Hard Times.*

After studying the consequences of hundreds of past financial crises in many countries, Kenneth Rogoff and Carmen Reinhart concluded that, on average, asset market collapses are deep and prolonged, with house prices falling 35 percent over a period of six years and equity prices by 55 percent over three and a half years after a crisis begins. Crises also, on average, have nasty consequences for the economy as a whole. Unemployment typically increases by 7 percentage points, over a period lasting four years, while output falls 9 percent on average over two years. Government debt explodes, rising by an average of 86 percent.

Yet this picture disguises huge variations in the impact of financial crises. Some bubbles do serious harm, while others have negligible effect on economic growth or employment. For example, Tulipmania and the South Sea Bubble really only count as hiccups in the advance of Dutch and British capitalism in the seventeenth and eighteenth centuries, respectively. More recently, the U.S. economy has survived the savings and loan crisis, the 1987 stock market crash, and the implosion of Long-Term Capital Management with little effect on growth or jobs. The dot-com crash of 2000 resulted in a long decline in stock prices, but again the knock-on effects in the real economy were small. Similarly, the 1907 crash was followed by a recession, but the fallout in the banking system was contained and the U.S. economy recovered quickly.

Although the crash of 1873 looks at first glance to be an exception, the long economic depression that followed it had little to do with the crash itself and more to do with the deflationary consequences of the gold standard. The Great Depression of the 1930s was different, which makes it perhaps the most important case study for politicians in what not to do after a financial crisis, although Japan's experience in the 1990s provides a similarly cautionary tale. The lesson from both these events is that there are times when government should act quickly to try to revive the economy by spending heavily.

THE ROAD TO HOOVERVILLE

The response of policymakers to the snowballing crisis that began in the autumn of 1929 could not have been more different from President Obama's urgency. Rather than worrying about the jobs, savings, and dreams of the American people, the treasury secretary at the time, superrich financier Andrew Mellon, prescribed tough medicine: "liquidate labor, liquidate stocks, liquidate the farmers, liquidate real estate . . . . purge the rottenness out of the system." This was the economic orthodoxy of the time: if prices had risen too high, be they for assets, wages, or consumer goods, market forces meant they had to fall. The economic theory of the time said that there was no alternative route to recovery. As a result, Mellon and his president, Herbert Hoover, lacked the intellectual tools needed to tackle the problem.

In many ways, Hoover (who had always been skeptical about the booming stock market and suspicious of Mellon's free-market fundamentalism) should have been the right man to be in charge in the crisis. He had made his mark organizing the successful aid effort to the starving population of Europe after World War I, as head of the American Relief Administration. After the war he went into politics and served with distinction as commerce secretary to President Coolidge, winning plaudits for leading the relief effort after serious flooding in Mississippi in 1927.

Yet Hoover had few levers to pull when the contraction of the U.S. economy, which had started before the Wall Street crash in 1929, accelerated in 1930. His administration had moved quickly to cut taxes, but the federal government was only a tiny part of the economy in those days, and this fiscal stimulus was to prove just a drop in the bucket.

Whatever small benefit the economy received from Hoover's tax cut was reversed when he signed the Smoot-Hawley Tariff Act in 1930, which sharply raised trade barriers and triggered protectionist retaliation around the world. This legislation had started out as a sop to American farmers and was working its way through Congress before the Wall Street crash. As the economy slowed, congressmen from industrial constituencies widened the scope of the bill to protect the interests of their voters. The final draft contained nearly 900 tariff increases. More than a thousand economists, including Irving Fisher, the godfather of monetary economics who had blithely predicted that share prices had reached a stable plateau just before the crash, unsuccessfully petitioned Hoover to veto the legislation. Economists still argue over whether the collapse in world trade from 1929 on was caused by protectionism or just a symptom of the global recession, but Smoot-Hawley cannot have helped.

As poverty and hunger spread, Hoover belatedly turned to the voluntary sector to manage the relief effort, under the leadership of such organizations as the Rockefeller Foundation and the American Red Cross. (In the same way, he tried to rescue the banking system in 1931 by urging the larger banks to rescue their weaker brethren, rather than through direct government intervention.) But this was a general economic crisis, not a localized humanitarian emergency, and charity was not sufficient to the task.

Hoover lost the 1932 presidential election to the Democrat Franklin Delano Roosevelt, winning only six states. The popular version of history is that the ineffectual Hoover was replaced by the dynamic FDR, who launched the big-government New Deal that saved the day. But the reality was more complicated.

By the end of 1931, as the economy plummeted, even Hoover had conceded that the time for voluntary solutions was past. In January 1932, having failed to persuade the bankers to save themselves, he established the Reconstruction Finance Corporation (RFC) to funnel public money into the banking system. By contrast, the Democratic platform for the 1932 election included an attack on the rising public deficit, which called for not an economic stimulus but an "immediate and drastic reduction of governmental expenditures" to restore fiscal balance.

The flagship New Deal legislation of FDR's "first hundred days" was mainly a hodgepodge of regulatory and welfare measures. By today's standards it would not qualify as a stimulus package and in dollars spent (even in real terms) did not compare with Obama's fiscal boost in early 2009.

The reboot of the banking sector in 1933, which had been

designed under Hoover, demonstrated FDR's gift for brilliant polit-ical communication. In an effort to restore confidence in the finan-cial system, the nation's banks were closed for the week after the March inauguration. Only those that the government judged to be sound would be allowed to reopen. This plan may have been drawn up under Hoover, but the execution was all FDR's. In his innovative first radio "fireside chat" with the American people, the new pres-ident reassured listeners that "my friends, it is safer to keep your money in a reopened bank than under the mattress." He explained that depositing cash back in the banks was part of the recovery pro-cess because the bank "puts your money to work to keep the wheels of industry and of agriculture turning around."

The bipartisan plan worked. Confidence returned and dollars flowed from under mattresses, from socks, from jars in the kitchen back into the banks, easing the capital crisis in the finan-cial system.

Despite this success, the economy was still in the grip of defla-tion. Falling prices meant that households and companies had become ever more indebted, even though they were not taking out new loans. The total of private and public debt in the United States as a proportion of national income hit 300 percent in 1933, a level not reached again until 2008. Prices would not rise again until the economy recovered, and without higher prices the econ-omy would not recover—unless prices could be pushed up arti-ficially by devaluing the dollar.

On April 19, 1933, FDR took the dollar off the gold standard, against all the counsel of his economic advisers, one of whom pre-dicted "the end of Western civilization." (Ironically, ahead of his inauguration, speculation about Roosevelt's intention to take the dollar off the gold standard had caused gold to flow out of the country. Hoover had pleaded with FDR to pledge his allegiance to the gold standard, to stop the speculation that was actually worsening the banking crisis.) To their surprise and everyone's delight, the president's gamble worked. Wholesale prices leaped 45 percent over the following three months, the stock market surged, and companies began borrowing and investing again. The recovery had started, producing a 40 percent increase in national income and a doubling of industrial production during FDR's first term in office.

FDR had as little interest in the technicalities of economics as did his wartime ally Winston Churchill, but whereas Churchill was bullied back onto the gold standard in 1925, FDR held out against the economists in 1933 when he took the dollar off gold. FDR's intuitive grasp of the need to restore confidence and to flush money out from under the nation's mattresses was codified in economic theory soon afterward by the man who had tried hardest to save Churchill from his error in 1925, the economist John Maynard Keynes.

The General Theory of Employment, Interest and Money, published in 1936, was Keynes's intellectual and popular masterpiece, bringing together his insights on economic management with a lucid analysis of the causes of economic stagnation and how to emerge from it. His great insight was that the self-correcting mechanisms in a market economy can, in extreme circumstances, break down.

Keynes was a believer in the importance of psychology in economics. According to his biographer, Robert Skidelsky, Keynes saw money as a measure of "mistrust of the future." Hence the more pessimistic households become, the more the economy risks falling into a "liquidity" trap as households hoard cash rather than spending and investing it. According to the conventional economics of his day that Keynes attacked, cutting interest rates would encourage borrowing, to spend or to invest, which would help the economy to recover. Yet if prices were to stagnate or fall,

Keynes observed, this mechanism would break down, due to what he called "the uncontrollable and disobedient psychology of the business world."

When an economy is stuck in a liquidity trap, the interest rate cannot solve this problem, because in practice it cannot really fall below zero. (A few economists argue that negative interest rates are possible, and perhaps desirable. But if banks started charging, through negative interest rates, to take care of citizens' savings, depositors would probably just move their money under the mattress. Nor are banks likely to start paying people to borrow.) The result is stagnation, which in turn may cause households to tighten their belts and save more, which means less economic activity, which slows the economy even further. This latter problem, described by Keynes, is known as the "paradox of thrift"— individual households acting rationally in hard times collectively extend the duration of those hard times by refusing to spend.

In retrospect, what Keynes described seemed to be a pretty good fit with the way the U.S. economy had sunk into the Great Depression and struggled to get out (and elements of what he described are present in the current crisis). Half a century later, those extreme circumstances appeared again in an unexpected place: Japan.

LAND OF THE STAGNANT SUN

The recovery of the Japanese economy after World War II amazed the world. Helped by a low exchange rate and massive U.S. military expenditure in Southeast Asia to support the war efforts in Korea in the 1950s and Vietnam in the 1960s, Japan blazed a trail of export-led growth. Between 1960 and 1973 the Japanese economy grew by 9.6 percent a year, twice the average of the advanced economies of Europe and North America. Even after the 1973 oil shock that should have hit the hardest in a country that had to import most of its energy, Japan's growth was better than most, averaging 3.8 percent a year until 1989.

In the 1980s, America regarded Japan much as it does China today—as a rival for global economic dominance. Then, in 1990, out of the blue, the Japanese economy stalled and stubbornly refused to restart, due largely to a string of errors by the government. A decade of stagnation followed that seemed to bear out Keynes's nightmare scenario.

Japanese industry was relaunched after the war by competing on price in low-tech markets. It quickly moved into ever more sophisticated markets, importing technology from around the world and improving on it. By the 1980s, Japanese brand names such as Toyota and Sony had become renowned for their quality and price. The growth of these companies was funded according to a model created by Finance Minister Hayato Ikeda in 1952 in which banks, rather than the stock exchange, would be the main source of capital for industry.

The British and American model of capitalism was built on the joint stock company, the Dutch invention of the seventeenth century, and the sale of shares through stock exchanges. Most large corporations are publicly listed on the stock exchange because this is the best way to tap into large pools of capital. The problem with this system, in Ikeda's view, was that it is too short-term, focused on profits today to satisfy shareholders rather than building for the long term. Building Japanese capitalism on bank lending to corporations would, he hoped, avoid the volatility and short-termism of stock market financing.

Under strong government direction, Japan's banks established close, even cozy, relationships with their industrial borrowers and lent freely for the long term, supported by Japanese citizens' willingness to save rather than consume. The stock market existed but never developed as a mechanism for raising much capital. Its main purpose was to allow the industrial conglomerates and banks to hold shares in each other, which made the system even stabler.

It seemed to be working. Export-led growth meant that Japan ran trade surpluses year after year, and, like China today, by the 1980s Japan was the world's biggest creditor. This was achieved not just through industrial innovation and productivity but by a deliberate policy to keep the value of the yen low and thus Japanese exports competitive. Worrying about this trade imbalance (in an echo of America's recent relations with China), the U.S. government leaned on the Japanese to raise the value of the yen to reduce the Asian nation's trade surplus. Japan was more compliant than China. In 1985 senior officials from the world's leading economies met at the Plaza Hotel in New York City to decide what to do. Following what became known as the Plaza Accord, the value of the Japanese currency rose steadily from ¥260 to ¥150 against the dollar by 1986.

The spending power of Japanese companies in America and the rest of the world shot up, sparking a wave of real-estate and other asset purchases overseas. Fearing that the loss of competitiveness would lead to a drop in exports and an economic slump, the Bank of Japan repeatedly cut interest rates to stop the yen appreciating further and to provide cheap credit to industry. It was at this point that a domestic asset bubble in shares and real estate started to inflate, powered by cheap and plentiful credit.

The other factor inflating the bubble was the Japanese financial sector's efforts to diversify in response to deregulation that had been introduced under pressure from America. Looking for new ways to make money, Japanese banks invested heavily in real estate, which they saw as a sure bet that could not fail. They also began experimenting with sophisticated financial instruments such as derivatives. At the same time, the banks carried on lending money to their traditional clients without much due diligence regarding the outlook for returns.

Moral hazard may have played a part in this strategy. Since the days of Ikeda, the Japanese government had been active in directing the economy. As borrowers and lenders entered uncharted waters, they may have assumed that the Japanese government would never let the banks fail.

Asset prices in Japan spiraled upward. By 1990 the value of all shares traded on Japanese stock exchanges was greater than that of those traded in America—in a country with a population and economy half the size. Real-estate prices soared as well. It was even rumored that the value of the land under the Imperial Palace in Tokyo was greater than the market value of all the land in California.

At the end of 1989, however, the Bank of Japan decided it was time to deflate the bubble. It began to raise interest rates steadily, from 2.5 percent to 6 percent in August 1990. This strategy worked. By October 1990 the Nikkei 225 had fallen by nearly 50 percent from its peak and real-estate prices were in a tailspin, eventually falling 70 percent. As the economy slowed, Japanese companies that had invested heavily in real estate turned to their banks seeking "temporary" loans to ease their cash-flow troubles. Fearing the collapse of their clients, the banks lent freely, widening their exposure to the sinking real-estate market. The banks were now being hit by a double whammy: Four-fifths of the loans that they had extended were reckoned to have been backed by real-estate collateral that was declining in value. And much of their own capital, which had always been kept to a minimum to encourage lending, was held as shares in other firms, which were declining in value as stock prices fell.

Toxic assets were piling up in Japanese banks. Yet their managers refused to confront reality—presumably because that would have meant forcing some of their clients into bankruptcy. Instead they opted to wait for real-estate prices to rise again, once the crisis had blown over, by hiding the true extent of their losses. Embarrassing files were hidden away from regulators, and, as at Enron a decade later, troubled assets were parked in subsidiary companies where they could be kept off the balance sheet and away from prying eyes. "Freezing bad loans at a time when land prices are declining is like putting rotten meat in a freezer" was how one banking expert later described the policy of the banks.

Meanwhile, as worries about the soundness of the banks spread, depositors withdrew their money, putting it in the post office or under their futons. This only deepened the crisis in the banking system. In 1993 the Japanese banks were forced by regulators to own up to $120 billion of bad loans against only $34 billion of capital. Most observers thought this underestimated their bad loans. Yet there was no consensus on how to resolve the crisis. Neither the banks nor the government wanted to force a wave of insolvencies. Equally, the banks did not have the capital and the government did not have the will to clean up the toxic assets. The result was a stalemate as banks continued to hide bad loans off their balance sheets and pay dividends as if everything was normal.

This state of denial could not last forever. The chill wind of reality was felt in late 1994 when two poorly run Tokyo credit cooperatives (the Japanese equivalent of savings and loan institutions) collapsed and had to be bailed out. More credit cooperatives failed, and the problem spread to larger mortgage lenders, which were saved only with taxpayers' money, pumped in because the government feared that letting them fail would lead to contagion spreading across the entire financial sector. In the absence of a government-backed deposit insurance scheme, spooked savers continued to pull their money out of the banks.

The Japanese economy did not melt down, unlike America's in the 1930s. It experienced stagnation, not depression. Yet the duration of the Japanese recession, and in particular its prolonged deflation as prices fell, has been taken by the Nobel Prize–winning economist and *New York Times* columnist Paul Krugman to be an example of Keynes's liquidity trap.

When the asset bubble burst in 1990, the Bank of Japan kept interest rates high for several months, fearing that asset prices would take off again if it cut rates too quickly. By the time the bank lowered rates again, confidence had so drained out of the economy that this easing of monetary policy failed to have any impact, even as interest rates reached zero. According to Krugman, this failure to respond quickly enough, caused by "an odd combination of smugness and fatalism—and by a noticeable unwillingness to think hard about how things could have gone so very wrong," was the reason for the stagnation.

Keynes had argued that massive government spending was the only solution to a liquidity trap and that it was the act of spending money that mattered more than what it was spent on. In typically polemical style, he said that, as a cure for economic stagnation, government could even stuff old bottles with banknotes and bury them in the ground for the private sector to dig up again.

The Japanese government did eventually respond to the slowdown with higher public spending. Its budget went from a surplus of 2.9 percent of national income in 1990 to a deficit of 8.7 percent of national income by the end of the decade. This spending, which included plenty of useless infrastructure (roads to nowhere and the like) that Keynes would have approved of, may have prevented a slide into a deeper recession or even a 1930s-style depression. (The fact that the world did not go into a phase of protectionism at the same time may have helped: there was no Japanese Smoot-Hawley Act, while the rest of the world generally lowered trade barriers during the 1990s.) Yet, according to Krugman, Japan's efforts at a fiscal stimulus never went far enough fast enough to get the economy out of the liquidity trap. (Raising the rate of consumption tax in 1997 did not help.) Hence the stagnation. Krugman pointed to Japan's experience to argue for a quick and decisive stimulus in America after the crash of 2008. By the middle of 2009, he was among a growing number of economists calling for a second stimulus because the first had not been big enough.

Only in 2001 did Japan finally launch a radical policy to stop deflation and escape the liquidity trap. Interest rates had been cut to zero two years previously, but cheap money had failed to get banks to lend again or prices to rise. The Bank of Japan's plan, known as "quantitative easing," was to pump nearly $300 billion of free money into the economy through the banking sector by buying up bonds. By 2005 this seemed to be working. Economic growth returned, and by 2006 prices had stopped falling.

It is still hotly debated whether quantitative easing was the cause of the recovery. Critics of the liquidity-trap thesis point out that pumping money into the economy does not work if the banking sector is still unable to lend—it's like pushing on a string. And there is an alternative theory that might explain the recovery: at the very moment that the Bank of Japan began to print money, the Japanese government finally began to tackle the problem of the insolvent banks.

For nearly seven years, the government had colluded with the banking sector in denying the scale of the toxic-asset problem. It hoped that economic recovery would revive asset prices and restore the banks' balance sheets to health. By 1997 it began to realize that this denial could not go on forever. In the spring of that year, the Nippon Credit Bank had to be rescued with a capital injection, which included public money. Then, in July, the financial crisis hit Japan's Asian neighbors, denting confidence and reducing trade. In the autumn of 1997 the stockbroker Sanyo Securities defaulted and then the Hokkaido Takushoku Bank failed. Then another brokerage firm, Yamaichi Securities, collapsed. The Bank of Japan pumped liquidity into the banking system to stop the slide, but this did nothing more than paper over the enormous cracks in the banks' balance sheets.

In 1998 the government announced a $300 billion rescue package for the banks. However, this admission of the enormity of the problem sparked a run on one of the more exposed financial institutions, the Long-Term Credit Bank (LTCB), which had to be taken into temporary state ownership. But, at last, a strategy was emerging.

The first step, echoing one of FDR's New Deal initiatives, was to restore the public's shattered confidence in the banks and to lure money out from under the futons by strengthening the system of deposit insurance. Then a new regulator was created, since renamed the Financial Services Agency, to get tough with the banks in a way that the former regulator, the Finance Ministry, had never done.

This still left the problem of what to do with the ailing banks. America had dealt pretty effectively with the failure of hundreds of savings and loan institutions through its Resolution Trust Corporation. Yet, as the U.S. treasury secretary in 1998, Larry Summers, commented at the time, the S&Ls were just "a small amount of stuff in a big lake." The problem now facing policymakers in Japan—as it would do again in America and many other countries in 2008—was that the whole banking system was rotten.

In 1999, nine of Japan's biggest banks were given an injection of public money as an incentive to merge into four "megabanks."

With some reluctance, the government also took the radical step of selling the publicly owned LTCB to a group of American investors for $1 billion, only because no Japanese bank wanted to take on their ailing sibling. The deal was underpinned by an agreement for the government to take over the bad loans of LTCB. But, fearing that the government would not own up to the extent of the rot in the bank's assets, the investors also insisted that they be allowed to hand back to the government any bad loans that they discovered over the next three years, under a kind of refund policy.

LTCB was relaunched in 2000 as Shinsei Bank. Investors' fears were quickly realized, as they found more than $7 billion of bad loans hidden away. This discovery was met with the usual political furor, gaijin bashing, and official obfuscation when Shinsei's foreign owners tried to exercise the refund agreement. By 2002, Shinsei was outperforming its peers in the Japanese banking sector, but the investors recognized that it was going to be a long and painful process to get a return on their money.

In 2003 the Japanese government finally created a vehicle to clean up bad loans. By 2005 the banks had started paying back the public money and, at last, increasing lending. It is almost impossible to know whether the recovery of the Japanese economy from 2005 was caused by the bank restructuring or quantitative easing, or both. Strong world growth that boosted Japan's exports certainly helped.

The global economic slowdown that followed the financial crisis of 2008 dealt a severe blow to this fragile recovery. The Japanese economy contracted even more sharply than America's or Britain's because it was so dependent on export markets, which suddenly dried up. The specter of deflation reappeared. This time, the Japanese government's response, like that of governments elsewhere, was to swiftly cut interest rates almost to zero and keep credit flowing, accompanied by a fiscal stimulus. Clearly, some valuable lessons had been learned.

The Japanese experience is a powerful illustration of why a government should act quickly and decisively when the financial sector is close to collapse—and before the economy stagnates. By muddling through and allowing the problems of the banking sector to go unresolved for too long and then failing to decisively reflate the economy, Japanese policymakers locked their economy into a decade of stagnation. In contrast, when the Nordic countries of Europe were hit by a similar crisis in the early 1990s, a decisive government response that was painful in the short term led to a rapid resolution of the problem.

SHORT-TERM PAIN . . . LONG-TERM PROSPERITY

The Nordic countries of Sweden, Norway, and Finland epitomized the high-tax, tight-regulation, big-government model that was dominant in Europe until the 1980s, when a resurgent free-market philosophy began to push a wave of deregulation. As in Japan, the sleepy financial sectors of these countries used their newfound freedom to innovate and compete with each other, leading to a lending boom in the late 1980s. This credit bubble was inflated by strong inflows of foreign capital, attracted by high interest rates set by the central banks as they tried to keep a lid on inflation while their economies roared ahead and asset and real-estate prices shot up.

In 1990 these forces went into reverse. Interest rates in the rest of the world, which had been cut dramatically after the 1987 stock market crash, had begun to rise, drawing capital away from the Nordic countries. The slowing world economy (and for

Finland in particular, the collapse of one of its main trading partners, the Soviet Union) reduced demand for Nordic commodity exports, such as oil and wood. The boom had also pushed up costs in the Nordic countries, reducing their competitiveness in the battle to attract mobile international capital.

As in the emerging-market crisis later that decade, the confidence of international investors suddenly disappeared. The Nordic currencies came under speculative attack as the foreign capital that had flowed in during the 1980s began to rush out again. To defend their currencies against devaluation, the Nordic governments were forced to push interest rates ever higher. In consequence, the costs of servicing the borrowing binge of the 1980s increased sharply and the Nordic economies started to melt down. The banks were hit by massive debt defaults and their balance sheets were burdened with mounting toxic assets. In Sweden, loan losses jumped from 0.3 percent of total loans in 1989 to 7 percent in 1992.

Finland was hit hardest by the crisis. In September 1991, its main savings bank, Skopbank, teetered on the brink of failure. As other banks refused to lend it money, the Bank of Finland stepped in, nationalizing Skopbank. The Finnish government pumped capital into the banking system and moved quickly to guarantee deposits. In the end, this rescue package cost 9 percent of gross domestic product (GDP).

Sweden and Norway took a similar approach, committing public money quickly and taking some of the banking system into public ownership, costing each country about 3.5 percent of GDP. Painful restructuring of the banks, orchestrated by institutions modeled on America's Resolution Trust Corporation, followed during the 1990s. In the end, the Nordic governments were able to sell off most of their stakes in the banks, largely to foreign investors, which helped to defray the net cost of the rescue. The

Norwegian government even turned a small profit on its rescue efforts when it later denationalized the banks.

Each of the Nordic countries experienced sharp recessions, but, unlike Japan, they recovered quickly. (Sweden and Finland helped their own recoveries by devaluing their currencies, shortly after the British pound was knocked out of the European Exchange Rate Mechanism in 1992.) With their small economies open to international trade and capital movements, the governments of Sweden and Finland realized that denial was not an option. Unlike Japan, which hoped that its banks were facing only a temporary crisis of liquidity that would pass when the value of their assets recovered, the Nordic governments quickly acknowledged that their banks were insolvent and needed new capital. With a de facto public guarantee to those banking systems in place and with public money available, the restructuring process was managed transparently. This meant that investors were confident that they knew the real condition of the banks, and so regarded providing additional capital as less risky than if the situation had been more opaque, which helped the three financial systems to recover quickly.

EASIER SAID THAN DONE

The behavior of most governments in the aftermath of the economic crisis that started in 2008 certainly suggested that they had learned some lessons from the past about how to respond when disaster first strikes. However, they may not have learned some of the hardest lessons. Certainly, there was no shortage of governmental activism, all of it ostensibly designed to minimize the

immediate economic impact of the financial meltdown by chan-
neling the spirit of Keynes and not that of Andrew "Liquidate"
Mellon. This activism had three encouragingly familiar themes:
increased government spending, looser monetary policy, and
bank restructuring. But doing the right thing was easier said than
done.

Government deficits widen automatically in recessions as tax
revenues fall and expenditures on social security rise. This is generally regarded as a good thing, an "automatic stabilizer" for the
economy, provided that public borrowing remains at levels accept-
able to the capital markets. Usually governments try to make sure
that their borrowing does not get out of hand, keeping their
deficits to a few percentage points of national income. But after
the 2008 crisis began, fearing the speed and depth of the recession, governments in many countries increased public expenditures as never before. Obama's stimulus package of nearly $800
billion was the biggest in cash terms, but Japan and China spent
much more when measured as a percentage of their national
income. Even then, economists such as Paul Krugman worried
whether this would be enough, reasoning that a global recession
would require a massive global stimulus. ·

This strategy raised all sorts of questions that policymakers had
largely ignored during the previous two decades of relatively strong
growth and low inflation that economists had dubbed the Great
Moderation. The most pressing issues concerned how to spend the
stimulus money to ensure that each dollar had the maximum
impact (the biggest "multiplier effect," in the economic jargon).
Free marketeers wanted the money to go to tax cuts. Keynesians
warned that this would be of little use in a liquidity trap because
households would just cling to the cash rather than spend it.

Governments generally took this advice and pushed most of

the money out through public expenditure. Some worried about wasteful, unproductive expenditure. Others, such as Krugman, Keynes's self-appointed apostle, argued that this was irrelevant. Government just needed to push the money out the door as quickly as possible, he claimed, recalling his master's dictum about burying cash in bottles. The word "stimulus" suggests a precise, predictable act, but in reality, it was a game of high-stakes poker in which the only thing ruled out was not taking part.

Investors were thus being asked to buy unprecedented amounts of government debt in a context of massive uncertainty about whether the stimulus would work, how long it would continue, and what strategy, if any, governments would ultimately take to return the public debt to prudent levels. What they did know is that governments often find it much easier to increase spending than to cut it, and that inflating their way out of debt (by reducing its value in real terms) has at times in the past been a more politically palatable option than reducing borrowing by raising taxes.

There was thus much debate about what the policy of stimulus would do to the credibility of various countries in the capital markets. Would investors be willing to finance ballooning government deficits? In Britain, there were reports of a spat between the prime minister and the governor of the Bank of England, who feared that the government was borrowing too much. Meanwhile, Wall Street veterans worried that the credit-ratings agencies might downgrade American government debt, which is regarded by investors as the ultimate risk-free, triple-A investment. Such a downgrade, it was feared, would plunge the capital markets into a deeper crisis than ever before.

That may be why the strategy of monetary loosening was pursued with even greater determination than the fiscal splurge. Starting with the Federal Reserve, central banks in the industrialized world moved quickly to slash interest rates close to zero, encouraging people to spend and invest rather than hold on to cash. Even so, this did not do enough to entirely remove the prospect of deflation. Urged on once more by the Keynesians, whose economic models predicted that an (impossible) interest rate of –5 percent would be necessary to stop deflation, the central bankers turned to more-radical techniques. The United States, Britain, and eventually the eurozone, among others, joined Japan in trying different forms of quantitative easing, to increase the amount of money in the economy and get credit flowing again. However, Ben Bernanke, the chairman of the Federal Reserve, stopped short of taking to the air with sacks of money to scatter over the public, failing to live up to his nickname "Helicopter Ben," which he had earned by promising, if necessary, to do just that (an idea he had borrowed from Milton Friedman).

If credit is the lifeblood of the economy, then the financial sector is its beating heart. Japan's experience in the 1990s suggested that the central banks' efforts to increase the amount of money in circulation would be ineffective if the financial sector could not, or chose not to, pump it around. Getting the banking system working again as quickly as possible is thus crucial to stimulating the economy and preventing slowdown from turning into depression. Ultimately, the only way to do that is to solve the problem of the toxic assets on bank balance sheets that paralyzed their lending activities.

But if the challenges of fiscal and monetary policy were tough, those posed by the banking sector were even harder. This was arguably the most difficult part of the economic rescue package.

The basic difficulty lies in judging whether banks are in crisis due to temporary illiquidity problems or to something more fundamental. If the issue is illiquidity—banks cannot raise cash to lend, perhaps because the price they can sell their assets for has plunged—then the government can provide the cash they need via the central bank, until the liquidity drought passes. If the problem is more basic—the assets have plunged in price because they are fundamentally not worth as much as they were, and banks cannot raise cash because the market thinks they are in danger of bankruptcy—things will not improve until the banks' balance sheets are strengthened. This is the world of "zombie banks," in which lending will not resume unless the banks are detoxified and recapitalized, one way or another.

Judging between a liquidity problem and the nastier alternative is especially hard for government, in part because banks, which have far better information than government about the true value of their assets and liabilities, have every incentive to claim that their troubles stem from illiquidity and nothing worse. This in turn plays to the natural tendency of government to cast any problem in the rosiest possible light, to avoid alarming the voting public. No government wants to trigger a collapse in confidence in the banking sector by exaggerating the problems, as happened in America in 1931.

This may explain why the response of the U.S. government, under both George W. Bush and Barack Obama, to the crisis in the banking sector that began in 2007 and got much worse in September 2008 tended to be more Japanese than Nordic. First came the denial. Hoping that the problems revealed by the credit crunch were simply due to temporary illiquidity, from 2007 the Federal Reserve made plenty of money available through the Discount Window, leaving market forces to sort out the good banks from the bad. Various efforts were made to encourage banks to come up with a private-sector solution that would remove toxic assets from bank balance sheets without costing the taxpayer a dime—but these got nowhere.

As the crisis worsened, the government's liquidity strategy was used as an excuse for failing to acknowledge the evidence that most banks were for all intents and purposes insolvent, remaining in business largely because the public believed the government would not allow them to fail. It was only after Lehman Brothers was disastrously allowed to collapse that the U.S. government was shaken out of its denial and forced to address the fundamental insolvency of the banking system. The government may have hoped that by letting Lehman go bust, it would demonstrate that the strategy of providing liquidity had worked: an insolvent bank would have failed, but the rest would have demonstrated their solvency by carrying on regardless. Instead, Lehman's bankruptcy demonstrated the opposite: that, absent the guarantee of government support, the markets regarded most of the other banks as insolvent, too.

As the financial system melted down, Treasury Secretary Hank Paulson converted to a policy of aggressive government support for the banks. Within a matter of days he asked Congress for a $700-billion blank check to sort out the mess. There was certainly plenty wrong with this plan. However, when legislators chose to reject his proposals, they were motivated less by technical concerns than by preelection populist point-scoring about the cost of the package—a shortsighted decision that significantly worsened the panic, which in turn ensured that Congress approved the money at the second go-around soon after.

Even then, the actions of the American authorities lacked the clarity of the Nordic nationalizations—in large part because nationalization is a toxic concept in Washington, D.C., viewed by Republicans and Democrats alike as tantamount to betraying the essence of American capitalism. This concern was understandable—nationalization has often been a disaster due to bureaucracy and politically motivated interference in management decisions. Yet, as a temporary measure in a crisis, with a clear exit strategy, executed by a government with the self-discipline not to meddle, nationalization would probably have been the least worst option.

The price of this refusal to go the whole way (even when the government took control of Fannie Mae, Freddie Mac, and AIG, officials used euphemisms such as "conservatorship" instead of the blasphemous "nationalization") was that the government condemned itself to playing an unnecessarily complicated game. It had to maintain the fiction of the banks remaining private institutions, while in fact the government's commitment to stand behind them was the only reason they were able to stay in business. At the same time, it had to attempt to orchestrate the restructuring of bank balance sheets without the ability to act decisively that full nationalization would have brought.

Both Paulson and his successor, Timothy Geithner, struggled to figure out how to play this game, frequently changing strategy in ways that seemed almost designed to confuse the markets. At times, they favored buying toxic assets off banks; at other times, recapitalizing them by buying their equity. They also tried to partner with private investors to buy toxic assets from the banks—a strategy that runs the risk of being more expensive than if the government alone bought them. Private investors will drive a hard bargain, as did the vulture funds that bought failed S&Ls' assets. While this has the attraction of bringing private-sector expertise to bear on valuing the assets—which banks have every incentive to exaggerate—it also means that if such a plan were to work, the private investors could earn large profits, which otherwise might have gone to the taxpayer.

In early 2009 the British government tried to cut through this pricing problem with its "asset protection scheme," which insured the banks against losses on their toxic assets rather than taking these assets over. This appealed to most of the banks, but it had the disadvantage that it did little to make the banks face up to their problems or get them lending again. The taxpayer, as the guarantor of the banks, was also made responsible for the risks of the entire financial sector, putting yet another burden on the creaking public finances.

The U.S. government also behaved inconsistently in deciding which investors to help or punish in different bailouts. In some cases, such as Bear Stearns, shareholders were allowed to retain some value in their investments, which was better than the nothing allowed shareholders of, say, Wachovia, when its ownership was transferred to Wells Fargo. Different treatment was meted out to different types of shareholder and bondholder, too. Shareholders of Lehman got nothing (probably rightly), while Lehman bondholders were treated less kindly than their counterparts at Fannie Mae and Freddie Mac. Some banks were forced to accept government money they did not want under Paulson's Troubled Asset Relief Program, known as TARP, to ensure that those which did need the money were not stigmatized for accepting it. Then ostensibly scientific but in practice highly subjective "stress tests" that analyzed how a bank would fare in (supposedly) extreme market conditions were used to force some banks to raise a lot of additional capital, and others small amounts of capital or none at all.

Nationalization, done fast the Nordic way, might have been an insult to American capitalism, but it might also have been the best way to get it working again. By nationalizing banks, a government can inject capital directly into the banking sector and determine banks' lending decisions, to make sure that as much of the money as possible reaches the consumers and businesses who need credit, and thus keep the economy going. The taxpayer can do best from this, because the government does not have to sell off toxic assets at the bottom of the market. Instead, these assets can be separated from the operations of the bank, and both the "good bank" (the ongoing, profitable bit) and "bad bank" (its toxic assets) can be sold off when market conditions are appropriate. This may even generate a profit to taxpayers, as the Norwegian denationalizations did in the 1990s.

Admittedly, that represents a best-case scenario—not least given the risk that public ownership will lead to the politicization of operational decisions. Even with government shareholdings that did not amount to full nationalization, the rescued American banks soon generated ire in Washington over pay, bonuses, and corporate entertaining, as well as their "unpatriotic" offshore activities.

President Obama said he was "choked up with anger" when he heard that bailed-out insurance giant AIG was going to pay $165 million in bonuses to its executives. In Britain, the political debate was dominated for weeks by a lucrative pension deal in the termination package struck by the government with Sir Fred Goodwin, the former boss of the failed Royal Bank of Scotland. The public outrage at these decisions may have been understandable, but it did not help get the banks working properly again.

Keynes understood that psychology is fundamental to the way that economies respond to crises—the longer governments wait to act decisively, the more uncertainty and pessimism builds up among consumers and investors that can delay a recovery. The sluggish response of the Hoover administration in the early 1930s certainly worsened the Great Depression, although the government at least had the excuse that the economic orthodoxy of the time provided little guidance on what to do.

The Japanese government in the 1990s had no such excuse. A failure of commercial and political leadership delayed stimulus measures and allowed the banks to postpone facing up to their problems until it was too late and the economy had stagnated. In contrast, the governments of the Nordic economies moved swiftly and decisively. The public rescue packages and government guar-antees of their banking systems crucially enjoyed bipartisan polit-ical support. This sent a clear and credible signal to investors and depositors that helped restore confidence in the banks.

Regardless of the long-term consequences for public finances, governments deserve credit for quickly pulling the levers of fis-cal and monetary policy after the crisis of 2008, with massive boosts to public expenditure, interest-rate cuts, and, in some cases, quantitative easing of the money supply. Yet they hesitated to take quick action to clean up the banks, a lack of decisive action that threatened to render their other efforts less effective. And that was just the first response to the crisis. Fixing the longer-term flaws in capitalism highlighted by the current crisis may provide an even sterner test for the world's governments.

5

THE REFORMER'S CHALLENGE

Don't throw out the baby with the bathwater

L*e laissez-faire, c'est fini"* was French president Nicolas Sarkozy's almost gleeful verdict on the financial crisis of 2008. European leaders had long railed against the Anglo-American faith in free markets (somewhat ironically known by the French term for "let do"), in contrast to the more regulated, bigger-government version of capitalism practiced on the Continent. The economies of Europe were badly hit by the crisis, yet their leaders claimed that they had been largely innocent victims of deregulation in the English-speaking world. (Well, they would say that, wouldn't they?) They pointed a finger especially at the reckless speculation in financial markets that had threatened the stability of the global economy and their own prosperity.

Before world leaders gathered for the crucial G-20 summit in London in April 2009, the governments of Continental Europe demanded comprehensive new regulations for the financial sector. Sarkozy had even threatened to walk out if the Americans and Brits refused to clamp down on their cavalier capitalists such as hedge funds. At the summit, each of the world's twenty most economically significant countries pledged to strengthen their own regulatory systems, to work together to crack down on tax-haven countries (for reasons not entirely clear), and to find ways to produce a more coordinated regulation of the global financial system.

America was already working on it. Not long after Lehman Brothers collapsed, prompting the government bailout of the banking system, people had started saying that Washington, D.C., was now the "financial capital of the world." Having unexpectedly seized control from New York City, the politicians on the Potomac had lost no time in trying to reshape the governance of the financial system to their liking. Even before the G-20 summit, Timothy Geithner, America's new treasury secretary, had pledged the biggest expansion of government regulation in the home of laissez-faire since the 1930s. As he had explained to Congress, his reforms would be far-reaching—the "new rules of the game," not "repairs at the margin." There would be four main themes: containing systemic risks; protecting consumers and investors; streamlining the regulatory structure; and promoting international coordination.

Having saved the banking system at great cost to American taxpayers, Geithner's top priority was to minimize the systemic risk that this sort of mess would ever occur again. One way to do this, he argued, was to tackle the tendency of banks to take on too much risk in the good times, leaving them exposed in the bad times. Banks had long been required to hold a cushion of capital to protect them from losses, in proportion to their risk exposure from lending and other activities. However, this cushion did not change with the economic cycle. In the future, Geithner said, banks should increase the relative size of their capital cushion during booms so that they would be better protected from the inevitable busts when the cycle turns down. By forcing banks to stash away capital rather than lend it out, he hoped that booms in credit would be restrained, making busts less likely.

He also planned to widen the regulatory net to include pools of capital outside the banking system, including President Sarkozy's bête noire, the hedge funds. These had not been regulated in any meaningful way before the crisis. Large hedge funds would, Geithner said, be required to register with the Securities and Exchange Commission (SEC), which many did already, and to provide it with information about their assets and leverage. If the SEC deemed them "systemically important," in that their failure could have serious consequences for the financial markets as a whole, large hedge funds could become subject to "stringent" capital requirements similar to those imposed on the banks.

Geithner further proposed to control systemic risk through greater oversight of complex financial derivatives, such as the credit default swaps that had effectively bankrupted AIG. In particular, he would target the "over-the-counter" (OTC) market, in which financial institutions privately entered into derivative contracts that were not obliged to be disclosed or registered with any public exchange. OTC derivatives accounted for a large chunk of the booming global derivatives market and especially of the newer, more complex, and riskier derivatives. In the future all derivatives would be subject to government oversight, said Geithner. "The days when a major insurance company could bet the house on credit default swaps with no one watching and no credible backing . . . must end."

More and better regulation is an easy mantra for those who blame deregulated financial markets for the crisis. Indeed, most supporters of the laissez-faire approach to markets would also concede that regulatory failures contributed to the crisis, and should be addressed at least in part by implementing better regulation. Yet—and here's the rub—although delivering more regulation is easy, delivering better regulation is fiendishly difficult, as Geithner and President Obama discovered in June 2009 when their regulatory reform bill got a decidedly lukewarm reaction.

The crisis provided plenty of evidence of the difficulty of regulating well—and, make no mistake, for all the talk of its "deregulated" markets, America had plenty of financial regulation throughout the buildup to the crisis. In 2008 alone, the SEC issued 671 enforcement actions against various offenders. It is far from clear whether the more tightly regulated parts of the financial sector, such as banks, did any better than those which were lightly regulated, such as hedge funds. As Geithner admitted, "There were failures where regulation was extensive and failures where it was absent."

Crises are often turning points for regulatory policy as governments try to figure out what went wrong and how to prevent a repeat. What is needed is a thoughtful analysis of the causes of the mess, not a rush to judgment. Any remedies should take into account the inevitable costs and failures of even the best-designed regulations—which can include discouraging or otherwise hindering wealth creation. Few staff at regulatory agencies have much experience of working in the financial sector, so they may lack street smarts. Regulators also tend to be at an economic disadvantage as they struggle to stay on top of those whom they regulate—namely, they can rarely afford to pay staff as much as they could earn working for a bank, which means the best talent on average works for the regulated rather than the regulator.

The urge to regulate should also be tempered by a recognition of the ability of markets to learn from their mistakes, which in some circumstances may even make regulatory reform unnecessary. Yet the risk is that short-term political priorities will get in the way of sensible policymaking. Playing the blame game can be easier and go down better with voters than making subtle changes to regulation.

Often the easiest regulatory options are the least effective ones. For instance, as the financial storm clouds gathered in the summer of 2008 and bank shares started to fall alarmingly, the SEC and Britain's Financial Services Authority (FSA) each introduced a ban on short selling of bank shares that was, at best, irrelevant to the problem.

Short selling had increased because many investors, particularly hedge funds, thought that bank share prices would fall. But this was largely a symptom of the toxic assets piling up on banks' balance sheets, not the cause. Banning short selling may have made the crisis worse by undermining the risk-management strategies of many financial firms, including the banks themselves, which made them even weaker. "Knowing what we now do, I imagine it's not a step we would take again," admitted the then chairman of the SEC, Christopher Cox, later. The ban, introduced under pressure from the Fed and the Treasury, was supposed to break the cycle of panic selling of bank shares but only served to coagulate the already illiquid credit markets.

The ban on short selling had, however, been a way for regulators to appear to be doing something about the maelstrom in the markets. It also played to the desire of politicians to satisfy public bloodlust by blaming hedge funds for the mess. Fortunately, the ban was easy to remove and caused little long-term damage. The bigger danger is that once the immediate panic is over, politicians—in America and elsewhere—will introduce new regulations that are more damaging and far harder to remove.

This will be further complicated by national and regional politics, which may lead to very different approaches to regulatory reform despite the pledges of the G-20 leaders to work together. Still, this may have the benefit of allowing market testing of which of the different strategies works best as the American and British regulatory models diverge from each other and from those of Continental Europe.

Despite his enthusiasm for the end of laissez-faire, President

Sarkozy (along with his fellow world leaders) would do well to consider the consequences of a very French financial crisis that took place in 1720, the same year as the British South Sea Bubble. The politicians in London had responded to their crisis with a ban on short selling (nothing much has changed in the past three hundred years) that was soon ignored as British capitalism steamed ahead to global financial dominance. In contrast, the political response in Paris to the crisis caused by the French Mississippi Company was to abandon financial innovation to such an extent that the system never really recovered before it was swept away by the French Revolution at the end of the eighteenth century. However, as the Mississippi Company crisis resulted from a Briton encouraging French investors to speculate on trade with what is now the United States, perhaps Sarkozy will dismiss that historic regulatory disaster as merely another Anglo-American conspiracy.

STIFLING REGULATION . . . FOMENTING REVOLUTION

As he passed through the cheering crowds in the narrow rue Quincampoix in Paris in 1719, John Law threw gold coins from the window of his carriage. The throng of ecstatic investors loved the Scotsman, France's de facto finance minister, the self-styled economic savior of the nation who was going to make them all rich. However, the adulatory feelings were not mutual. As the crowds scrambled for the coins, Law's hired hands poured buckets of slops on them from the rooftops as a mark of his contempt for the greedy speculators.

At the time, the shares in his Mississippi Company were riding high, but within months their price would plunge. Law would enter French history as probably the biggest crook of all time. Indeed, he probably deserves much of the blame for the deep Gallic hostility to financial capitalism. Nonetheless, he should also probably be remembered as one of the great visionaries of economics.

Born and raised in Scotland, Law had moved to London as a young man. There he developed a reputation as a playboy and gambler, before he was forced to flee after he killed another city dandy in a duel (which the other man had instigated). He continued his gambling lifestyle on the Continent, where his keen mind turned to the possibilities of the new financial capitalism that was flourishing in Holland. Inspired by new ideas about economics, he returned home to Scotland, then still a sanctuary from English justice, to write up his insights.

Law had come to understand the limitations of basing money on a finite supply of precious metal. His 1706 book, *Money and Trade Consider'd*, was an early masterpiece of monetary economics. Law explained how an imbalance between the demand for money and the supply of money could affect prices and thus the productivity of the entire economy. For a poor country such as Scotland that lacked reserves of gold and silver, therefore, unemployment was caused "not for want of Inclination to work, or for want of Employers, but for want of money."

This insight may seem obvious today, but it was not for the economists then or, indeed, for the next century, who remained trapped by the idea that poverty was solely a manifestation of idleness that required punitive solutions such as forced labor. For Law, poverty was instead the result of a failure of economic policy. The answer to Scotland's or any other bullion-light country's financial problems was simple—abandon gold and silver and create money entirely from paper.

Having found little enthusiasm for his ideas in Britain, Law moved to France, where the long wars and extravagant living that had earned Louis XIV the name "the Sun King" had also weighed France down with enormous debts that it could not service. The country faced economic stagnation because of a lack of gold, and the Crown faced a financial crisis because of its debt mountain. Law claimed to have the solution—although his initial approaches were rebuffed by a Catholic royal court suspicious of the Protestant foreigner.

After Louis XIV died in 1715, the French court was more open to new ideas. The following year Law was given permission to issue paper money through his new Banque Générale. Years of debasing the currency to make France's reserves of gold and silver go further had so undermined public trust in the coinage that Law's paper money was quickly accepted as a more reliable means of exchange (although gold and silver continued in use as well). The credibility of his banknotes was further strengthened in 1717 when tax collectors were required to use them when paying money to the treasury.

Despite this success, Law did not want to remain a mere banker. He was determined to prove that his ideas could save the French economy. His opportunity came in 1717 when he was granted control of the Mississippi Company, France's trading monopoly with its colonies in the New World. This had been chartered a few years earlier but had failed to live up to its promise. Following a strategy later copied by the British South Sea Company, Law decided that most of the stock of the Mississippi Company (renamed the Company of the West) would be offered in exchange for outstanding government bonds. With much of this government paper trading at only 20 percent or 30 percent of its face value, holders were only too grateful to swap their bonds and annuities for shares in the company.

To give the share price a boost and to inject some cash into the money-starved French economy, Law's next move was to convert the Banque Générale into the Banque Royale. The new bank would issue notes based not on its own capital but in the name of the Crown. Such was Law's credibility that these notes were readily accepted by the public. Many of these notes were soon invested in Mississippi Company shares.

When shares in the company had first been sold in 1717, they traded below their face value of 500 livres. By July 1719 the price had topped 1,000 livres. As with the South Sea Company, these initial gains were not unreasonable. After all, the Mississippi Company had taken over French companies that traded with other parts of the world, greatly improving its future earning prospects.

Law's plan moved into overdrive. Paper money, in the form of banknotes and shares in the Mississippi Company, was in wide circulation. Yet the government was still saddled with 1.2 billion livres of debt. The Mississippi share issues had, by August 1719, raised only a little more than 100 million livres, less than a tenth of what the Crown needed to get out of the red. The company had by now been further enriched by being granted a lucrative concession to collect taxes. Law's grand plan was to use these earnings as the basis of a massive share offer in exchange for all the outstanding government paper.

The attraction of this swap to government bondholders was a chance to participate in the booming market in Mississippi Company shares, which seemed to offer the certain prospect of massive capital gains. The company's share price had passed 2,000 livres at the start of August 1719, en route to over 5,000 livres in mid-September. From mid-September to mid-October 1719, the company issued 324,000 new shares at 5,000 livres each, raising more than 1.5 billion livres. Yet the share price kept rising, reaching 10,000 livres by the end of the year.

Law pumped up this bubble by offering a range of incentives. Investors had to make only a 10 percent down payment to buy shares. Anyone having trouble meeting the payment installments was given extensions and credit. Investors nervous that prices would not rise were threatened, on the one hand, by being told that future share issues would be restricted to existing stockholders, and encouraged, on the other hand, by being offered a guaranteed buyback at 9,000 livres. With this price floor limiting the downside risk, it seemed that the market could go only one way, and money poured in from across Europe. Such was the frenzy of buying and selling at the rue Quincampoix that, it was said, a hunchback earned a living by letting people use his hump as a writing desk.

By early 1720, Law presided over a huge financial-industrial conglomerate, to which was added the honor of his appointment as *controlleur général des finances,* a position now known as prime minister. At this moment of triumph, his scheme began to collapse under its own weight. The paper money issued by the Banque Générale had engineered a welcome increase in the money supply of France, which had helped to kick-start the stagnating economy. But the flood of notes from the new Banque Royale had started to cause inflation. As prices rose, holders of gold and silver realized that they could buy more with it abroad than at home and started to shift it out of the country. Law responded by imposing a ban on the export of bullion—the eighteenth-century form of capital control—but this was no more than a stopgap measure; never a solution.

In May 1720, Law took a more radical step, attempting to deflate the bubble he had created by declaring that the value of banknotes in circulation would be halved. This, he hoped, would restore credibility to the currency. But the French Parlement was opposed to the devaluation and blocked the edict. The market swung from euphoria to panic. Fearful investors switched their money from Paris to London, where the South Sea Bubble was in full swing.

With confidence in its banknotes gone, the Banque Royale quickly collapsed and the value of Mississippi Company shares slumped. In October 1720 the French government abandoned paper money entirely and returned to using gold and silver coins. Law, after a brief spell in prison, fled the country, dying in Venice in 1729.

The story of the Mississippi Company is typically lumped together with the chicanery of the South Sea Company. Yet the similarities in their business models should not obscure their fundamental differences. Law's sin was not fraud but overambition. France provided the perfect laboratory for a grand macroeconomic experiment: it was mired in debt that it could not service and in a state of near monetary breakdown. England, by contrast, had already discovered the secrets of sound public finance with the creation of the Bank of England in 1694, long before the South Sea Company had tried to muscle into the business of financing public debt. Until 1719, Law's project was, in fact, hugely successful in establishing monetary stability.

As part of a wider economic program, Law had also designed regulatory reforms and public works intended to accelerate the development of the French economy, and he had funded almshouses across the country to provide assistance to the poor. In contrast to the miserable failure of the South Sea Company's commercial activities, the Mississippi Company's trading business proved to be a success. The value of French overseas trade quadrupled between 1716 and 1743.

In the end, the more centralized structure of government in France allowed Law to concentrate too much power and push the experiment too far. He simply printed too much money too fast. Yet even in exile, Law hoped to return to France to salvage the financial system, although the scale of the collapse meant that was never likely to happen. Instead, France undid all his financial innovations and returned to the moribund system of finance that Law had tried to replace. It was the eventual bankruptcy of the Crown that forced the convening of the Estates-General in 1789, which triggered the French Revolution.

It would be an exaggeration to blame Law for this political upheaval decades after his death. Yet the backlash against financial innovation that followed the collapse of the Mississippi Company certainly did prolonged damage to the country's economy, helping to create the conditions where revolutionary sentiment took hold. Perhaps things would have turned out differently had the French responded to the bursting of their bubble in the same pragmatic way that the British reacted to the bursting of theirs. But they did not, and in the end, Law's legacy, as one historian puts it, was that "France was permanently inoculated against credit operations."

Law's error of looking for economic salvation in the money-printing press was to be repeated two and a half centuries later during the economic turbulence of the 1970s. This time the result was a previously unheard-of phenomenon of simultaneously rising unemployment and inflation known as "stagflation." It was during this decade that politicians came to realize that the rules, regulations, and red tape in which they had swaddled the economy since the Great Depression had become a financial straitjacket restraining economic growth.

LETTING THE MARKET RUN FREE

The year 1973 opened with a stock market slide that went on to last nearly two years, during which the Dow Jones Industrial Average lost nearly half its value. Shares on the London Stock Exchange fell even further, and a banking crisis forced the Bank of England to bail out several financial institutions. This was also a year of turmoil in the global monetary system. The U.S. government's policy of printing money to finance its adventures at home and abroad eventually brought down the Bretton Woods system of fixed exchange rates.

Oil was then, as now, priced in dollars, so the devaluation of the U.S. currency in 1973 enraged the increasingly powerful oil-producing countries of the Middle East, which suddenly found that they could buy a lot less for each barrel of oil they sold. The Organization of the Petroleum Exporting Countries (OPEC) decided to fight back by exercising the market power it enjoyed as a cartel. On October 15, oil ministers from the Arab states announced that they would drive up the price of oil by 70 percent by restricting supplies, blaming America's support for Israel in the Yom Kippur War for their decision. As a result, the industrial world, which was already in recession, now had to cope with soaring energy prices. The governments of the industrialized countries reacted by throwing fiscal and monetary prudence to the wind. They spent money they did not have by borrowing it, printing money to repay the debt—all justified in the name of John Maynard Keynes.

After World War II, a consensus had formed in support of so-called Keynesian economics. This argued that it was government's job to manage the economy through active tax and expenditure policies. According to this approach, governments faced a straightforward choice between unemployment and inflation. Spending more and taxing less would push down unemployment and push up prices. Cutting back on spending combined with more taxing would keep inflation down—but at the price of higher unemployment.

By managing the demand for goods and services through public expenditure, Keynesians believed that governments could permanently banish the breadlines of the 1930s by keeping the economy at full employment. They responded to the economic slowdown of the early 1970s by arguing that governments should spend more, financed by borrowing if necessary, even though this would mean higher inflation. To their surprise, and everyone's loss, the expected trade-off between inflation and unemployment did not occur. Rather than moving in opposite directions, unemployment and prices began to rise together.

This phenomenon, which soon got its "stagflation" moniker, had been predicted by the then cultish but widely disbelieved guru of monetarist economics, Milton Friedman. He had warned that by constantly pumping money into the economy, governments did not cause people to produce more. On the contrary, he argued, the public would begin to anticipate increases in prices and wages, an expectation of higher inflation that would become self-fulfilling, especially if they demanded higher salaries so they could afford to pay the anticipated higher prices.

Once established, this inflationary expectation would be hard to purge from the system, Friedman warned. His prescription was that, instead of trying to push down unemployment through inflationary public expenditure, governments should first squeeze inflation out of the system. They could then stimulate growth through deregulation that freed up markets to work more efficiently by cutting through red tape.

With Keynesianism obviously failing, during the 1970s and early 1980s policymakers around the world adopted various forms of Friedmanite monetarism to fight inflation. From 1979 this effort was led in America by Paul Volcker, then chairman of the Federal Reserve, who aggressively increased interest rates to drive inflation out of the economy. This it did. However, it also led to a severe recession in the early 1980s. Margaret Thatcher's government in Britain followed similar policies after her election in 1979, with similar consequences.

Defeating inflation was but phase one of Friedman's plan. Phase two was to cut the economy free from the regulations that had stifled economic growth since the New Deal. This effort began in the citadel of capitalism, the stock market.

Taming the excesses of the stock market had been a top priority for FDR and his New Dealers. In particular, they set out to end the perceived widespread mis-selling of securities that was believed to have contributed to the 1929 crash. The 1933 Securities Act introduced new rules to force companies to disclose more about their finances. The following year, Congress passed the Securities Exchange Act, which established the SEC as a dedicated agency of government to oversee the new rules. Its first head was Joseph Kennedy, founding father of the Kennedy political dynasty. "It takes one to catch one" was reportedly FDR's response to an aide who expressed surprise at this appointment. After all, Kennedy, unlike today's regulators, had made a fortune on the stock exchange in the boom years through insider trading (and later, it was claimed, through bootlegging) but was now charged with cleaning the place up.

Strict regulation of the financial markets would be the norm for the next forty years. However, by the 1970s, there was a growing realization that the market had become bogged down by too many rules. Deregulation started in New York in 1975 with the removal of distinctions between brokers (who took buy and sell orders from the public) and jobbers (who executed trades on the exchange floor but did not interact with the public), abolishing brokers' fixed commissions on share transactions; in addition, permission was given for foreign firms to enter the market. (London followed suit in 1986, with its "Big Bang" deregulation.) The broad thrust of this deregulation was to encourage competition. And as competition increased, profit margins for brokers and other market players were squeezed, efficiency improved, and innovation surged.

One of the most notable innovations was the creation in the 1980s of the "junk bond" market, which allowed companies that would not previously have been considered sufficiently creditworthy to issue debt. This debt, which paid higher yields to reflect its greater risk, became a huge source of funds for "leveraged buyouts" (LBOs), in which investors borrowed money to launch (often hostile) takeover bids for public companies listed on the stock market.

This activity was hugely controversial and contributed to the public suspicion of the confident, thrusting, deregulated financial markets of the 1980s that was captured in the 1987 film *Wall Street*. This movie was famous for a speech claiming that "greed is good" by Gordon Gekko, an investment banker played by Michael Douglas, modeled on the insider trader Ivan Boesky. In real life, Boesky (whose actual words in a University of California commencement address in 1986 were that "greed is healthy") amassed a fortune of $200 million by buying up shares in corporations that were about to be taken over, based on tips from insiders.

Regulators had largely turned a blind eye to insider trading in the past, but, perhaps because Boesky was so brazen, in this case they chose to act. Boesky plea-bargained his sentence down to three and a half years, of which he served three, and a

$100 million fine, by informing on the so-called junk bond king, Michael Milken.

Milken had pioneered the market for high-yield junk bonds at Drexel Burnham Lambert, the Wall Street investment bank where he worked. To his supporters, Milken was a great financial innovator who created a new way for investors to bounce out poor managers and improve returns. To his critics, including the then U.S. attorney for New York, Rudy Giuliani, he was a crook. Early in 1989, based on Boesky's testimony, Milken was indicted on a host of charges, including racketeering and insider trading. In the end, the major charges were dropped when he agreed to a guilty plea on six securities and reporting violations. Milken spent nearly two years in jail. Although Drexel Burnham Lambert agreed to pay a $650 million fine, it went bust shortly after, in 1990. It is still hotly debated whether Milken's conviction really reflected any serious wrongdoing. The junk bond market, soon rebranded as the "high-yield debt market," continued to thrive, becoming an integral part of the global financial system— although it was hit hard by the credit crunch that began in August 2007.

The Boesky/Milken affair was fairly typical of the SEC's track record over its first seventy-five years, which has been decidedly mixed. It has caught a few villains and prosecuted a few people who may have been innocent. It has certainly not eliminated fraud, as the discovery of Bernie Madoff's Ponzi scheme in December 2008 demonstrated all too clearly (over several years the SEC had failed to act on tips about Madoff's wrongdoing, perhaps because he was a respected member of the Wall Street establishment). More fundamentally, it failed adequately to address the systemic risks that led to the crisis of 2008. For example, the SEC was the lead regulator of the securities arms of investment banks, including Lehman Brothers, yet it failed to sound the alarm. These events demonstrated that the New Deal legislation and institutions had failed to keep pace with financial innovation.

A JIGSAW OF REGULATION

The 2008 crisis exposed several gaping holes in the regulatory system. One was the split in responsibilities between the SEC, which had oversight of securities, and the regulator that was supposed to be keeping an eye on derivatives, the Commodity Futures Trading Commission (CFTC).

Like the SEC, the CFTC was a product of the New Deal (in this case the 1936 Commodities Exchange Act, amended in 1974). The name itself highlights the problem. Futures contracts had first become popular in the agricultural commodities markets as a way for farmers to pre-agree to the price at which they could sell their crops when the harvest came (just as the tulip growers of the Netherlands had done in the seventeenth century). The early futures markets in America were in commodities such as wheat and pork bellies. Over time, however, the derivatives market came to be dominated by purely financial rather than agricultural products.

Innovation in derivatives began after the collapse of the Bretton Woods exchange-rate system in the early 1970s. International companies faced a new risk as the value of currencies floated freely against each other, sometimes fluctuating wildly. In 1972, Leo Melamed, a former lawyer, spotted a business opportunity helping companies to hedge these new currency risks and launched currencies-futures contracts on the Chicago Mercantile Exchange, one of the two big agricultural futures markets in Chicago (the other being the Board of Trade). Companies and financial institutions that traded abroad quickly discovered the benefits of these futures contracts, which allowed them to fix the exchange rate at which they would do business in the future. The market boomed.

The next phase of the great wave of innovation in derivatives was the market for swaps, which created a new opportunity for arbitrage. For example, interest-rate swaps allowed borrowers with floating (variable) interest rates to swap their future payment obligations with borrowers with a fixed interest rate. This allowed company finance directors (and speculators) to change their risk exposure depending on their view of where rates would go.

The credit default swap (CDS) built on this idea. Managing the risk of default is fundamental to finance, so the market for CDSs—which acted as a form of insurance for creditors against the risk of a firm to which they lent going bust—grew at an explosive rate. In 2007 alone, the nominal value of CDSs issued was over $60 trillion.

The vast majority of CDS contracts were made over the counter (directly between financial institutions) rather than through exchanges. This meant that the CFTC, the derivatives regulator, did not have direct oversight of all of the huge derivatives market. The parties to CDSs came from across the financial system and were each regulated according to the rules of their particular sector. As a result, although the insurer AIG was one of the biggest players in the CDS market, it faced no supervision by the CFTC— which may be why, unlike Wall Street investment banks, it had no capital cushion in case of losses on its CDS exposures, a lack of protection that proved disastrous when the markets crashed in 2008. Regulation of insurance was a state affair, so most of AIG's business was overseen by the New York State Insurance Commissioner, although the Office of Thrift Supervision, an arm of the U.S. Treasury Department, was supposed to be keeping an eye on the activities of its financial products division, which traded in CDSs. With such fragmentation of the regulatory system, neither the SEC nor the CFTC had a complete view of the systemic risks that were being built up by the boom in derivatives.

One proposal for reform, that derivatives currently executed over the counter should have to pass through an exchange or "central counterparty," seems sensible at first glance, but in practice it could deal a severe blow to financial innovation, especially if "pass through" is taken to mean anything more intrusive than publicly disclosing the transaction. Most securities markets begin as OTC because they are not yet sufficiently standardized, and their risks not yet well enough understood, for them to trade on an exchange. The OTC market is where bespoke financial securities are traded and new sorts of securities are piloted and refined, until what investors and issuers want is sufficiently clear and standardized. Cut out the OTC phase and it will be far harder to launch innovative new securities. (Some might say, "So what?"—just as the French government did, no doubt, before it banned paper money after the Law Panic three hundred years ago.)

Merging the CFTC into the SEC, creating a "super regulator," would make more sense. It is true that competition between regulators can sometimes promote efficiency, as markets move to wherever there is the best combination of regulation and freedom to innovate. Yet these benefits must be set both against the ability of market participants to exploit differences between regulators and against the danger that the fragmentation of regulation will mean that no regulator has a complete picture of what is going on in the market it regulates. That danger seems to have been a real one in the derivatives marketplace.

Admirers of regulatory competition might point to the sharp differences of regulatory philosophy that existed between the CFTC and the SEC. The CFTC regulated by setting out clear principles that market participants were expected to abide by, without going into great detail about what "abiding" meant. The SEC, by contrast, is a stickler for detailed rule making that can often seem entirely devoid of any underlying principles. This is said to have encouraged a culture among those it regulates of a narrow focus on complying with individual rules, regardless of whether the behavior in question makes much sense. It may also explain the rather patchy enforcement record of the SEC, which has too often been guilty of failing to see the forest for the trees.

Whether or not America creates a superregulator—the Geithner-Obama proposals in June 2009 backed away from that idea—hopefully future American regulation will be based on a principles approach rather than the SEC's legalistic, box-checking ways. Ideally, top regulators will no longer be lawyers but instead be people who understand how markets work—the modern equivalent of the poacher-turned-gamekeeper Joseph Kennedy. Thanks to the crisis, there may be plenty of well-qualified candidates looking for a new job.

A MARRIAGE MADE IN . . . ?

New York's Waldorf-Astoria Hotel has played host to many merger announcements over the years, but few were as euphoric as that which took place on April 6, 1998. Even the journalists in the room stood and cheered when two modern-day titans of capitalism, John Reed and Sandy Weill, announced what was then the biggest deal in American banking history. The merger of Reed's Citicorp with Weill's Travelers Group, to create the new Citigroup, made headlines not just because of the size of the deal, which was valued at

$140 billion, but because it marked the death knell of the system of banking regulation created during the Great Depression.

Justifying the merger, Reed promised that Citigroup would be "the model of the financial services company of the future." Citicorp had served individuals and business and was the only successful global brand in consumer banking at the time, with branches in more than a hundred countries serving mostly better-off individuals. It was also one of the world's leading credit-card operators. Travelers' business was peddling everything from property insurance and mutual funds to shares. Bringing these two different businesses together would create a global financial supermarket offering a comprehensive range of products through a wide variety of distribution channels.

In the end, the marriage turned out to be a spectacular failure, and Citigroup was the big American bank that regulators most feared would go bust during the market crash of 2008. In November, the U.S. government rescued Citi with a massive injection of funds, and in February 2009, it took a 35 percent shareholding in the financial giant.

The merger had been rocky from the start. The cold and distant Reed was soon driven out by the hot and in-your-face Weill and his newly recruited ally in the executive suite, Robert Rubin, formerly treasury secretary under Bill Clinton. While Rubin stayed at Citigroup until after the markets crashed (along with his reputation for financial savvy), Weill was forced to step down in 2003 under pressure from then New York attorney general Eliot Spitzer, who was pursuing alleged wrongdoing at Citigroup during the dot-com bubble.

Such was the gravity of Citi's legal problems that Weill was succeeded as chief executive by his lawyer, Chuck Prince. In the summer of 2007, Prince achieved notoriety by responding to a question about whether Citi should scale back its lending due to the bubble by saying, "As long as the music is playing, you've got to get up and dance," then adding, "We're still dancing." He became one of the first major casualties of the credit crunch that began soon after, being forced to retire in November 2007. The challenge facing his successor, Vikram Pandit, was widely seen as figuring out how to break up Citigroup—a task that became more urgent after the government took its stake in the company.

The merger of Citicorp and Travelers had created a financial supermarket of the kind that legislators were trying to stop when they voted through the Glass-Steagall Act in 1933. This New Deal legislation, which banned banks from providing commercial and investment banking services together, was still in force in 1998 when Reed and Weill announced their deal. But they, rightly, did not expect any obstacles. Glass-Steagall was, by that time, widely seen as out of date, and, besides, Citicorp's well-funded lobbying efforts had been one of the main reasons the act had stayed on the statute books, efforts that ended with the announcement of the deal. In 1999, Glass-Steagall was consigned to the dustbin of history by Congress. From then until the fall of Lehman Brothers, the rule on Capitol Hill seemed to be, whatever (de)regulation Wall Street wants, Wall Street gets.

So what had changed in the decades since Congress had introduced these regulations? The Wall Street boom that turned to bust in 1929 and the wave of bank failures that followed it starting in 1930 prompted an inquisition by Congress to find out what had gone wrong. Much of the blame, it said, fell on the "universal banks" that offered investment services to customers as well as the usual checking accounts, savings accounts, mortgages, and small loans.

Congress found these institutions guilty of three offenses.

First, the universal banks had used their access to customers through branches and brokerage offices to push stock market investments at the American public, which, supported by easy credit, had fueled the speculative frenzy behind the boom. Second, they had sold risky shares to unwary citizens who knew no better (a bit like sellers of subprime mortgages). Third, their fragile investment banking divisions had undermined the solid commercial banking part of the business, making universal banks more vulnerable to shocks and prone to failure than those that stuck to commercial banking alone.

The problem was that most of this was untrue. Yes, the banks had sold investment products to banking customers and, in some cases, lent them money to speculate. But it has never been shown that the role of universal banks was big enough to cause the widespread mania, rather than being a symptom of a mania that was going on anyway. In terms of the risk profile of their products, universal banks had a reputation and relationship to maintain with their clients for commercial banking services, so they appear to have been more conservative in their choice of stocks than were the stand-alone investment banks. Moreover, diversified universal banks were, in fact, better able to deal with the market meltdown of the 1930s than those that chose to stick to either commercial or investment operations.

In passing Glass-Steagall, Congress may have been driven less by the facts than by a populist prejudice against big banks. America had long preferred its banks to be small, local, and, well, inefficient. Fear of powerful national banks motivated much of the resistance to Alexander Hamilton's proposals for the First Bank of the United States and inspired President Andrew Jackson to kill off the Second Bank. This suspicion reemerged at the start of the twentieth century under the Progressive banner and its attacks on the "money trust," most notably the JP Morgan firm. (Glass-Steagall was responsible for the split between the firm's commercial banking activities, which remained with JP Morgan, and its investment banking, which continued as a new firm, Morgan Stanley.) In 1927, as the speculative mania of the Roaring Twenties gathered pace, Congress had passed the McFadden Act, which effectively blocked the development of interstate banking until the 1980s. Even after World War II, Harry Truman's administration went after the investment banks on antitrust grounds, although by the early 1950s the government had given up this effort owing to a lack of evidence.

While the deregulation of the financial sector that started in the 1970s and gathered pace in the 1980s was driven in part by an ideological commitment to free markets, it was reinforced by the growing struggle of the banking sector to cope with the weight of so much regulation as well as its growing recognition of its ability to buy favorable legislation in Congress. The consequence of the existing New Deal regulation was a high cost of compliance spread across a vast number of banks (America has long had more banks per capita than any other industrial country), most of which were too small to bear this burden.

All this regulation imposed a heavy cost on customers in poor service (despite the occasional exception) and poor value for money. It also encouraged cheating. Another provision of Glass-Steagall was Regulation Q, which capped the interest rate payable on savings accounts and effectively drove the savings and loan institutions into an expensive crisis for the taxpayer as they sought out new, risky ways of making money.

Something similar happened in Japan after it introduced the same rule, capping interest rates on deposit accounts for some banks in 1980: with deposits harder to come by, the banks tried to squeeze more profit out of the capital they did have and turned to real-estate speculation that ended with the asset price collapse later that year. Regulation often has unintended consequences.

Ultimately, rules such as Regulation Q and the separation of commercial and investment banking under Glass-Steagall, as well as the restrictions of McFadden, were eased because the crippling effect they had on America's banking industry became impossible to ignore. The fact that the far bigger, universal banks of Europe and Japan were becoming increasingly powerful globally, and threatened to dominate an industry that America expected to lead, may have helped concentrate minds in Congress.

The fact that Citigroup was one of the banks worst hit by the financial crisis, and became one of the biggest recipients of taxpayer support, gave plenty of ammunition to those who blamed the crisis in part on the scrapping of Glass-Steagall. Yet while big universal banks such as Citigroup may have been more expensive to rescue, this was an equal-opportunity crisis for financial institutions of all types. The performance of banks during the crisis seems to have had more to do with the way they were managed. Indeed, the problems at Citigroup arguably owe far more to a dysfunctional corporate culture that had formed soon after the merger and never improved than to the fact that it was a universal bank.

Turning back the clock and returning to the era of Glass-Steagall was one of the most popular suggestions for regulatory reform after the crisis, regardless of how impractical such a move would be given today's global capital markets and the complexity of financial products. It has also been proposed to go further and carve up the financial system between "narrow banks," which take deposits but can only invest the money in low-risk assets, and other institutions, which could take bigger risks but whose investors would not receive deposit insurance. This, it is argued, would insulate everyday banking from a crisis like the one in September 2008.

The lesson of history, however, is that boring banks that do not take risks often find themselves challenged by new sorts of financial firms that take slightly more risk in order to pay higher rates to customers. (That was why the banking trusts grew so rapidly in the early twentieth century, before the crisis of 1907.) Once enough customers switch from the boring, regulated bank to the new, riskier "shadow banks," a powerful political pressure builds to extend the deposit-insurance safety net to the new banks. On the other hand, if somehow regulation means that the shadow banks do not emerge, an economy reliant on narrow banks for its risk capital will not fund many of the bright ideas of its entrepreneurs. Glass-Steagall and variations on it should remain in the legislative graveyard.

The other big reform idea is not to regulate what banks do but to regulate their scale. "If a bank is too big to fail, it is too big" goes the easy mantra. It's true that mergers and acquisitions had created a banking industry dominated by a small number of mega-institutions. But is size, itself, the problem? Clearly, the failure of a bank the size of Lehman Brothers came as a massive shock to the markets, but that just makes the U.S. authorities' decision even more extraordinary. Bailing out a large bank is also more costly, but it may be cheaper and simpler than having to bail out a number of smaller banks that fail as contagion spreads around the financial system. So the question is whether bigger or smaller banks would be safer. That, as in the 1930s, is not evident from the facts. Again, the fate of banks in this crisis seems to have been, most of all, a test of how they were managed. Tougher rules to ensure competition in the banking sector should drive better management, which would probably mean smaller banks. Setting an arbitrary limit on the size of banks, however, looks like treating the symptom rather than the disease. The real challenge is how to get the whole banking sector to manage risk better, particularly risk to the whole system, which they failed to do in the run-up to this crisis.

The problem with systemic risk—that is, the risk built up by lots of individual decisions that do not, individually, seem risky but as a whole could bring down the system, as happened with mortgage-backed securities—is that it is, well, systemic, so no individual bank has enough information to assess the problem. A popular suggestion has been to give this role to a regulator, who will monitor the risk and then tell banks to, say, cut back lending or increase their capital base if necessary.

This is tricky stuff. An overzealous regulator, knowing that his or her reputation depends on avoiding crises, would be too cautious, jumping at financial shadows and constantly meddling in business decisions. A regulator captured by the industry, on the other hand, would be too permissive and no protection at all. Both would be subject to the charge of unfairness, as each bank protested that it was being misunderstood and hard done by compared with its rivals.

Any regulatory solution begs a question about which financial system is being regulated. Take Citigroup, for example. It was the world's largest and most diverse financial institution, with operations in more than a hundred countries, selling just about every financial product that has ever been invented. Probably every financial regulator in the world considered Citi, to some degree, his or her problem. Yet in a sense nobody truly regulated Citi, a global firm in a world of national and sometimes sectoral watchdogs. The same was true of AIG, GE Capital, UBS, Deutsche Bank—indeed, any financial firm operating across borders.

It is hard to imagine any country ceding oversight of its banks to a new global superregulator—and anyway, given the extraordinary complexity of financial regulation and the vast differences in the detail of regulation from one country to the next, such a global regulator would have its work cut out. A better option, at least in theory, may be for national regulators, who understand the local rules better than anyone, to cooperate with each other fully and transparently, sharing as much information as possible about the firms they each regulate so that they can build up an accurate picture of global risks.

Yet, ironically, such cooperation seems to have been in place in the years before the current crisis. In January 2007, leading central bankers and financial regulators meeting at the World Economic Forum in Davos, Switzerland, expressed general contentment at their ability to work together, and agreed that although there was more risk in the financial system than made them feel comfortable, it was well diversified and so there was very little danger of losses causing a systemic crisis. Only one regulator, from the SEC, dissented, worrying—rightly, as it turned out—that risk could prove to be much more concentrated in the banking sector than anyone else in the room thought possible.

Why was everyone else so wrong? It was probably not a lack of international cooperation but owed rather more to the confidence the regulators had that those running the banks had a strong self-interest in collectively keeping the financial system healthy. The important lesson as we look forward is that the regulators' (ultimately misplaced) faith in the effectiveness of the risk-management models was itself the product of an initiative to deal with risks that straddle two or more countries: the Basel system of bank-capital requirements.

SURE FOUNDATIONS?

On June 26, 1974, the otherwise undistinguished Herstatt Bank in Cologne, Germany, went bust owing money to counterparts in New York, the settlement system for international payments having failed to complete a deal due to a problem related to the differences in time zones. The first reaction of the liquidators was that the American creditors would simply have to get in line for payment along with everyone else. Yet senior bankers soon realized that a failure of the payments system in this way would undermine confidence in international financial flows. To stop that from happening, the deal was honored. After that near miss, regulators and central bankers around the world agreed to establish standards to ensure that international deals between banks were no longer exposed to this "Herstatt risk." Alas, the standards they established, which included requiring banks engaged in international payments to have sufficient reserves of capital to guard against potential losses, turned out to have perverse consequences that ultimately contributed hugely to the financial crisis.

Years of painstaking negotiations about international banking rules finally produced, in 1988, the Basel Capital Accords, named after the Swiss city that is the seat of the Bank for International Settlements (BIS), the banker to the world's central bankers and a bit of a private club where they can shoot the breeze about all things monetary. As the BIS's name suggests, it was set up in 1930 to manage international payments related to Germany's reparations after World War I. It was nearly scrapped at the Bretton Woods Conference, in part because of controversy about gold received from Nazi Germany, but was saved when FDR, who was strongly in favor of abolition, died in 1945. (Saving the BIS was a rare victory for Keynes. Abolition had been agreed to by the negotiators at Bretton Woods over British objections after a late switch in the American position. Keynes read this as a sign of double-crossing by the U.S. negotiators and stormed into Treasury Secretary Morgenthau's office, threatening to quit the conference. Morgenthau agreed to delay a final decision, which, when it came, fell to FDR's less hostile successor, Harry Truman. Keynes was so agitated by the incident that he fell ill. False reports circulated that he had suffered a heart attack, and some German newspapers even published an obituary.)

Broadly, the Basel Accords required any bank doing business across borders to hold a capital cushion of at least 8 percent of its lending. If banks wanted to trade internationally, they had to keep enough cash stashed away to ensure that their counterparties in other countries would always get paid.

Why 8 percent and not 5 percent or 10 percent? Why indeed. This was a fairly arbitrary figure. There is no right answer. Strikingly, in response to the current crisis, there have been calls, including from former Fed chairman Alan Greenspan, to raise the capital requirement (and thus lower the amount of leverage/credit creation that banks can do) to perhaps as high as 15 percent. This would certainly be a more conservative requirement, though a case can surely be made that it would be too conservative.

The 8 percent requirement posed a particular problem for Japanese banks as they tried to implement the Basel Accords. Their business had been based on almost incestuous lending relationships with industrial conglomerates, which they judged were very low risk, and this meant they needed to hold relatively little capital in reserve (in some cases well below 4 percent of the value of assets). To meet the new requirement, Japanese banks therefore shored up their capital base by buying up real estate and equities, which were much riskier. This asset-buying spree had the opposite effect to that intended by the signatories to the Basel Accords. It further inflated Japan's asset price bubble of the late 1980s and ensured that the banks' balance sheets were in a parlous state when the bubble burst in 1990. With no way of plugging the hole in their balance sheets and needing to meet the Basel capital-adequacy standards, Japanese banks resorted to creative accounting that denied the severity of the problem and to reducing lending.

The Asian financial crisis of 1997–98 further highlighted a serious flaw in the Basel Accords—namely, that they failed to take into account the differences in the riskiness of different sorts of bank lending. Some loans, such as to a rich government like America's or a blue-chip company like Toyota, are inherently less risky than others—for example, those to an emerging-market government, a highly leveraged real-estate development, or an unproven social media start-up company. A well-designed capital-adequacy regime would require less capital to be set aside against losses on the first two loans than on the rest. The Basel Accords had made some effort to take into account these differences in riskiness, but the Japanese and Asian crises showed that this was inadequate. The regulations used categories of risk that were too undifferentiated: banks had to set aside as much capital against a loan to Microsoft as to a Hungarian dot-com, as much against a loan to America as one to South Korea. Banks also discovered ways to use derivatives and other securities to allow relatively risky loans to qualify for a low-risk, low-capital treatment. Even in the late 1990s, some forward-thinking regulators worried that a large part of the growth in the use of derivatives and securitization by banks was driven by the desire to finesse the Basel risk rules.

In 2004, after much controversy and delay, new capital rules were agreed, under the imaginative name of Basel 2. These new rules of the game tried to be more flexible and market-oriented to avoid the kind of distortions that the original Basel Accords had created. Although Basel 2 was barely in use by 2008, it relied on two mechanisms that failed dramatically that year: banks' own risk-management models and the ratings agencies.

Regulators believed that banks had a strong self-interest in managing their risks sensibly. Basel 2 therefore assumed that the banks' risk-management models accurately reflected reality and that the banks understood well their exposures to other financial firms and to the systemic risk of the overall financial system. In reality, the self-interest of making a quick buck in many cases outweighed the deeper self-interest of being a healthy long-term business.

Part of the problem was that banks, under pressure to improve their ratio of capital to assets but wanting to lend to eager borrowers, had a choice between the tiresome business of slowly attracting more deposits from savers and simply reducing the risks on their balance sheets. Many banks chose the latter and boosted their profits through the wonders of securitization and off-balance-sheet finance.

It also turned out that big financial firms had increasingly used similar internal risk-management systems. These were sensitive to movements in the markets, and they caused their users to respond in similar ways, so the few big firms that dominated the markets increasingly moved as a herd. The resulting lack of diversity of opinion pushed the banks into the crisis and worsened the liquidity crunch after the crash. Some bank regulators had argued that this danger was not all that significant because the underlying risks taken by financial institutions were quite different even if their risk-management systems were similar. If only. Getting better risk models is now a priority for the banks.

Basel 2 did not leave everything to the banks. Credit-ratings agencies had a crucial role in judging the riskiness of assets, especially those that had been securitized. The contribution of the ratings agencies to the crisis made that role look mistaken. The outsourcing of due diligence on risk assessment proved to be misguided. Whether out of a short-term focus on profit maximization from rating as many securities as possible or out of sheer incompetence, securities were often rated using woefully optimistic risk models. This was particularly true of securitized assets that were given triple-A ratings. The defining characteristic of a triple-A security is that Anybody buying it should feel confident that it is extremely low-risk. It is a "widows and orphans" investment. That is why so many investors failed to do their due diligence on these securities—due diligence that would probably have revealed the inadequacy of the risk models. In this respect, the ratings agencies were the weakest link in the financial system—and as the crisis confirmed, the financial system is only as strong as its weakest link.

The failure of ratings agencies has led to proposals that they should no longer be allowed to be paid by those they rate. But in that case, who would pay for the ratings? Another proposal is for the government to oversee the ratings process—though this would certainly bring problems of its own, ranging from the potential for underfunding the ratings process due to tight public-sector budgets to the danger that a rating would be interpreted as a government guarantee of the riskiness of a security, which might add to moral hazard in the financial system. If anything, part of the solution may be to reduce government involvement in the ratings process. The Basel process elevated Moody's, Standard & Poor's, and Fitch to approved ratings agencies—handing them a de facto oligopoly. Perhaps it would be better to deregulate the market, to encourage a more competitive ratings industry. Of course, that would require the users of ratings to ask some probing questions about the risk models used by the different rating agencies—but some questioning of the assumptions used in risk models, and indeed a healthy degree of skepticism, could only be a good thing.

REGULATE IN HASTE, REPENT AT LEISURE

In the aftermath of the crisis that followed the fall of Lehman Brothers, there was a real danger that the offices of the world's financial regulators would echo with the sound of stable doors being slammed shut after the horse had bolted. After every crisis, the first reaction of the politician is to propose tougher regulation. Yet this is a dangerous path. Regulation introduced in a hurry inevitably imposes considerable costs but often fails to solve the problems it is meant to. The Sarbanes-Oxley Act was introduced following the collapse of big companies such as Enron and World-Com. It was supposed to greatly improve the internal risk controls in firms. It certainly cost a fortune to implement and comply with. Yet it did nothing to prevent the massive failures of risk management by financial firms that was at the heart of the latest crisis.

It may be far-fetched to suggest that governments today could be as daft as France's was in the eighteenth century and try to reverse all financial innovation. But there were plenty of politicians wanting a return to basic banking, limited to taking deposits and making loans, ignorant of the economic cost of regulating financial intermediation back into the nineteenth century. The crisis was also used as an excuse to fight other battles. Within Europe, Britain's position was weakened as the champion of a more free-market model of capitalism than France or Germany. The advocates of more state-led capitalism did not pass up the opportunity to try to constrain hedge funds and other, similar manifestations of the Anglo-Saxon economic model.

Even in America, there was a real danger that rather than learning how to better manage financial innovation, regulators would try to slow it down or stop it entirely, by curbing hedge funds and the use of financial derivatives—no doubt driven by members of Congress citing Warren Buffett's description of derivatives as "weapons of mass financial destruction." Yet if anything was clear from the market reaction to the crisis, it was that users of derivatives would in the future take a much more informed and skeptical view of their usefulness, without any prodding from government. The same went for lending to hedge funds. Nobody in finance wanted a repeat of the crisis, which personally cost them so much.

Rather than fighting yesterday's battles by trying to fix symptoms of the crisis, a better solution is to fix the causes. Better management of banks through the discipline of more competition would help. That is going to be a particular challenge for governments, since the bailout and rescue process led to a series of mergers that concentrated ownership in the banking sector even further. It may be tempting for cash-strapped governments to do little about this problem if they think that bigger banks will get a better price when denationalization finally comes.

Everyone knows that bank risk management has to improve, but here the answer is not micromanagement by regulators. The problem that needs to be fixed is that no single market participant, currently, can see the big picture. There is a need for a regulator—new or existing—that will use its neutrality to collect commercially sensitive information that no bank would currently put in the public domain and then aggregate that information to give an overall picture of how risk is building up in the system. By publishing a regular systemic risk assessment, the regulator would not only be helping the banks themselves to run better risk-management models. This information would also help shareholders, ratings agencies, and other banks to scrutinize the riskiness of individual financial institutions.

There remains a danger of inappropriate regulation being

introduced that either misses the point, like much of the New Deal regulation that largely tackled phantom problems in the U.S. financial sector for decades, or tackles yesterday's problems rather than tomorrow's. Even if regulators build up defenses to prevent a recurrence of the factors that caused the crisis of 2008, will they be ready for the next challenge that financial innovation throws up?

Financial markets and how they are regulated certainly need to change. To avoid the mistakes of the past, the public debate needs to move beyond the blame game on to a frank, informed, and considered discussion of what really went wrong and what really can be done to fix it. Proposals for new regulation must be rigorously stress-tested to determine their costs in terms of unintended consequences.

This will require a mature public debate as well as political vision and courage. Getting America's legislators to reduce the fragmentation of its regulatory system would be a remarkable achievement, let alone agreeing to better regulation at a global level. The financial sector itself, and the leaders of capitalism more broadly, must take responsibility and reassess the values that have underpinned the boom of the past thirty years. There is also a fundamental challenge to the economics profession, which failed to provide the tools to bankers or to regulators to understand the risks that were building up in the system. Are the dismal scientists ready for that challenge?

PART TWO

THE ROAD FROM RUIN

6

ECONOMICS WITH A HUMAN FACE

Toward a less dismal science

Practical men, who believe themselves to be quite exempt from any intellectual influences, are usually the slaves of some defunct economist," observed the late, great British economist John Maynard Keynes in 1936. Ironically, the defunct economist to whom the practical men (and women) instinctively turned during this latest crisis was none other than Keynes himself.

In early 2009, as the economy slumped, *Time* magazine called Keynes the "trendiest dead economist of this apocalyptic moment . . . the godfather of government stimulus." *Newsweek* provided a cheat sheet explaining that Keynes ("rhymes with brains"), among other things, believed that "big government is good government" and that "markets fail when left to their own devices." It also noted, incidentally, that his lifestyle was "ahead of its time" (he was bisexual) and that "for an economist, he ran with a cool crowd" (he married a ballerina, and his friends included Virginia Woolf and Pablo Picasso).

Keynes would certainly have seen clear parallels between the credit-crunched economy of 2009 and that of the Great Depression, when he wrote his seminal work, *The General Theory of Employment,*

Interest and Money. Indeed, as a description of how a loss of confidence can lead to a credit crunch, it is hard to improve on his writing about the "liquidity trap"—in which people become so scared of being hit with losses on illiquid assets such as stocks and bonds that they switch en masse to the one truly liquid asset: cash.

Likewise, what Keynes called the "paradox of thrift" seemed eerily familiar. The paradox describes a situation in which lots of individuals behaving rationally by increasing their savings as an economy deteriorates actually produce a worse outcome in the aggregate than if they had each been less personally prudent. That is because the flip side of their increased saving is less spending, which when added up across the economy means less demand overall and thus less income to save from. His recommendation, in both cases, that the government should spend more in situations where aggregate demand is not sufficient to generate full employment certainly seemed right on message in 2009, both as a description of what happened and as a statement of what, in terms of economic theory, should have happened.

Ironically, Keynes himself would probably have objected to being intellectually exhumed as the spokesperson for big government. Even when he was alive, he bristled at followers who called themselves "Keynesians" yet in his view bastardized his ideas. Given the later problems with the policies of economic "fine-tuning" implemented by these followers in government, he was right to keep his distance. The failure of government spending in many countries to produce anything better than the "stagflation" of the 1970s meant that barely had President Richard Nixon declared himself a Keynesian in 1971 (forever misquoted as "we're all Keynesians now") than these ideas were consigned to the intellectual wilderness for a generation.

Today's self-declared Keynesians like to quote the great man's critique of stock market capitalism, that "when the development of a country becomes a by-product of the activities of a casino, the job is likely to be ill done." Few of them seem actually to have read *The General Theory* or to have understood the nuances of his case for greater government activism at times of high unemployment.

When Lehman Brothers went bust on September 15, 2008, Keynes surely would not have shared the schadenfreude of many a born-again Keynesian at the sudden discrediting of faith in free markets—the previous conventional wisdom of practical men, behind which was another defunct economist, Adam Smith. The eighteenth-century Scotsman had posthumously dominated the previous thirty years with the laissez-faire ideas he had set out in 1776 in his *An Inquiry into the Nature and Causes of the Wealth of Nations,* in which he famously attributed the superior performance of market forces to the workings of an "invisible hand." Contrary to his popular image as a fan of big government, Keynes favored government action to boost demand in certain dire situations because he believed that it was the only way to preserve a mostly market-based economy. Keynes wanted the invisible hand to be given plenty of scope to work its magic. As he put it, his goal was to "cure the disease" of high unemployment "whilst preserving efficiency and freedom." This should also be our goal today.

Keynes certainly would have been critical of responding to a crisis simply by returning to old orthodoxies. In *The General Theory,* he wrote about the bigger difficulty lying not so much in developing new ideas as in "escaping from the old ones." For Keynes, an irritatingly mercurial intellect, being open-minded was a duty. As he once challenged a questioner, "When the facts change, I change my mind. What do you do, Sir?" However, probably through experience, he was skeptical about the open-mindedness of others, noting that "there are not many who are influenced by new theories after they are twenty-five or thirty years of age, so that the ideas which civil servants and politicians and even agitators apply to current events are not likely to be the newest." *Plus ça change* . . .

Moments of crisis, such as the 1930s and today, provide the opportunity for significant new ideas to break through. The stagflation crisis provided the breakthrough opportunity for a free-market school of economics that was built on the assumption that people made their economic decisions in ways that were rational. Having seen government fail, practical men such as Alan Greenspan, the chairman of the Federal Reserve, placed their faith in lightly regulated markets as the driving force of the economy.

That faith, which dominated policymaking around the world for the best part of thirty years, ultimately proved misplaced. Yet there is a chance for today's generation of practical people to embrace a new and better economic paradigm. Ironically, this should include at its core an idea that both Keynes and Smith shared, though they lacked the tools to develop it beyond the anecdotal: the notion that people are not fully rational. Smith believed that psychology played a big role in economic activity. He attributed the willingness to take risks to what he called "overweening conceit." Likewise, Keynes understood that apparently inexplicable mood changes could have huge economic consequences. He called the irrational optimism that drives people to act "animal spirits."

In the past couple of decades, academic economics has made significant advances in understanding how people do not always behave in simplistically rational ways, individually or collectively. Three broad areas of new thinking have emerged to explain why firms and individuals can be irrational: the first admits that even rational individuals have to act on limited information; the second looks at the tensions and conflicts within institutions and the networks they form; the third delves into our psychological and neurological drives. Together, economic thinkers have started to explain how otherwise inexplicable events, such as bubbles and crashes, can occur, with devastating economic consequences. Bringing these ideas into the policymaking mainstream may be our best hope of preventing, or at least minimizing the impact of, future crises. But first we need to understand where the idea of rational economic man and perfect markets came from.

THE BIRTH OF *HOMO ECONOMICUS*

"Imagine an ideally perfect instrument, a psychophysical machine, continually registering the height of pleasure experienced by an individual," wrote the British economist Francis Edgeworth in 1881. This "hedonimeter" would be able to measure in real time the happiness of every individual, he hoped. "From moment to moment the hedonimeter varies; the delicate index now flickering with the flutter of the passions, now steadied by intellectual activity, low sunk whole hours in the neighbourhood of zero, or momentarily springing up towards infinity. The continually indicated height is registered by photographic or other frictionless apparatus."

Having measured the happiness of each individual, Edgeworth argued, it would be possible to map changes in total happiness throughout the population. It would not be merely selfish pleasure that was measured: if a person gained altruistic pleasure from helping someone else or seeing that person experience happiness, the hedonimeter would flicker higher. Economic policy could then be designed to maximize total happiness—or, as the philosopher John Stuart Mill christened it, "utility"—and the success of that strategy could be demonstrated empirically with the hedonimeter.

Edgeworth was one of a group of economists, led by Alfred Marshall, the "father of modern economics," who transformed their subject in the second half of the nineteenth century by arguing that the purpose of economics is to understand utility and how to increase it. The key was to look at the different alternative uses to which scarce resources could be put and calculate how much extra happiness—"marginal utility"—would arise from shifting resources from one use to another.

Until then, "classical" economists had tended to focus on the cost of resources used in production, rather than the benefit that the production created for consumers. The "marginal revolution," as it is known, gave mainstream economists new intellectual tools to fight the Marxist movement, which was growing strongly in the late nineteenth century, partly in reaction to the high unemployment arising from the long economic depression that began in 1873. Marx had based his ideas on classical economics. His "labor theory of value," which underpinned his analysis of the weaknesses of capitalism, argued that the value of production should be determined by the amount of labor needed to produce it, not by how much consumers benefit from it or are willing to pay for it.

The hedonimeter was never built—not surprisingly, as it would have required technology that is still beyond us today. The marginal revolutionaries quickly lost interest in exploring the workings of the human mind. Attempts were made, decades later, by another great economist, Irving Fisher, to measure utility indirectly, by observing how people spent their money rather than attempting to peer inside their heads. But by the 1940s, mainstream economists had largely given up trying to measure utility, or concerning themselves with the complexities and irrationalities of human psychology.

Instead, the postwar years were marked by the emergence of a new wave of economists who were dedicated rationalists. The dominance of rationality went hand-in-glove with the growing use in economics of mathematics, which also happened to be much easier to apply if humans were assumed to be rational—*Homo economicus* rather than *Homo sapiens*. Advances in computing technology allowed the new models to be tested on data that were piling up in unprecedented quantities. Increasingly, engineers and physicists turned to economics as a fertile field of study. Vast computerized models of the economy were built and were used for forecasting.

Rational behavior was understood to have several components. At a minimum—what economists called "narrow rationality"—*Homo economicus* was assumed to be trying always to maximize his general happiness. In other words, given a choice he would take the option with the highest "expected utility." And he would be consistent in his choices: if he preferred apples to oranges, and oranges to pears, he also preferred apples to pears. A broader definition of rationality added the notion that a person's beliefs were based on logical, objective analysis of all the available evidence.

Economists became gripped by what, with hindsight, might be called "physics envy," a belief that combining complex mathematical models, megabytes of computing power, and mountains of data could turn economics from a soft social science into a hard science. This belief survived the failure of so-called Keynesian fine-tuning, when governments tried top-down management of the economy based on massive computerized forecasting models that turned out to be not very good. (As the old joke goes, "Economists have correctly predicted nine of the last five recessions.")

The failure of Keynesianism shifted the consensus among policymakers toward a more decentralized, market-based economics. Inspired by Milton Friedman's monetarism, government narrowed its focus to keeping inflation in check, initially by tightly controlling the money supply. Adam Smith's invisible hand was granted its freedom through policies of deregulation, competition, and privatization, all of which reflected a belief in the superior rationality and efficiency of the market.

Macroeconomic policy, notably in America and Britain, was shaped by believers in the theory of "rational expectations." This said that rather than forming expectations on the basis of limited data drawn from past experience, the public took into account all available information. The theory did need everyone to be rational. It relied on the assumption that optimists and pessimists exist in equal measure and therefore cancel each other out, making the aggregate of all public expectations rational even when individuals were not (a bit like "Lincoln's First Law," that "you can't fool all of the people all of the time"). This public rationality included making an accurate assessment of government policy. Thus, when governments announced that they would do whatever was necessary to bring down inflation, people would adjust their expectations accordingly.

In the same way, from the mid-1970s, Wall Street investment firms, too, increasingly fell under the spell of the "efficient market hypothesis," an economic theory that says that the prices of financial assets such as shares and bonds are rationally based on all available information. Drawing on rational expectations, the theory said that even if there are many stupid investors, they would be driven out of the market by rational investors who could profit by trading against the investments of the foolish. As a result, economists scoffed at the notion that investors could consistently earn a higher return than the market average by picking shares. At the time, this rational view seemed like a dose of sanity, since most Wall Street money managers did nothing but compete on promises to beat the market, which few of them did for long, if ever. Yet this theory also drove economists into an ultimately catastrophic belief that since markets are rational, bubbles cannot form.

The influence of the efficient market hypothesis owed much to the fact that it proved to be a useful tool in the world of finance. Until then, the prices of financial derivatives such as options had mostly been set using little more than gut instinct. No wonder the mathematically rigorous Black-Scholes formula for pricing options, devised by Fischer Black, Myron Scholes, and Robert Merton in the early 1970s, caught on fast, spawning a new sort of Wall Street professional, the financial engineer. These engineers designed derivatives and securitizations, which (until the recent crash) made the banks ever richer and fatter—while economists argued reassuringly that this growing profitability was evidence that applied financial economics was making the banking system, and the economy as a whole, safer as well as better off.

Admittedly, some academic economists had started to question the purest version of the efficient market hypothesis as early as 1980, when Sanford Grossman and Joseph Stiglitz (the latter later won a Nobel Prize) pointed out a paradox: If prices reflect all information, then there is no gain from going to the trouble of gathering it, so no one does. A little inefficiency is necessary to give smart investors an incentive to drive prices toward efficiency. Nonetheless, most economists took this to mean that although markets would sometimes be inefficient, mispricing would not last for long, so it did not shake their faith in the efficient market hypothesis.

As we shall see, some economists started to have serious doubts after the stock market crash of 1987, which the hypothesis said should not have happened—but which actually turned out to be aggravated by the portfolio insurance designed by believers in the efficient market theory. A decade later, Merton and Scholes themselves provided an even more graphic example of the gap between their rational models and reality when Long-Term Capital Management, a hedge fund of which they were cofounders, went bust in 1998.

Yet these real-world contradictions of the theory, which stirred up plenty of debate among academic economists, did not cause policymakers to abandon their support for economic policies based on rational *Homo economicus*. (They behaved much as Keynes thought the classical economists had done faced with the start of the Great Depression. Referring to Euclid, the father of geometry, Keynes commented that "the classical theorists resemble Euclidian geometers in a non-Euclidian world, who discovering that in experience straight lines apparently parallel often meet, rebuke the lines for not keeping straight as the only remedy for the unfortunate collisions which are occurring.")

The greatest central banker of the day, Alan Greenspan, was suggesting that markets might not be completely rational when he coined his catchphrase by publicly asking in 1996, "How do we know when irrational exuberance has unduly escalated asset values, which then become subject to unexpected and prolonged contractions, as they have in Japan over the past decade?" Yet, when push came to shove, he never allowed the possibility of "irrational exuberance" in the markets to affect his decisions at the Federal Reserve.

Why? Even if he had tried to burst the bubble, the massive hikes in interest rates that would have been necessary to puncture the mood of "irrational exuberance" would probably have done in Greenspan's reputation and his career. How could he prove to his own satisfaction or to the public that such drastic measures were really necessary, when the efficient market hypothesis, which said that the regulator could not outsmart the market, still enjoyed such currency?

Greenspan took comfort in his belief, again reflecting the rational conventional economic wisdom of the day, that if there were a bubble and if it burst, he had the economic tools to revive the economy fast. Taking action to stop a bubble from forming would be horribly painful—probably causing a recession, at least—so why bother, given that the messy aftermath of a bubble could easily be put right, with judicious interest-rate cuts and other measures?

And after all, despite the occasional wobble, the rational model seemed to be working in practice. Indeed, as Greenspan explained at a congressional hearing in October 2008, when asked why the financial crisis had shocked him, "I had been going for forty years or more with very considerable evidence that it was working exceptionally well."

The U.S. and global economy had enjoyed decades of high-growth, low-inflation "Great Moderation" to such an extent that in September 2007, Christina Romer (whom Barack Obama later appointed chair of his Council of Economic Advisers) declared that "better policy, particularly on the part of the Federal Reserve, is directly responsible for the low inflation and the virtual disappearance of the business cycle in the last twenty-five years." Meanwhile, share prices had continued, albeit with an occasional wobble, their long bull run that began in 1982. The profits of financial firms soared ever higher. All of which enabled policymakers to convince themselves that everything was working just fine—until suddenly it wasn't.

The Great Moderation ended in 2008 when the economy plunged into a cataclysmic downturn following the bursting of precisely the sort of massive bubble in asset prices that the efficient market hypothesis said should not happen. At the congressional hearing in October 2008, grilled by a committee that used to fawn over him, Greenspan confessed that he had made a "mistake" in believing that banks would look after their own rational self-interest. Although this was not the full-blown mea culpa reported by the press, when asked, "Were you wrong?," Greenspan replied, "Partially."

Yet Greenspan should have known better. Academic economists had long since rediscovered an interest in everything that did not fit the rational models of *Homo economicus.*

THE LIMITS OF REASON

"It is time for a profound rethinking of how financial markets work. The prevailing paradigm of the efficient market hypothesis has been proven wrong," says George Soros, clearly enjoying his moment of glory. "I first predicted the financial crisis in 1987, again in 1998, and, finally, the third time. I am the boy who cried wolf three times," says the controversial billionaire hedge-fund boss. He has been used to having his theories dismissed by academic economists, but in February 2009 at Columbia University, a library full of them (including two Nobel Prize winners) was hanging on his every word. Although in a moment of modesty he conceded that "I did not anticipate how serious it would become," his unambiguous message was "I told you so."

Another "boy" who in the aftermath of the crisis was quick to remind everyone that he had cried wolf was Nassim Nicholas Taleb. The former trader had become famous for his warnings that the complex mathematical models of the rocket-scientist financial engineers did not work because they failed to capture the complexity of the real world. The title of his book *The Black Swan* alludes to the widely held view in Europe for centuries that swans were always white, which was proved to be wrong when black swans were discovered in Australia. Taleb argued that throughout history, the world has been changed by unexpected, unpredictable "black swan" events. In his view, the banking sector simply ignored the possibility of "black swan" extreme shocks that could, and eventually did, bring down the system. He blamed the crisis on the dependence of the financial sector on models, since "economic papers that rely on mathematics are not scientifically valid. Not only do they underestimate the possibility of 'black swans' but they are unaware that we do not have any ability to deal with the mathematics of extreme events."

Taleb certainly had a point that what should have been "once-in-a-thousand-years" events (such as the 1987 crash and the collapse of LTCM), if the economists' models were to be believed, seemed to keep cropping up every few years. Yet he offered few solutions, beyond caution. To Taleb, the globalized world was a complex place, packed full of unforecastable dangers, in which the only safe course of action would be to take far fewer risks, especially by borrowing far less.

While Taleb has been dismissive of mainstream economics (and most mainstream economists are dismissive of him in return), Soros wants to change economics, and at Columbia University his views were being taken seriously. He believes that he came up with a new paradigm decades earlier, and that his alternative economic theory, called "reflexivity," had finally been proved right by the crisis. He threw down the gauntlet to the gathering of dismal scientists: "Yet this hasn't been accepted as the new paradigm. There has been no research done on it. Why is that?"

Reflexivity has two main components, Soros says. First, markets always distort and misinterpret all the available information. There is always bias and fallibility. Second, mispricing has ways of affecting the fundamentals that market prices are supposed to reflect. The most dramatic example of how these "feedback mechanisms" can distort is bubbles. As Soros sees it, every bubble involves a trend that prevails in reality, and a misconception or misinterpretation of the trend. Sometimes the misinterpretation accelerates the trend, reinforcing the misinterpretation. The crisis that began in 2007 was "due to a super bubble that has been developing since the early 1980s and has finally reached a turning point." In Soros's view the efficient market hypothesis had been a major cause of misinterpretation by the market, which had fueled the super bubble for so long.

Despite his complaints about being ignored, for the past couple of decades some mainstream academic economists have been developing new economic paradigms that have much in common with Soros's reflexivity, including misinterpretation, network effects such as feedback loops, and actions that are, or appear to be, irrational.

One school of thought says that although people are essentially rational, their rationality is limited or "bounded" due to not having enough information to make a fully rational decision, which can produce apparently irrational outcomes. There is nothing new in economics about the idea that people must make decisions based on imperfect knowledge. Frank Knight gave his name to "Knightian uncertainty" thanks to his 1921 book, *Risk, Uncertainty and Profit*, which noted that most business decisions involve a step into an unknown that is to some degree unmeasurable. Keynes, too, observed that "human decisions affecting the future, whether personal or political or economic, cannot depend on strict mathematical expectation, since the basis for making such calculations does not exist."

The idea of "bounded rationality" was first proposed over half a century ago by the economist and psychologist Herbert Simon in his 1957 book, *Models of Man*. He was largely ignored during the boom in full-rationality economics. His ideas have since been found to create valuable opportunities for economists to experiment with models in which people have to make decisions with varying levels of information or varying degrees of accuracy in the information they do have.

Using these techniques, economists have developed models of bubbles in which incomplete information leads lots of people to rationally overestimate the value of shares, which thus rise in price. As prices rise, the investors see those higher prices as proof that their initial optimism was correct, encouraging them to buy with even greater confidence, pushing prices up further and continuing the bubbly cycle—until eventually the error becomes clear. Such informational "feedback loops," in this case at least, lead people who are acting rationally further away from the fully rational outcome, rather than helping them to learn more about true value—in the short run, anyway.

Perhaps the clearest example of this problem during the crisis that began in 2007 was how the mathematical models used by financial firms to manage their risks—such as value at risk (VAR) models—actually made matters worse. According to Nobel laureate Myron Scholes, risk managers at investment banks generally believed that they had sufficient control of the risks they were taking, "but they needed to know what everyone else was doing to see the aggregate picture." It turned out that, unknown to each other, everyone was doing very similar things. So when their models started telling them to sell, they all did—driving prices down further and triggering further model-driven selling. In short, their limited information about systemic risk in the market left them far more exposed to risk than they thought they were.

Another way in which economists have argued that investors acting rationally can expand bubbles rather than burst them, at least for a while, is based on what has become known as the "greater fool theory," the belief that you can safely invest in an asset because you will be able to find a greater fool than you to take it off your hands. The theory says that even if prices start to overheat, it may be rational for smart "momentum" investors to go with the flow for a while, buying the overpriced assets and thus helping to inflate the bubble rather than burst it. They would do so knowing that prices were irrational, but as smart investors they would expect to be able to get out at the top of the market, while less accomplished "fools," who believed that the rising prices made sense, would remain in the market and suffer losses when the bubble burst. (Inevitably, some who believe themselves to be smart investors, such as Sir Isaac Newton during the South Sea Bubble, discover they were not as rational as they thought and are still in the market when it crashes.)

Bounded rationality offers important insights into how limits on information can cause rational economic actors to behave apparently irrationally. Evidence has also been stacking up that distorted and perverse incentives within institutions can likewise drive rational actors to behave madly.

INSTITUTIONAL IRRATIONALITY

The efficient market theory was based on a faith in the effectiveness of the institutions of the markets—from banks to regulators. The theory's supporters did not believe that everyone trading in a market was fully rational. Instead, they assumed that the institutions of the market would allow rational investors to overcome the irrational "noise traders" (as Fischer Black dubbed them) and so keep prices accurate. This belief was widespread. Macroeconomic policymakers, for example, assumed that when the

Federal Reserve cut interest rates, banks would simply pass on interest-rate cuts to borrowers (and depositors) without focusing on the microeconomics of how that would happen, how quickly, and whether this process would work at times of market stress.

This faith in the effectiveness of the market was all the more surprising because one of the most active areas of economic theory in the past thirty years has been in regard to why institutions fail to function properly. This theory focused on "agency" problems that arise when shareholders hire a professional ("agent") to run their firm and that professional pursues his or her own personal interests rather than those of the shareholders.

This was not a new idea. "Being the managers rather of other people's money than of their own, it cannot well be expected that they should watch over it with the same anxious vigilance with which the partners in a private copartnery frequently watch over their own," observed Adam Smith in *The Wealth of Nations*. In the 1920s, this analysis was updated and expanded by Adolf Berle and Gardiner Means, who concluded in their great study, *The Modern Corporation and Private Property*, that the only solution to the conflicts of interest created by separating ownership and management was for control of big public companies to be exercised through "a purely neutral technocracy, balancing a variety of claims by various groups in the community and assigning to each a portion of the income stream on the basis of public policy rather than private cupidity."

The sort of "stakeholder capitalism" described by Berle and Means was the opposite of the free-market vision that Michael Jensen and Will Meckling believed in when they turned their attention to the agency problem of the separation of ownership and control in the 1970s. It would be perfectly rational for managers of public companies to manage in their self-interest, not in the interests of shareholders, concluded Jensen and Meckling.

A manager who has little or no investment in his firm would have little incentive to maximize its value, and every incentive to use it for his own ends. The smaller the ownership stake a manager has, the more likely he is to channel corporate resources in directions that give him value (perks, empire building through mergers and acquisitions, and so on), and the more effort and resources that shareholders have to devote to monitoring the manager's behavior to stop him from feathering his nest at their expense (these are known in the jargon as "agency costs"). Taken to its extreme, a boss without shares might build a comfortable but profitless empire that squandered cash on shareholder-value-destroying acquisitions. This bleak picture was a fairly good description of industrial conglomerates, which were common at the time.

Ironically, Jensen (and most of his fellow economists) did not apply this agency-cost analysis to financial firms, although this would have highlighted the inefficiency of the financial markets. Instead, he argued that financial markets were efficient—and that extending that efficiency to industrial companies would help solve their agency problems. In 1978 he even claimed that "there is no other proposition in economics which has more solid empirical evidence supporting it than the efficient market hypothesis." In short, if markets are efficient, so that share prices reflect all available information, that includes information about agency costs.

Jensen reasoned that shareholders should make it clear to managers that they are expected to increase their company's share price as proof that they are reducing agency costs. If the share price fell, that would be regarded as evidence of increasing agency costs, all else being equal. Better still, shareholders should explicitly link managerial pay to the share price, making managers into owners by paying them (partly) in shares or, as became extremely popular during the 1990s, in share options. Jensen also praised leveraged buyouts (LBOs), takeovers by investors using mostly borrowed money, as a way to reduce agency costs. By taking into private ownership a firm that had been traded on a public stock market, an LBO allowed the new owners to link the remuneration of managers to increases in the value of the firm. Taking on mountains of debt also meant that the firm was pre-committed to massive interest payments, which gave managers much less freedom to squander money in unproductive ways. Even the possibility of becoming the target of a hostile LBO bid would encourage existing managers to improve returns or risk losing their jobs.

Unfortunately, stock market bubbles—and the possibility that managers could pump up the short-term value of their companies through actions that hurt long-term value—made Jensen's solutions look far less attractive. Jensen eventually described schemes that paid executives with share options as "managerial heroin" that encouraged a focus on short-term highs, regardless of any potentially destructive long-term consequences. Once a firm's shares became overvalued, it was in managers' interests to keep them that way, or to encourage even more overvaluation, in the hope of cashing out before the bubble burst. Doing this not only meant being less than honest with shareholders, or being creatively optimistic with corporate accounting. It also encouraged behavior that actually reduced the value of some firms to their shareholders—such as making an acquisition or spending a fortune on launching an Internet arm simply to satisfy the whims of an irrational market. (This looks like a pretty good description of what was going on at Enron.)

Eventually, it dawned on economists that the financial markets were full of institutions rife with agency problems—and that this could fatally undermine the efficiency of markets.

Efficient market theory assumed that if asset prices moved

away from their fundamental value, market forces would drive them back again. If prices fell below the fundamental value, smart investors would keep buying the assets until the price was right again. If prices got too high, smart investors would be able to borrow all they needed to short the assets and drive them back down to the right level. But what if lenders are run by managers who are risk-averse and so will not lend all that the smart investors want to short-sell the assets? In that case, the smart money will not be able to bring about market efficiency. This is quite a likely scenario—and there is plenty of evidence that the further asset prices move away from fundamental value, the harder and costlier it gets to borrow to bet against the trend, however irrational.

If managers of nonfinancial companies are paid in ways that encourage them to pursue short-term profits, rather than to maximize long-term shareholder value, why wouldn't the same be true of financial firms? It should be no surprise that when their bosses are rewarded handsomely for every strong quarter, investment banks take on too much leverage to increase their bets. Likewise, if the boss of a ratings agency, which is supposed to be an impartial judge of credit quality, has a contract that allows him or her to get rich fast if the business grows fast, it should be no surprise that the agency risks hurting its reputation by giving a triple-A rating to subprime mortgage securities on which it has little performance data, but clear evidence of strong, lucrative demand from investors.

Short-termism was certainly a factor in the run-up to the crash of 2008, and it helps explain some of the recklessness of bank executives. It is easy to attribute these undesirable, short-termist actions to stupidity or greed. Yet, as a growing number of economists now argue, thinking about this behavior as a consequence of badly designed institutions and incentives may help us prevent similar problems in the future through reforms to corporate governance and managerial culture (see chapter 9).

Economists are also discovering agency problems in the institutions through which government oversees markets. For instance, politicians may want to be seen as getting tough on banks—or on how much bankers are paid—because they think it will win them votes, not because they think it is the right thing to do. The growing activism of elected state attorneys general in pursuing alleged financial wrongdoing may owe much to the fact that this can be an effective platform for an ambitious politician with an eye on a higher office (for example, Eliot Spitzer, who prosecuted firms such as Merrill Lynch and AIG when he was New York's attorney general, which helped him later become governor).

On the other hand, the theory of "regulatory capture"—whereby firms that are regulated form such a close bond with their regulator that they start to manipulate regulation to their advantage—has long been applied to industries such as telecoms and pharmaceuticals, but it has only recently been used to explain the favorable treatment given to some financial firms before the crisis (and, indeed, in a few cases, after it). Yet agency problems within regulatory institutions are rife, and of the sort that could easily contribute to regulatory capture. For instance, staff at regulatory agencies such as the Securities and Exchange Commission may be motivated more by getting noticed so that they can get a lucrative job in the private sector than by doing what is in the best interests of the users of the marketplace they regulate.

It is essential that careful thought be given more broadly to incentives and institutional design when creating or reforming financial regulators and central banks. For example, maybe a future chairman of the Federal Reserve would have been more willing to take action against bubbles than Alan Greenspan was if the Fed no longer had its (at least sometimes) conflicted mandate to simultaneously control inflation and maintain full employment.

The lack of a good understanding of these economic problems helps to explain why policymakers were caught by surprise when financial firms suddenly stopped cooperating with each other in August 2007, contributing to the credit crunch, and why governments failed to realize how little impact they would have when they tried to increase the supply of credit to the economy by pumping money into the banking system. They were wrong-footed when banks focused on using the money to help themselves survive, rather than passing it on to firms and people that wanted to borrow. Economists certainly need to look again at their macroeconomic models to take better account of things like how the banking system really operates and how credit really flows around the economy.

It is certainly possible that the behavior described in examples such as these is rational. If so, there is a big opportunity: by figuring out how to change the incentives for bankers and regulators, we can prevent some of the problems that caused the current crisis. The harder task is taking into account why, and when, people are sometimes plain dumb. New thinking in economics is helping with that, too.

INSIDE THE ECONOMIC MIND

A man is stretched out inside an MRI machine. He is not sick— he is taking part in an economic experiment. A series of investment options, some riskier than others, are projected onto the inside of the machine. An economist asks him to choose among them, and as he does so, the MRI tracks where the blood flows inside his brain.

The MRI is no hedonimeter, though it is a step in that direction. In the past few years it has given birth to neuroeconomics, a new discipline that draws on the insights of neuroscientists who have discovered that different bits of the old gray matter are associated with different sorts of emotional and decision-making activity. The amygdalae are an example. Neuroscientists have shown that these almond-shaped clusters of neurons deep inside the brain's medial temporal lobes play a key role in the formation of emotional responses such as fear.

Among other things, neuroeconomists have argued that releases of dopamine, the brain's pleasure chemical, may indicate economic utility or value. There is also growing interest in new evidence from neuroscience that tentatively suggests that two conditions of the brain compete in decision making: a cold, objective state and a hot, emotional state in which the ability to make sensible trade-offs disappears. The potential interactions between these two brain states are ideal subjects for economic modeling.

Already, neuroeconomics is giving many economists a dopamine rush, as they see the possibility of transforming economics, by providing a much better understanding of everything from people's reactions to advertising to decisions to go on strike. If it can help us to explain some of the rash decisions taken by bankers in the run-up to the crash of 2008, it should clearly be a priority for economic research, although, with neuroscience still in its infancy, its breakthroughs may not come fast enough for today's policymakers.

A more immediate source of insight into bubbles and other behavior that also does not fit the narrowly rational models is another relatively new school of economics, which draws on psychology.

Psychologists have compiled a long list of common behavioral traits that seem at odds with the rationality of *Homo economicus*. For example, people appear to be disproportionately influenced by the fear of feeling regret and will often pass up even benefits within easy reach to avoid a small risk of feeling they have failed. They are also prone to cognitive dissonance: holding a belief plainly at odds with the evidence, usually because the belief has been held and cherished for a long time (such as in the efficient market hypothesis, perhaps, or the Great Moderation). Psychologists sometimes call this "denial"—and there was clearly a lot of that around during the bubble years, even inside the Fed. Following the bursting of the bubble, there was a serious risk that denial would take hold in the political system, locking in old, orthodox ways of thinking.

Then there is anchoring: people are often overly influenced by outside suggestion. They can be influenced even when they know that a suggestion is not being made by someone who is better informed than they are. Perhaps most relevant of all to the formation of bubbles is the huge amount of evidence that people are persistently, and irrationally, overconfident about their own abilities. Asked to answer a factual question, then asked to give the probability that their answer was correct, people typically overestimate this probability. This may be due to a "representativeness heuristic": a tendency to treat events as representative of some well-known class or pattern. This gives people a sense of familiarity with an event and thus confidence that they have accurately diagnosed it. Such confidence can lead people to "see" patterns in data even where there are none. A closely related phenomenon is the "availability heuristic": people focus excessive attention on a particular fact or event, rather than the big picture, simply because it is more visible or fresher in their mind. (This may explain the misplaced popular expectation that, because they had been making headlines by continuously increasing in value, real-estate prices would never fall.)

Another delightfully human habit is "magical thinking": attributing to our own actions something that had nothing to do with us, and thus assuming that we have a greater influence over events than is actually the case. (Was the phenomenon of all those central bankers crediting central banks with delivering the Great Moderation a case of magical thinking?) For instance, an investor who luckily buys a share that goes on to beat the market may become convinced that he is a skillful investor rather than merely a fortunate one. He may also fall prey to "quasi-magical thinking"—behaving as if he believes his thoughts can influence events, even though he knows that they cannot.

Most people, say psychologists, are also vulnerable to hindsight bias: once something happens, they overestimate the extent to which they could have predicted it. Closely related to this is memory bias: when something happens, people often persuade themselves that they actually predicted it, even when they did not. (Could this be true of some of the many economic Dr. Dooms who claimed, after the event, to have predicted the full severity of the economic meltdown of September 2008?)

None of these insights is especially startling—these phenomena are around us (and inside our own heads) all the time—which makes it all the more surprising that economics assumed them away for so long. Milton Friedman is partly to blame, for pointing out that every economic model is unrealistic by definition, as it is a model, and arguing that the key test of any model is not how closely it reflects reality but how "useful" it is. Yet there are strong reasons to hope that incorporating these various irrational factors into mainstream economics can make it far more reliable and useful.

The challenge was laid down more than ten years ago by one

of the pioneers of behavioral economics, Robert Shiller, whose insights into how markets can deviate from rationality had a major role in inspiring Alan Greenspan's "irrational exuberance" speech. Indeed, *Irrational Exuberance* was the title of Shiller's prescient 2000 best seller about the widespread assumption that the stock market would rise forever. "Psychological anchors for the market hook themselves on the strangest things along the muddy bottom of our consciousness," he warned just before the dot-com bubble popped. Shiller called on economists to dispense with the comfortable assumptions of the efficient market hypothesis and "grapple with these messier aspects of market reality." Some have started to do so.

A NEW PARADIGM EVOLVES

As *Homo economicus* and efficient markets are laid to rest, are we left with anything but a view of financial markets as irrational casinos that need to be subjected to direct government control? Big-government Keynesians may want to turn back the clock to an era of strict regulation that stops banks, hedge funds, and other financial institutions from innovating their way into trouble. Yet the great man himself would probably be getting excited about the new tools available to economists and policymakers to better understand how markets work and how markets can work better. Rather than retreating into old orthodoxies, economists need to get on with the hard work of turning the new insights from areas such as behavioral economics into practical policy.

What is striking about these new approaches is that they do not fully reject the old paradigms. Even Daniel Kahneman, a psychologist whose Nobel Prize in 2002 signaled the acceptance of behavioral economics by the mainstream, has argued that economists should not give up the rational model entirely. "As a first approximation, it makes sense to assume rational behavior," he said. Instead, economists should abandon rationality only "one assumption at a time. Otherwise the analysis will very soon become intractable; the great strength of the rational model is that it is very tractable."

Reflecting on the implications of the market meltdown for the battle between the efficient market rationalists and the behavioralists, Richard Thaler, a leading behavioral economist, concluded that "in some ways, we behavioral economists have won by default, because we have been less arrogant." Those rationalists who denied that prices can get out of line or ever have bubbles now "look foolish." Likewise, those economists who said there have been big advances in risk management since 1998 look pretty dumb.

Yet Thaler concedes that in some ways the bubble and meltdown strengthened the efficient market hypothesis. There are two parts of the hypothesis, he says—the "no-free-lunch part, and the price-is-right part." In his view, the no-free-lunch part still stands, "as we have learned that some investment strategies are riskier than they look and it really is difficult to beat the market." It is the idea that the market price is the right price that is now completely busted. Unfortunately, this "is much more important than the first part, because we rely so much on market prices to efficiently allocate resources in the economy."

So where do we go from here? The new paradigm needs to bring together these different strands: rationality, bounded rationality, institutional and network theory, and behavioral economics—drawing on each when it works best in modeling reality.

One particularly promising attempt to make economics better reflect reality is based on replacing physics envy with evolutionary biology envy. Shaping economics by understanding how systems evolve makes far more sense than trying to turn it into hard science, with universal, unchanging laws similar to those of physics. This new approach, known as the "adaptive market hypothesis," assumes that markets, financial instruments, institutions, firms, and individuals interact within a dynamic evolutionary system governed by a process of "economic selection" similar to Darwinian natural selection. (In one application of this approach, financial markets are characterized as an ecosystem in which dealers are like herbivores, speculators are carnivores, and floor traders and distressed investors are "decomposers.")

In this dynamic, adaptive system, individuals make choices based on past experience and their "best guess" as to what might be optimal. They learn by receiving positive or negative reinforcement from the outcomes of their decisions. They are neither fully rational nor psychologically unhinged. Instead, they work by making best guesses and proceeding by trial and error. They tend to develop rules of thumb to help their decision making—those "heuristics" mentioned by behavioral economists—which typically work well when the economy is relatively stable but can lead to bad choices at times of change.

Andrew Lo, one of the economists behind the adaptive market hypothesis, calls the inappropriate actions that sometimes follow from the use of these rules of thumb "maladaptive," in the same way that a fish flopping about on dry land might look irrational but is in fact simply taking a tried and tested technique that worked in water and applying it in the wrong context.

In a similar way, the financial crisis triggered by the failure of Lehman Brothers had much in common with what goes on in other complex networks such as pandemic panics like SARS, the destruction of rain-forest ecosystems, and the blackout along

America's East Coast in 2003 as the electricity grid seized up. In a speech in April 2009, Andrew Haldane, director of financial stability at the Bank of England, highlighted the similarities: These "events were manifestations of the behaviour under stress of a complex, adaptive network. Complex because these networks were a cat's-cradle of interconnections, financial and non-financial. Adaptive because behaviour in these networks was driven by interactions between optimising, but confused, agents."

In the early years of the twenty-first century, financial institutions pursuing strategies of diversification and risk management that they believed made themselves and the system stronger created a financial system "exhibiting both greater complexity and less diversity," concluded Haldane. He thinks that experts on similar networks from outside the financial world, such as engineers and ecologists, would have spotted that "complexity plus homogeneity did not spell stability; it spelt fragility."

The challenge is to apply those insights to making markets work better. The world of finance has been turned upside down since the financial crisis of 2008. It is no surprise therefore that there is so much "maladaptive" behavior going around as people stick to tried and tested orthodoxies to understand this new world. But it is new thinking, to help us adapt effectively, that is required. Keynes would be having a ball.

THE OPPORTUNITY IN THE CRISIS

Economists now have the opportunity, and obligation, to raise their gaze, to come out from their specialized silos and work together (where necessary, also with those from disciplines outside economics) on developing a new, improved economic paradigm: Macroeconomists must understand finance, and finance professors need to think harder about the context within which markets work. And all of them need to work harder on understanding asset bubbles and what happens when they burst.

But already some of the fundamentals of this new paradigm are clear. If bubbles are driven by irrational choices by individuals, then policymakers should "focus on making the world easier," argues Thaler. One way to do this, for example, is to define more carefully the financial choices that people have to make. For behavioral economists, the typical problem with financial innovation is not the innovation per se but that people too often suspend their critical faculties when they embrace it, or are confused by it, and thus push their use of the innovation beyond what is prudent.

One of Thaler's earlier attempts to apply behavioral economics to saving has had impressive results. Recognizing that people find it harder to save money they already possess than to promise to put aside money they might have one day in the future, he designed the Save More Tomorrow scheme. This gets people to commit themselves to saving a slice of any future pay increases. Where implemented, the plan has already brought about sharp increases in saving rates. In the same way, economists—maybe Thaler himself—should try to devise ways of framing other choices that help to reduce unthinking herding and other irrational behaviors by homebuyers and investors.

These insights could also be applied to managing the complex dance between financial institutions and regulators. There must be ways of what Thaler calls "nudging" banks to behave more rationally, rather than resorting to the old regulatory tactic of simply throwing sand in the wheels of financial intermediation by, say, breaking banks into tiny inefficient pieces or imposing higher capital requirements on them. There is a risk, as Peter

Fisher, a former regulator and crisis fixer at the New York Fed and U.S. Treasury, puts it, of "a misplaced focus on more expensive airbags, whereas a greater focus on good driving, brakes and steering is just as, probably even more, essential."

Central banks face a particularly tough challenge in figuring out how to deal with bubbles, now that the possibility of their existence is no longer seriously questioned. The crisis means that central bankers can no longer wash their hands of bubbles as Greenspan did. On the other hand, no central banker should want to get involved in setting prices in equity, housing, or commodity markets. Again, Thaler argues that behavioral economics shows there is a middle way—an opportunity for governments to "lean into the wind a little more" to reduce the volatility of bubbles and crashes. Take real-estate markets, for example. One warning sign of a housing bubble is a growing gap between valuations of property to buy and property to rent. To address this, the government could create a sort of automatic stabilizer, argues Thaler, by requiring the giant mortgage lenders Freddie Mac and Fannie Mae to alter the ratio of down payment to purchase price required for a mortgage in step with the ratio of home values to rent. In other words, as property prices rise relative to rent, homebuyers would have to put down a higher percentage of the purchase price to buy their home, thus making it harder for them to blow air into a bubble.

Another interesting idea would be for the Federal Reserve to publish annually what it believes is a rational range of prices for shares. If share prices rise above that range, regulators could "lean against" the trend by altering market rules to make it easier for investors wishing to short shares to borrow. If prices fell below, the regulator could make shorting more difficult. This would be a halfway house between the public mention of the possibility of a bubble, which was all that Greenspan felt a Fed chairman should do, and using interest rates to try to stop or burst the alleged bubble, which he judged a step too far.

This type of nudging could also be used to influence the behavior of banks. One obvious area where irrationality creeps in is in the cyclicality of lending, where bad times fade from memory ("disaster myopia") and bankers extrapolate recent good loan performance into the future. As a result, the banks impose easier conditions on their borrowers in good times than would be justified by looking at the cycle as a whole, fueling the bubble. A popular proposal for regulators to address this behavioral bias would be to create countercyclical capital requirements for banks. This would make them increase the size of their capital cushion relative to their loans the longer the cyclical upswing went on. This is certainly an idea worth exploring; in Spain (which has a version of such capital requirements), it may have helped some banks to avoid the worst excesses of the recent bubble.

The smarter answers that we need may come not from regulation but from harnessing some of the insights from the new economics to financial innovation. Maintaining liquidity in a crisis is crucial to the effective functioning of the financial system, as the turmoil that began in 2007 made all too clear. Raghuram Rajan, a former chief economist at the International Monetary Fund, has proposed a financial innovation that comes straight out of the modern finance playbook to address the possibility of liquidity disappearing from the market for irrational reasons (such as excessive loss-aversion on the part of lenders).

Banks and other financial institutions that are significant enough to pose a systemic risk should be required to issue a new form of "contingent capital," he argues. Rather than enter into difficult negotiations with lenders at the worst possible time, a process that might even involve bankruptcy, which is what usually happens in a financial crisis, banks should be asked in the good times "to arrange for capital to be infused when they or the system is in trouble." This special kind of debt, which should not be prohibitively expensive because the money is raised in the good times, would include a special clause to convert it into equity in the case of a crisis. This conversion would give an immediate boost to the health of the financial institution, by reducing how much debt it had to service. Of course, the risk to the lender of its loan turning into shares would be reflected in the price of this debt. The market prices of these securities would therefore provide useful early warnings of impending financial crisis if they suddenly started to fall sharply. A key part of this proposal is that the conversion could take place only when both of two conditions were met: first, the system is in crisis, either based on an assessment by regulators or based on pre-agreed objective indicators; and second, the bank's capital ratio falls below a certain value. The first condition is crucial, as it would ensure that banks that do badly because of mistakes they make, rather than because the system is in trouble, do not escape the consequences of their actions by converting their debt.

This idea fits well into the network approach advocated by the Bank of England's Haldane, who has proposed that the better mapping of the network might make the financial system stabler through improved data, improved analysis of that data, and improved communication of the results. This seems the perfect job description for the new systemic-risk regulator that was promised in several countries in the aftermath of the market meltdown.

Haldane was particularly keen on more use of "snowballing"—which means "constructing a picture of the network by working outwards from the links to one of the nodes." In early 2007, he says, it is doubtful whether many of the world's largest financial institutions were more than two or three degrees of separation from AIG. And in 1998, it is unlikely that many of the world's largest banks were more than one or two degrees of separation from LTCM. Rolling the snowball might have identified these financial black holes before they swallowed too many planets.

Network information is a classic public good, Haldane rightly observed. Not only is it in no one's individual interest to collect it, it is not remotely within anyone's compass. Compiling aggregate data is a job for the authorities. And having been collected, these data need then to be disseminated. In a crisis, the role of the government in communicating the right messages is absolutely crucial. Looking back at the panic that followed after the collapse of Lehman Brothers in 2008, Haldane reflected that "the financial crisis did not just dominate the news; it *was* the news. Only a hermit could have failed to have their perceptions shaped by this tale of woe. As woe became the popular narrative, depressed expectations may have become self-fulfilling." By communicating information about what is really going on in the network, a systemic regulator could ease this panic.

A proposal floated by Andrew Lo could help in this respect: the creation of a financial equivalent of America's National Transportation Safety Board. Just as the NTSB conducts an independent investigation into every civil aviation crash to see what went wrong, and if appropriate makes proposals to avoid a repeat, the Capital Markets Safety Board would send a team of highly trained financial experts to investigate every financial failure of any note, to see what caused it. This would be very different in nature from the commissions of inquiry that tend to be formed after the worst financial crises—and tend to be filled with the great and good, who are often motivated by politics more than getting at the truth. This way, failure could be studied carefully through an independent, technical lens, rather than from the perspective of blame and denial.

One of the most positive government responses to the Great Depression was the first comprehensive attempt to measure national economic statistics. The economic slump had revealed an alarming information gap; economic policymakers in effect had been driving blind. To develop reliable data on national income, consumption, and savings, the Department of Commerce commissioned Simon Kuznets, a Russian-born economist and former head of a statistics office in the Ukraine under the Bolsheviks, who was later to win the Nobel Prize. His first report on national income was delivered to Congress in 1937, and regular publication of a new measure, gross national product (GNP), began in 1942. Similar work was undertaken at the same time in Britain by two other subsequent Nobel Prize winners, James Meade and Sir Richard Stone.

The latest economic crisis has also raised important questions about economic statistics, though this time the issue is less their accuracy than their usefulness. GNP, and its successor, gross domestic product (GDP), have come to be seen as measures of economic progress. Yet, with hindsight, the U.S. economy looks less impressive today than its strong GDP growth from the early 1990s until 2007 had suggested. There is also a need to develop early-warning signals, which may require statistical offices to sacrifice more accuracy than normal in order to be timely.

At the very least, a new approach to national statistics is required that builds onto national income data meaningful measures of a country's balance sheet, and of its exposure to different sorts of risks. One potentially useful development would be for the government to commission and publish an annual risk report on the economy. Perhaps such a report in the early years of this century would have highlighted the growing importance of financial-sector income in GDP and asked tough questions about whether this was sustainable. Such a report would need to be produced by an independent body free from political pressure. There is a model and perhaps a candidate in America, the General Accounting Office, whose head, the Comptroller General of the United States, is protected from undue outside influence by being appointed by Congress to a fifteen-year term.

The crisis has also revived interest in finding a better measure of national economic progress than GDP. Kuznets himself said that "the welfare of a nation can scarcely be inferred from a measure of national income." He fell out with the Department of Commerce in the 1940s over its refusal to measure the value of unpaid housework, which he regarded as an important component of production. While the notion of "gross national happiness" launched in 1972 by the king of Bhutan has yet to be measured in a robust way, since 2007 economists at the Organisation for Economic Co-operation and Development have been engaged in a promising effort to augment existing national income data with statistics measuring the "progress of society."

In 2008, French president Nicolas Sarkozy launched a "commission on the measurement of economic performance and social progress," chaired by Joseph Stiglitz. This set out to develop a better definition of GDP (including nonmarket production, such as housework, which would please Kuznets); indicators of sustainable development and environmental well-being; and "credible measures on quality of life." This work is long overdue.

It is not just national economic statistics that require urgent attention. Glaring weaknesses have been revealed in accounting data for banks and other companies. In the financial sector, in addition to ideas about finding ways to improve market signals about risk, such as getting banks to issue contingent capital, the area ripest for change is accounting rules. The flaws of mark-to-market accounting were exposed by the crisis; revaluing assets to take account of falling prices, when combined with risk-management models and regulations that require selling by banks as the value of their assets declines, created a vicious circle that made the crisis worse. The use of mark-to-market accounting in this way made sense when the efficient market hypothesis seemed an accurate description of the world, but if we accept that market prices can be irrational, then to use these prices as the main basis of valuing a company's assets is to build our financial decision-making on shifting sands.

Current accounting rules also mean that investors and creditors have little more than a snapshot of a company at a moment in time that gives no indication of the firm's exposure to different sorts of risks. Just look at the way AIG turned from a financial-market hero to less than zero when its CDS business imploded. "Accounting is being asked to do something it was never meant to do," warned Robert Merton as far back as 2002. "It is like a road system built for when cars did 30 mph being used by cars doing 60—and then we wonder why there are accidents." After the high-speed pileup of 2008, we finally need to heed that warning, and modernize accounting.

Merton does not only blame the quality of the roads for the crash of 2008, he also thinks that bad driving played a big part. Chief executives and board members of financial institutions should be expected to have a working understanding of finance, he says. For a board member of, say, Citigroup to confess that he or she did not understand the complex instruments the bank traded should be unacceptable, just as it would be unacceptable for a board member of a pharmaceutical firm to say he or she did not understand the science behind the latest blockbuster pill. In short, even the best data in the world will have little value if people don't know how to use them.

These ideas are just a start, offering a flavor of what could be a new paradigm of economics. The crisis has prompted lots of gloom about the state of the dismal science. Commenting on macroeconomics in April 2009, Paul Krugman, then the newest recipient of a Nobel Prize, said that he feared that much of the work of the previous thirty years was "spectacularly useless at best, and positively harmful at worst." Yet just as the Depression inspired Keynes, and the 1970s stagflation led to a rediscovery of the virtues of markets and Adam Smith, this crisis brings with it a tremendous opportunity to help policymakers, financiers, business leaders, and other practical people do better. This time, however, finding a new paradigm for economics should not be viewed in terms of Keynes replacing Smith, or vice versa. Instead, the key to success for the new paradigm will be reuniting Keynes and Smith, and rediscovering their shared interest in the complexities of human behavior.

7

A NEW WORLD ORDER

The world must redesign how it is governed

A global crisis requires a global solution," pronounced the leaders of the world's twenty most economically important nations gathered in London in April 2009 as they unveiled their trillion-dollar plan to rescue the global economy. The G-20 conference was greeted by a wide range of protests about climate change and youth unemployment, focused on the City of London. Workers in the financial district were advised to stay at home, or to come to work in casual clothes, lest they be picked out as a banker and made a target for retribution. A small band of anticapitalist antiglobalizers provided the image the media wanted by smashing up a branch of the Royal Bank of Scotland, and the police provided the news story with their heavy-handed crowd-management techniques, which resulted in the death of a bystander.

The meeting itself was widely hailed as a success. The attendees pledged reforms to the global economic governance system, many of which had been deferred in the past as they were supposedly too difficult, and announced a financial stimulus package to get economic growth going again around the world. Yet what may have seemed bold moves to the world leaders were only the first stage of what will need to be a massive effort to tackle the fundamental imbalances that threaten the stability of a globalized world.

This G-20 declaration was doubly significant. It demonstrated the falsehood of the recently fashionable idea of a "decoupled" world in which the fates of the rich West and the emerging East were no longer intertwined: managing globalization remained the challenge for world leaders. But it also showed that the rich nations could not solve the crisis alone.

For the previous thirty years, the meeting that mattered most for global governance had been the annual summit of the G-8 (the world's seven richest nations plus Russia, thanks to its nuclear arsenal). In April 2009, the new powers of China, India, and even Brazil and South Africa (neither of which has nuclear weapons) were at the table, too, as equals. By bringing together developed and developing countries without the numbing bureaucracy of the United Nations, the G-20 had emerged as the world's new forum for practical world government.

When the financial storm broadsided New York in the autumn of 2008 with the collapse of Lehman Brothers, the world was quick to blame the failings of U.S. capitalism and make dire predictions about the fate of the American economy. Yet smugness soon turned to fear as the world realized that America's almighty sneeze was going to give nations across the globe the mother of all colds. Countries such as China had raked in billions of dollars and enjoyed booming economic growth because of, not despite, America's willingness to spend. With the "spender of last resort," as America had become known, suffering, factories across China and other exporting nations started to close. Tata, an Indian industrial conglomerate that had only recently made headlines for its plans for world domination, had to put the launch of its new low-cost car on hold. The sovereign wealth funds of oil-exporting nations that had been splashing cash around to buy up the crown jewels of American finance and industry suddenly looked somewhat less flush, while Russia's treasure chest was quickly emptied as the price of oil slumped and the nation's economy ground to a halt.

The economic crisis was likewise a huge setback for the world's poorest people, millions of whom had started to climb out of deprivation during the boom years. The managing director of the World Bank, and former finance minister of Nigeria, Ngozi Okonjo-Iweala, complained that African countries were "innocent bystanders" at the financial crisis. But this was no succor to poor diamond miners in the Democratic Republic of Congo, one of the world's unluckiest countries, who lost their jobs when the hedge funders and their wives slashed their bling budgets and stayed away from the jewelry stores on Fifth Avenue and Bond Street. The World Bank predicted that in 2009 nearly 50 million people in the developing world would be pushed back into destitution by the economic slowdown.

As he urged his fellow leaders to agree on an ambitious agenda, the beleaguered host of the G-20 summit, British prime minister Gordon Brown, reveled in the first positive headlines he had received in more than a year at home—where he had been widely blamed for his handling of the economy. Everyone toasted the magic touch of new American president Barack Obama. Certainly, some praise was due the world's statesmen, given the often disgraceful track record of their predecessors, who had all too frequently dropped the ball at similar international meetings at moments of crisis.

In 1933, in economically desperate times similar to the ones the G-20 leaders faced in 2009, sixty-six nations gathered in London to try to save the world economy as the golden foundations on which it was built crumbled. In an atmosphere of mutual recrimination as each country accused the others of "beggar thy neighbor" policies, the summit was a dismal failure. The U.S.

delegation was as colorful as it was inept: the typically inebriated Senator Key Pittman of Nevada threatened another member of the delegation with a pistol when they disagreed about the merits of the remonetization of silver, while Congressman Samuel D. McReynolds of Tennessee spent his time trying to get his daughter presented at the royal court. These antics were immaterial to the outcome. America, which dominated the supply of gold, had just devalued the dollar and was determined to look after only itself, infuriated by what it saw as Britain's selfish unilateral decision to drop off the gold standard two years earlier. France, which was keenly buying gold to protect itself from a perceived threat from its neighbor Germany, played for short-term political gains. Germany's only interest was to avoid a reimposition of the financial reparations that had been imposed on it in 1919 as punishment for World War I. When President Roosevelt sent a cable dismissing the conference's rather feeble plan to restore monetary stability as a "specious fallacy," everyone knew the game was up.

America's intransigence in 1933 was perhaps no more than Britain should have expected after its own intransigence half a century earlier when the Great Powers had met once before, this time in Paris, to try to reform the gold standard (although Germany refused to participate, as it had just switched to gold, which it had no intention of giving up). At the 1878 conference, held as the global economy stagnated, the United States and France tried to get Britain, the dominant force in global finance, to agree to a relaxation of the international monetary order by allowing silver as well as gold to be part of the monetary base. Britain refused.

The perennial failure of efforts to get global agreements on financial issues has made regional solutions attractive in the past. Probably the biggest success, since the creation of the United States, has been the European Union, which now binds twenty-seven countries together in a single market where goods, capital, and people can move freely, with generous flows of aid from the richest members to the poorest. Sixteen countries within the EU have even joined together in a monetary union. (Other notable regional initiatives, none of which is anywhere near as substantial as the EU, include the North American Free Trade Agreement and the Association of Southeast Asian Nations.) But the achievements of European integration would not have been possible without American commitment and financial support at the outset, through the Marshall Aid program that bankrolled postwar recovery and through a military security guarantee.

European solidarity was sorely tested by the economic crisis of 2008. In February 2009, the European Commission was sucked into a row when France wanted to offer $8 billion worth of soft loans to the carmakers Renault and Peugeot-Citroën to protect jobs at their French plants. The Czech government protested that this was a breach of EU rules banning national governments from subsidizing their industries, fearing that the carmakers were being bribed to keep jobs in France at the expense of workers at subsidiaries in the Czech Republic. When some of the financially weaker member states, including Portugal, Italy, Greece, and Spain, started lobbying for a bit more European solidarity in the form of financial assistance, they got short shrift from the fiscally austere Germans, and, as a group, the four countries earned themselves the unflattering title of the PIGS (geddit?). For a brief period there was speculation that the eurozone could fracture.

The euro survived. Yet when some of the newer EU member states that had not joined the monetary union, including Hungary, Romania, and Latvia, ran into financing problems as global credit dried up in 2009, relief came not from their European partners but from the Washington-based International Monetary Fund, a product of the Bretton Woods Conference of 1944.

Bretton Woods is the great exception, the one glimmer of

hope from history that suggests that national leaders can show vision and courage to tackle global economic problems together.

The Bretton Woods Conference was the product of a particularly dire global crisis, World War II, which had forced extraordinary levels of cooperation between rival nations. Its deliberations were also underpinned by the unquestioned economic dominance of America, which meant that the U.S. negotiators were able to force a deal by dictating many of the terms to the representatives of bankrupt nations gathered around the table. The United States did not need to create a global consensus, since its only rival of any note, the Soviet Union, had pulled out of the process.

There was, admittedly, plenty wrong with what was agreed on at Bretton Woods. The new fixed-exchange-rate system creaked and then collapsed within thirty years because of the instability that resulted from using the dollar as the reserve currency. The new institutions of global economic management, the IMF and the World Bank, have had, at best, a patchy track record (although efforts to remedy their failings by creating an Asian IMF after the emerging-market financial crisis of 1997 quickly stalled). Nonetheless, for improving global economic governance, Bretton Woods remains the high point, so far.

Facing up to the current global crisis, the process that began at the London G-20 summit, will demand courage and imagination at least as great as that shown in 1944. This time America does not have the resources to push through a deal on its own by bankrolling everyone else. Its negotiating partners will want important concessions to sign on to any agreement that could be difficult for them to sell at home. Reaching a deal will not be just about technical economic questions, or even a matter merely of money: it will be about coming to terms with the new global balance of power in the twenty-first century.

The temptation to play for quick wins and ignore the real,

structural issues will be strong. Learning to share power and give up control can be difficult, as Britain discovered over the past century as it struggled to come to terms with no longer being the world's dominant economic and political power. Indeed, even now Britain, along with France, could be an obstacle to the creation of a new world order by clinging to the seat at the top table (such as permanent membership on the UN Security Council) that is no longer justified in terms of political and economic clout.

The first task of the global leaders, which they started to address in London in 2009, is to find a way to deal with the global financial crisis and the economic imbalances that contributed to it. Yet that crucial first step is only a start. The financial crisis of 2008 brought together all the main fault lines in globalization— financial, economic, resource, demographic, and political—that have been developing over many years. The United States is still the world's leading economic power, but it is no longer as dominant as it once was. At the G-20 summit, other nations began to question whether the American dollar could continue as the world's reserve currency. Many countries also felt they were innocent victims of a crisis caused by American economic mismanagement and wanted a fundamental change in the balance of global economic decision-making. All this came at a time when the world was trying to figure out how to build a global capitalist system that could deliver widespread prosperity by making trade and investment work for the poor. This task was already being made far harder and more complicated by an expanding global population competing for supplies of food and energy under the shadow of potentially catastrophic climate change.

Building a solid foundation for a global capitalism that can spread prosperity across the world will require our leaders to use this crisis to forge the international consensus needed to tackle all of these huge challenges.

REPLACING THE DOLLAR AS TOP DOG

On the eve of the London G-20 summit, Hu Jintao, the president of China, and Dmitry Medvedev, the president of Russia, surprised their fellow world leaders by calling for a new global reserve currency to replace the dollar. The case, set out in a speech by Zhou Xiaochuan, the head of China's central bank, was that any country that issues the world's reserve currency is "constantly confronted with the dilemma between achieving [its] domestic monetary policy goals and meeting other countries' demand for reserve currencies." It could not pursue different domestic and international objectives at the same time, he argued. (Through the English versions of his published speeches, Zhou emerged in 2009 as one of the most lucid commentators on the global economy.) Instead, it would "either fail to adequately meet the demand of a growing global economy for liquidity as [it tries] to ease inflation pressures at home, or create excess liquidity in the global markets by overly stimulating domestic demand."

China and Russia were addressing a familiar problem. When the Bank of England controlled the gold standard, other economies were buffeted by shocks coming from the British economy, as Wall Street discovered in 1907 when a hike in interest rates in London contributed to a liquidity crunch in New York. When control of gold passed to America after World War I, the same problem reemerged when the Fed tried to accommodate the needs of the global economy, and of the feeble British pound in particular, and eased monetary policy at the wrong moment. That fueled the stock market boom that ended with the Wall Street Crash of 1929. But at least in those days the pound and the dollar were anchored to gold, the supply of which governments could not much influence—which limited somewhat their ability to dominate the world economy (albeit at the cost of harnessing prosperity to the "hazards of mining").

The dollar became the world's reserve currency under the Bretton Woods system, the anchor against which the value of other currencies was fixed and the unit of account for most cross-border commerce. In 1960 the economist Robert Triffin identified a fundamental problem with this dollar standard of global finance: being the holder of the reserve currency for the world meant that America could live beyond its means indefinitely. When international finance was based on the gold standard, even when the pound was in its pomp in the nineteenth century, sloppy fiscal management by the British government would have led to a flow of gold out of the country, forcing an increase in interest rates to protect the value of the pound. The U.S. government faced no such discipline on domestic policy under the dollar standard, since the rest of the world had no choice but to accept dollars. This situation continues today, even after the collapse of the Bretton Woods system of fixed exchange rates, since the world still operates on a de facto dollar standard.

As a result of this "Triffin dilemma" (the mismatch of American and global monetary policy), the rest of the world has been left at the mercy of America's domestic monetary politics. In the 1960s and 1970s, the United States pumped liquidity into the world economy, which helped to fuel inflation. Then in the 1980s, when Fed chairman Paul Volcker pushed up interest rates to deal with domestic inflation, this sucked liquidity out of the world economy and tipped Mexico into a debt crisis. From the late 1990s, the United States again pumped dollars into the world economy, in part because of the spending and borrowing boom at home.

In the past decade, the mercantilist policies of countries such as China, which have undervalued their own currencies in order to run massive trade surpluses and build up their currency reserves, have also played a crucial part in creating this new "dollar glut." China's enthusiasm for reform of the global reserve currency reflects the fact that it recognizes the dangers of hoarding dollars. With $2 trillion worth of American paper in its reserves, by 2009 China was massively exposed to the U.S. economy: a fall in the value of the dollar would do serious damage to China's wealth. The dollar is the transmission mechanism whereby decisions made in Washington, for domestic reasons, send economic shock waves around the world. The crisis has shown that this mechanism also works in reverse, however, as the world's willingness to lend to America stoked the boom.

America is understandably reluctant to surrender the dollar's dominant position and to live by the same rules as everyone else. The dollar standard has ensured a plentiful supply of cheap credit from the rest of the world and greater freedom in economic policy than that enjoyed by any other country. But this freedom has also allowed America to postpone tough decisions and store up trouble for the future.

The U.S. government has been powerless to respond to the mercantilist policies of China and other emerging markets. It has been reduced to sending a procession of treasury secretaries to Beijing to exhort the Chinese to revalue their currency. That approach worked in the 1980s when it was Japan that was running huge trade surpluses on the back of an undervalued currency. Yet the Chinese have shown no interest in a new version of the Plaza Accord (although since 2005 they have let the yuan rise modestly against the dollar). The Asian financial crisis of the 1990s taught China and other emerging markets that they needed to protect themselves from the volatility of the dollar by running trade surpluses and hoarding foreign currency reserves. The exhortations of American treasury secretaries to do otherwise were mostly ignored.

In the end, the dollar standard created the global "savings glut" that resulted in the American economy becoming bloated with debt. The "exorbitant privilege" of controlling the world's reserve currency, as it was described by Valéry Giscard d'Estaing, Charles de Gaulle's finance minister in the 1960s (and later his successor as French president), has become more of an extraordinary liability for America in recent years.

John Maynard Keynes spotted this weakness at the Bretton Woods conference. Rather than the dollar standard, he proposed the creation of a global reserve currency, which he called the bancor, that would be based on the value of a basket of commodities. The bancor was to be the centerpiece of a new system of global finance called the International Clearing Union, which Keynes hoped would smooth out the imbalances in world finance, such as America's large and persistent trade surpluses that had destabilized the global economy in the interwar period.

Perhaps the timing for Keynes's proposal was not right, since America was then undisputed as the world's financier. At the Bretton Woods Conference, his advocacy of the bancor was dismissed by his American counterpart, Harry Dexter White, as simply Britain looking for excuses for its massive trade deficit. As far as White was concerned, the Brits just needed to take the economic medicine of consuming less and saving more to reduce their deficit.

Bruce Greenwald of Columbia Business School has pointed out that America today, with its massive trade deficit, is in a similar position to the one Britain occupied in 1944. China, however, by proposing a global reserve currency, is playing the Keynes role (although it has also done a fair amount of Harry Dexter White–style moaning about America's unwillingness to save). As the United Nations' expert panel on reform of the financial system, chaired by Nobel Prize–winning American economist Joseph Stiglitz, argued in 2009 on the eve of the G-20 meeting, now is the moment to correct this fundamental flaw in the global financial system.

Creating a global reserve currency is not the same as abolishing all national currencies and issuing notes and coins in the new currency. That was what the European countries did when they joined the eurozone, with established currencies such as the Italian lira, the French franc, and the German deutsche mark being withdrawn from circulation when the new currency took effect. A global reserve currency could be created through international agreements that have no implications for whatever currency is used within a country, though they would have huge implications for exchange rates between currencies.

China and Russia did not expect their proposals for a new reserve currency to be adopted in London. Yet the G-20 did take one small technical step in that direction by authorizing a $250 billion increase in IMF Special Drawing Rights (SDRs). The SDR was created under the Bretton Woods system to address the problem that the supply of gold in central bank reserves may not keep pace with economic growth. SDRs are therefore a kind of paper gold, allocated by the IMF to its members in proportion to the size of their economies. The G-20's agreement on an almost tenfold increase in the quantity of SDRs meant that every country now had bigger reserves than it did before the summit. With greater reserves, the world's central banks were effectively given more money by the international community, which they could pump into their economies. A number of central banks, including the Federal Reserve, were already printing money, through a process known as quantitative easing, to pump liquidity into their domestic economies. The new SDRs were, in effect, global quantitative easing.

For now, SDRs are merely an accounting tool used by the IMF for its transactions with central banks. The value of the SDR is also very narrow, based on a weighted basket of currencies made up only of the dollar, the euro, the pound, and the yen—a limited selection that reflects a bygone economic era. The Chinese have proposed widening the SDR currency basket to better reflect the balance in the world economy today. They also want the SDR to be used in international trade and finance. If these proposals were implemented, the SDR would be more representative of the real balance in the world economy and could be used as the unit of account for, say, World Bank loans or international bond issues. Like Sir Isaac Newton's move to make gold the basis of the pound nearly three centuries ago, these could be the first steps toward a new global reserve currency.

The cornerstone of any currency is the credibility of the authority that issues it—hence the push in recent years to create independent central banks that can fight inflation free from government interference. Although it was hard for them to give up the ability to use interest-rate cuts for political ends, a growing number of governments recognized that they could not trust themselves to use this power well and would be better off having a credible currency (as well as someone else to blame for killjoy interest-rate increases). Independent central banks have worked pretty well in terms of managing consumer price inflation in the countries that have them. Central bankers have, in general, acted swiftly in response to the crisis, cutting interest rates and then pumping money into the economy through quantitative easing. (They did less well in managing the asset price inflation of the bubble, however.)

So why not have a global central banker? There would be no need for economic harmonization, like that which the eurozone had to go through, because currencies would still be free to float

up or down against the new reserve currency. Transferring some
of the responsibility for monetary stability to a global technocrat
instead of a national technocrat would not be a huge leap—as
long as the global central banker was trusted. The success of a
global reserve currency would therefore depend on the credibility of the IMF. Currently, it lacks that credibility, however, and
restoring it will require a major overhaul.

BANKER TO THE WORLD

No country really enjoys a visit from the IMF. In good times, when
countries do not need its money, what the IMF has to say about
the health of an economy is an irrelevance, though occasionally
an irritating one. In bad times, it is a stern master, imposing harsh
economic conditions on a government in return for extending it
lifelines of credit. However, as Paul Krugman observes, "just
because people hate the IMF doesn't mean that it is doing its
job well."

The IMF's performance over the past sixty years has been
deeply flawed, for two main reasons. First, as developing countries rightly complain, it is not an impartial arbiter of sound
finance but highly capricious—controlled by America, with support from its friends in the G-8 (the so-called Washington consensus). As former Fed chairman Paul Volcker once put it: "When
the Fund consults with a poor and weak country, the country gets
in line. When it consults with a big and strong country, the Fund
gets in line. When the big countries are in conflict, the Fund gets
out of the line of fire."

The bias toward the rich countries is embedded in the IMF's

voting structure. This is tied to how much money each nation puts in—hence rich countries have the dominant voice. This has been reinforced by the unwritten, yet always honored, agreement that Europe gets to choose the head of the IMF, while America appoints the head of its sister agency, the World Bank. One of the first concessions that the economic crisis forced out of the rich countries is to end this murky conspiracy. At the 2009 G-20 summit in London, the leaders agreed that the presidents of the IMF and the World Bank should be appointed through "an open, transparent, and merit-based selection process." It would be naive to believe that these new rules would bring an end to diplomatic horse trading, or that a new passport for the head of the IMF will fundamentally change how it operates. Yet it would be a symbolic first step.

The second, more important failing is the IMF's lack of resources. A lender of last resort, as Walter Bagehot pointed out more than a century ago, needs to be able to lend freely and without fear of running out of cash. The IMF has always been woefully undercapitalized to play this role. It has enough money to cope with the day-to-day work of propping up a country here and a country there. But when big, systemic crises occur, it has to turn to the rich nations to help out. Unfortunately, that puts global financial stability in the hands of Congress, since America usually foots the largest share of any bailout bill.

When Mexico ran into one of its periodic financing crises in the mid-1990s, President Clinton was confronted with a dilemma. He knew he needed to help, but opinion polls showed that 79 percent of the American public were opposed to the idea. His treasury secretary, Robert Rubin, was forced to do some creative accounting to bypass Congress, using a special fund created to protect the dollar under the New Deal to help out the Mexican peso. The intervention worked, and the Treasury eventually turned a $500 million profit on the deal. But this is no way to run a global economy, as the Asian crisis that followed in 1997 made all too clear. Then, the IMF and the rich world failed to provide the money needed to stabilize the markets and instead pushed the painful costs of global adjustment onto the emerging economies themselves.

The G-20 in 2009 took a small step to strengthen the IMF, by pledging $500 billion of additional cash to support its loans to countries in need. Significantly, China offered to contribute to this pot, thereby ending the rich-country monopoly as funders of the IMF. The IMF itself also started to change the way it lends, offering more-flexible lines of credit rather than its traditional fare of "adjustment programs" that came with strict conditions and, invariably, sent out a warning to private investors to get their money out as quickly as possible. Yet, as welcome as these reforms may be, the IMF will never have the independence it needs as a credible lender of last resort while it has to go hat in hand to donors whenever there is a big problem.

An obvious way to fix this problem, albeit one that would represent a massive political challenge, would be for member countries to pool their currency reserves, so that this money would be available automatically to the IMF in times of crisis. Empowering the IMF in this way would force rich countries to start taking it seriously. That would be no bad thing if it helped prevent reckless policies.

Strengthening the IMF is more likely to happen if rich countries—perhaps even America—acknowledge that even they may one day need rescuing. Small countries such as Iceland discovered how vulnerable they are during the crisis of 2008. The exchange-rate flexibility of Britain, and of a few other medium-sized countries with their own currencies, helped to cushion the impact of the economic crisis there without triggering a damaging flight of capital from the country. Yet it is not clear how long this balancing act can be maintained, particularly as government debt soars. Might Britain have to accept that its relationship with the IMF has changed, and that it could need the support of an international lender of last resort in the future? The need for such assistance seemed inconceivable to the British in 2009—though Britain had had to call in the IMF once before, as its economy struggled during the stagflation of the 1970s.

The other job that has been proposed for the IMF is global financial regulator. (Other candidates for this role include the Bank for International Settlements, which managed the negotiations of the Basel Capital Accords, or an entirely new entity yet to be created.) National regulators cannot effectively manage the risks in a highly liquid global capital market, goes the argument. While this argument makes sense in principle, and there was much huffing and puffing at the G-20 summit in London about the need for a global financial regulator, little action seems likely in this area anytime soon, alas.

There are two obstacles to creating a global financial regulator. First, the diversity of the financial sectors in different countries means that "one size" is unlikely to fit all—global regulation would need to be varied to meet the needs of individual countries, which might be done better by national regulators.

Second, there are powerful national interests opposed to the creation of a single global regulator. International capital tends to go to wherever the conditions (regulations, taxes, and the like) are most favorable to it. Britain and Switzerland have been profiting from this "regulatory competition" for years, by offering light-touch oversight combined with a strong legal system to attract financial firms and their money. (Their critics accuse the two countries of leading a "race to the bottom" in terms of regulatory standards.) Singapore, Dubai, and other emerging-market financial centers are already greedily eyeing the wealth of the City of London, hoping that a tidal wave of crisis-inspired red tape in Britain will drive the business their way. Similar problems have long frustrated attempts by organizations such as the Organisation for Economic Co-operation and Development (OECD) to crack down on tax havens. Although it is easy for rich-country politicians to condemn them, the havens exist by exploiting international rules that also benefit at least one major economy, which typically blocks efforts to change those rules.

While monetary reform is urgently needed if prosperity is to return, any achievement on this front will be fragile unless the world also tackles the other urgent challenges it faces. Bretton Woods was only one part of the new system of global governance that was put in place after World War II. In addition to the United Nations, established in 1945, the postwar leaders also created the General Agreement on Tariffs and Trade (GATT) in 1947, to roll back the protectionism that had helped to damage the world economy in the 1930s. In the same year, the United States also launched its massive Marshall Aid program to rebuild the shattered economies of Europe. Trade and aid are crucial issues for the world economy today. We also face new challenges such as climate change—which will require dramatic changes in the global economy. By tackling these as interrelated problems that must all be solved as part of a new economic deal for the world, rather than as stand-alone issues, our leaders now have an opportunity to break the diplomatic logjam and write new rules for a prosperous world economy. The road from ruin runs through each of these challenges, starting with trade.

NO OPTION BUT FREE TRADE

From Haiti in the Caribbean to Bangladesh, Egypt, and across Africa, riots broke out around the world in 2008, for one reason: the high price of food. "There are food riots in countries where we have not seen them before," warned Josette Sheeran, the head of the United Nations World Food Programme. The surge of up to 40 percent in the cost of basic foodstuffs was due not to the usual drought, pestilence, or conflict but to population growth and prosperity, which had increased demand for food overall, and especially for costlier-to-produce sorts of food such as meat (which people tend to substitute for vegetables as they get richer). Talk of a global food crisis subsided as prices sank along with the global economy after September 2008, yet the underlying trend for demand, and prices, to rise will continue for as long as the world's population continues to grow and prosperity increases. According to the United Nations, global food production will need to increase by 50 percent by 2030 to keep up with demand. The irony is that this crisis might not be happening if the world could agree on sensible rules for agricultural trade—and that the biggest obstacle to a deal is the farmers themselves.

A freeze or even a reversal of trade liberalization was one of the worst dangers facing the world as it entered the economic crisis in 2008. In the months after the failure of Lehman Brothers, world trade actually shrank for the first time in nearly thirty years. As the global economy slowed in 2009, firms all over the world lobbied their governments for special treatment and protection.

The calls for higher trade barriers to offset the economic crisis created echoes of the Great Depression, when world trade declined by 66 percent from 1929 to 1934. In part this decline had been a symptom of the economic contraction already under way, but it was also caused by tariff hikes such as those ushered in by the U.S. Smoot-Hawley Act of 1930—a hugely controversial law that provoked retaliation from America's trading partners. As a result, the world economy got stuck in a lose-lose downward spiral of declining trade. It says something about the populist appeal of protectionism that, despite the experience of the 1930s, in 2009 legislators again reached for the quick fix. Congress, for example, slipped a "Buy American" clause into President Obama's stimulus package. (Happily, this was significantly watered down in the final version.)

If there is reason to hope that the international trading system will be more resilient this time, it is because of the reforms introduced to the governance of global trade since the Great Depression. In the 1930s, the only international forum where countries could tackle the problem of rising protectionism was the League of Nations. The brainchild of President Woodrow Wilson, the League had been formed in 1920 to promote a better world in the aftermath of World War I, but it lacked real power, in part because America declined to become a member due to opposition in Congress. At the end of World War II, world leaders set out to correct this failure by creating the General Agreement on Tariffs and Trade. This effort to deregulate international trade through a series of rounds of negotiations has been, at once, one of the biggest successes and biggest disappointments of global capitalism in the past sixty years.

There were only twenty-three countries at the first GATT meeting in Geneva, Switzerland, in 1947, at which participants began the process of cutting barriers to trade. This first Geneva deal (the Geneva Round, as it was known) led the way for further rounds that froze and then lowered trade barriers in a growing number of products and between ever more countries.

In 1995, GATT was renamed the World Trade Organization

(WTO), and the WTO's powers were enhanced. The WTO helped to fend off the protectionists in 2009, when many countries tried to find ways around its rules by using other means than tariff increases. It policed these measures, and leaders at the G-20 summit in London made the right noises about not retreating into protectionism. (Indeed, reviled as it is by antiglobalization protesters, the WTO has emerged as one of the better institutions of global governance. Unlike the United Nations, the 153 countries that are part of the WTO have to sign on to membership rules, and the WTO secretariat helps to make sure these are upheld. Big countries such as the United States do still use their greater resources to bully smaller countries, but they do not run the place by controlling the purse strings as they do at the IMF and World Bank.) Yet defending the status quo will not be enough. Developing countries were hit hard by a financial crisis that they had no part in causing, and the poorest were the least resilient to cope with the global slowdown. They need more help from the international trading system.

In 2001, the then 141 members of the WTO had begun negotiations known as the Doha Round (the round was launched in Doha, Qatar). The goal was to secure the benefits of trade for the poorest countries of the world. According to the World Bank, this trade deal could lift 100 million people out of poverty by finally tackling the obstacles to trade in agriculture—still by far the most nationally run and subsidized part of the global economy. Yet even before the markets crashed in 2008, little progress had been made toward a deal on agriculture.

Farmers have been a powerful lobby against free trade throughout the centuries. In the first half of the nineteenth century, Britain introduced tariffs under the "Corn Laws" to protect landowners' incomes from competition by cheap foreign imports. The move was opposed by the economist David Ricardo, whose theory of "comparative advantage" is one of the greatest insights of the dismal science, explaining how trade is not a "zero-sum" game of winners and losers but a potential win-win. Despite Ricardo's economic arguments, the farm lobby held sway in Britain from 1815 to 1846. Repeal finally came when Prime Minister Robert Peel, influenced by the writings of Adam Smith, sacrificed his career to push through legislation to end the tariffs. Food prices fell as cheap imports flooded in from North America's emerging agricultural sector.

The Corn Laws were a pernicious piece of economic sado-masochism that inflicted the pain of high food prices on the British public, slowed the development of the economy by keeping capital tied up in unproductive agriculture rather than allowing it to flow to new industries, and denied more-efficient farmers in other countries the chance to sell their produce. Sadly, the world is making the same mistake today. An estimated $300 billion a year of benefits for the global economy were up for grabs under the Doha Round. Poor countries stood to benefit by being able to exploit their agricultural potential, which was being stifled by unfair competition from less efficient but heavily subsidized farmers in the rich world. Poor people everywhere would benefit most from a more efficient global market in foodstuffs, since up to 80 percent of their meager incomes goes for food.

Doha was launched as a "development round" that would unlock the power of trade to help the poor. Yet the negotiations made little progress. Powerful agricultural lobbies in America, Japan, and Europe scared off reformers in the rich world. For example, in 2008 the mighty U.S. farming lobby got Congress to vote through more than $300 billion worth of subsidies to protect themselves from competition from the rest of the world (with much of that cash going to big, wealthy farmers, not poor dust-bowl share-croppers). The EU's system of subsidies under the Common Agricultural Policy is no better. There were also divisions in the ranks of developing countries as some big hitters, such as India, resisted reform. (India retains a unilateral ban on the export of rice, which is bad news for Indian farmers and for consumers in other countries.) The need to conclude these negotiations was enormous before the financial crisis. It is now more urgent than ever.

This is not merely about economics. What happens to trade could also have a big impact on global security. Tension is growing in many parts of the world as cash-rich countries such as Saudi Arabia and South Korea, as well as China, have rushed to buy up agricultural land to secure their food supplies in the future. In March 2009, Marc Ravalomanana was ejected from the presidency of Madagascar after popular protests against his government's decision to lease 2.5 million acres of farmland to Daewoo Logistics, a South Korean firm. Under this deal, Madagascar would receive $6 billion of investment in exchange, but the Madagascan public feared that Daewoo's plans to farm the land to feed people back home in South Korea would leave them hungry. Tension is also growing in many regions of the world over access to scarce water resources. These trends are likely to continue to worsen unless the world can move to a more rational basis for food security.

Harnessing the benefits of trade to increase production offers part of the solution to the global food crisis. Keeping trade flowing freely around the world will be essential to all our prosperity. The same is true of capital.

CAPITAL SANS FRONTIERS

"As we are unable to regulate fully the behaviour of gun owners, we have no choice but to restrict the circulation of guns more directly." Writing in the *Financial Times* in 2008, as the credit crunch in the U.S. economy went global, two respected economists, Dani Rodrik from Harvard University and Arvind Subramanian from the Peterson Institute for International Economics, stuck their heads above the parapet to argue that, just like guns, the spread of capital needs to be controlled. For "gun owners," with their alarming tendency to do bad, read "capitalists."

This view challenged the widespread orthodoxy, upheld by the IMF, that capital can add most to our prosperity by flowing freely. To Rodrik and Subramanian, that case was busted. "Financial globalisation has not generated increased investment or higher growth in emerging markets," they argued. "Countries that have grown most rapidly have been those that rely least on capital inflows." The time had come, they argued, to revisit the idea of putting up barriers to the movement of capital across borders.

Capital controls have been around for centuries, typically in the form of a ban on the export of bullion. By stopping subjects or citizens from shipping gold and silver out of a country to where it could be exchanged for more goods, governments were usually trying to maintain an artificial price level in their domestic economy that had been brought on by some kind of policy error (such as inflation caused by debasing the coinage). More recently, this type of capital control has been used in wartime, such as when the European powers suspended their adherence to the gold standard during World War I. Since capital controls distort the market, it was no surprise that a consensus emerged among economists during the market-loving past thirty years that capital should be allowed to flow freely around the world without obstruction or hindrance.

Yet the volatility of international capital has been a factor in many financial crises during this period, including the emerging-markets crisis of the 1990s. At the time, this led some policymakers, such as Prime Minister Mahathir in Malaysia, to revive the idea that a domestic economy should be protected from the whims of the global capital market. Some went even further, proposing that countries should work together to "throw sand in the wheels" of speculators by taxing international capital movements. This idea, called a "Tobin tax" after the Nobel Prize–winning American economist James Tobin, who first proposed it in the 1970s, came back into fashion during the crisis of 2008 as the financial contagion that started in the United States spread globally.

One country that felt it had no choice but to introduce capital controls during the crisis of 2008 was Iceland. Its experience illustrated that the desire to control the flow of capital is often the product of dumb economic policies. But not always. Particularly in moments of crisis, footloose international investors can be easily spooked into taking their capital to wherever it is safest. That is bad for riskier emerging markets and good for safer havens, particularly the safest haven of all, keeper of the dollar, the United States. Such defensive international capital flows explain why the value of the dollar surged even as the American economy collapsed in the autumn of 2008.

The case against global capital, as Rodrik and Subramanian put it, is that it seems to do little good and, sometimes, quite a lot of harm. That is certainly an argument that emerging-market economies such as China buy into as they shield their economies with capital controls and finance their economic development from domestic savings, not foreign capital. This development model, however, is based in effect on massive forced saving, and therefore deferred consumption, by the Chinese public. Such a policy of "jam tomorrow (maybe)" is tough on the hundreds of millions of Chinese still living in poverty, and is probably sustainable only because of China's authoritarian political system.

In most instances, capital controls are a poor economic policy

choice. True, for some small, poor countries, even tiny movements of capital could be disruptive, and capital controls may
make sense, but that is the exception, not the rule. Even so, some
countries will feel they must make that choice as long as the dollar's dominant position distorts the flow of money around the
world. Strengthening the IMF to more effectively support countries hit by liquidity crises during panics would help reduce that
pressure. China also uses capital controls to keep the value of its
currency low, which has boosted exports and helped build massive trade surpluses. China's capital controls, in this way, contributed to the global financial imbalances that were fundamental
to the current crisis. Getting China to drop these controls and
make its currency convertible as part of the deal to establish a
global reserve currency would be a significant contribution to
international financial stability. If we fail to end the domination
of the dollar and the weakness of the IMF, we face the danger of
continuing imbalances that will destabilize the world economy.

Capital controls, including the proposed Tobin tax, are not
just a threat to our prosperity because they contribute to global
financial instability. The rich world also needs new places to invest
its capital. The cost of caring for America's over-sixty population,
which is now about 10 percent of GDP, is expected to double to 20
percent in the next thirty years as the population ages. The problem is basically a lack of young, working people to support the cost
of older nonworking people. Raising retirement ages would help.
So, too, would making migration easier, so that people from poor
countries with excess labor can move to countries where workers
are in short supply. Yet whatever the economic benefits, migration
is sometimes socially, and always politically, disruptive.

If workers cannot move to where the factories are, then capital must flow from richer to poorer countries as investment, to
produce the returns needed to fund the retirements of the elderly

citizens of the West by providing jobs and income in labor-rich developing countries. This could be a hugely valuable win-win solution. We will all be losers if we erect higher barriers to the flow of capital around the world.

Yet while trade and investment offer the best route to global prosperity, they will take time to deliver it. Some countries will need a helping hand in the meantime. Marshall Aid was part of the postwar settlement that restored prosperity to Europe. The world needs the same spirit of generosity and imagination that gave birth to Marshall Aid to help some of today's worst economies get on their feet.

AID THAT WORKS

"Aid has not only often failed to meet its objectives; it has also rarely dealt with the underlying issues of poverty and weak societies." There was some tutting of indignation from those involved in providing billions of dollars of international aid when the president of Rwanda, Paul Kagame, expressed such skepticism about the rich world's efforts to help the poor in an article in the *Financial Times* in May 2009. Kagame, after all, had courted all the big donor countries, from America down, as he tried to rebuild a country recovering from the genocide of 1994, in which hundreds of thousands of people died in ethnic violence in a country with a population of just a few million. Rich countries had responded to Rwanda's pleas with lavish amounts of aid. The point that Kagame was trying to make was that aid is just that: aid. It is not development. Long-term sustainable economic development can only come if countries are well governed, with a vibrant private sector. Yet, done well, aid can help bring this about.

Britain does not think of itself as a recipient of aid. Indeed, most Britons are surprised to learn that their country was the largest recipient of Marshall Aid after World War II, getting about a quarter of the $13 billion assistance program. (Oddly enough, in 1947 many Americans did not even know about the U.S. government's pledge to fund the rebuilding of Europe. When Secretary of State George Marshall made the announcement, the Truman administration deliberately tried to keep it out of the American media for fear of a negative public reaction.)

Marshall Aid involved a quick injection of cash to kick-start the European economy, motivated largely by fears of Soviet expansion across the continent. By contrast, like the poor, aid to the developing world always seems to be with us. A chorus of disapproval has grown in recent years, criticizing aid as ineffective. Books such as William Easterly's *White Man's Burden* and Dambisa Moyo's *Dead Aid* have received considerable attention for highlighting what are certainly serious failures and abuses of the aid that has gone to the world's poorest countries over the past half century. These critics are right that aid has had a pretty awful track record. On the other hand, until 1989, much of this aid was driven by the need to win the Cold War, rather than by what was best to encourage economic development, so perhaps that's not surprising.

Advocates of more aid have responded to this attack by arguing that it did not achieve the success that was hoped for because there was never enough money to do the job. They may have a point. In the 1970s, the United Nations agreed that rich countries should spend 0.7 percent of their national income on international aid, a target that no large country has ever reached (the United States gave nearly 0.2 percent in 2008; former colonial powers such as Britain and France gave about 0.4 percent). A real danger arising from the current crisis is that rich countries will cut their aid budgets as a fiscal expediency, rather than on the basis of whether the funding allotted can achieve anything. By early 2009, Italy had already done so. Yet to abandon aid to the poorest people in the world would be particularly shortsighted during the world's first truly global economic crisis.

The traditional aid cartel of the rich world is, however, starting to break down as new donors from the emerging markets and oil-producing states have started to boost the amount of support they give to the developing world. Independent estimates suggest that China and Saudi Arabia are each giving around $2 billion a year, which is not significant yet (Western donors together give a little more than $100 billion) but could be if it continues to increase. However, as the Polish proverb says: "There's always a teaspoon of tar in every barrel of honey." Most of China's aid, in particular, is being used for political or commercial purposes, in some cases to shore up unsavory regimes in such places as Zimbabwe and Myanmar. Aid cutbacks in the West could hand China, as well as other new donors such as Venezuela and Russia, undue influence in the developing world. Africa has been an ideological battleground before, during the Cold War, and could be again. Failing to support democracy and market capitalism in Africa— just as the continent is starting to embrace both of these—would be a foolish mistake.

Of course developing countries need one day to end their dependency on aid. Yet reaching the point at which they will be able to do so will be much harder during a global economic slump. Aid can play a countercyclical role by helping to protect some of the most vulnerable people on the planet. Using it in this way is more than altruism: the economic shock waves from the financial crisis have the potential to inflame conflicts that could cause instability in some of the most geopolitically important parts of the world. That could limit the access of rich countries to resources, or even threaten their security, through the rise of international terrorism. An investment by the rich nations in peacekeeping and conflict prevention in the Third World, for example, could be a very good one.

The other role that aid can play is in laying the groundwork for trade liberalization and financial reform to work their magic. Too many developing countries, though by no means all (as some critics of aid argue), are held back by toxic political systems in which the elites do little or nothing for ordinary people. Sadly, "democratization" has become something of a dirty word in parts of the world that arguably need it most, because of its recent association with military adventures by the Western powers. That should not deter the world's democracies from redoubling their efforts to promote everywhere property rights and freedom of expression, particularly through a free, independent media. Global economic progress will be quicker and more equitable if it is built on sound political foundations in the developing world.

SUPERSIZED GLOBAL GOVERNANCE REFORM

When he is not getting an earful of abuse from some visiting American treasury secretary, Wen Jiabao has spent much of his time since becoming premier in 2003 overseeing China's embrace of capitalism. Such has been his enthusiasm for this task that in January 2009, when he addressed hundreds of global business leaders at the World Economic Forum in Davos, Switzerland, it was he, not the businesspeople, who raved about Adam Smith. Indeed, he said, he had been "rereading" one of the Scottish high priest of capitalism's greatest works. Rereading? Not many of those in the room could truthfully claim to have read Smith even once.

Smith is best known for coining the phrase "the invisible hand" to describe the superior efficiency of markets and for his book *The Wealth of Nations.* However, it was his other great work that Wen had been rereading, *The Theory of Moral Sentiments,* which celebrates the natural human capacity for sympathy toward others, which, Smith says, generally stops people from becoming excessively selfish.

Maybe Premier Wen was struck by Smith's discussion of why we care less for people we do not know, which he illustrates by asking if we would have the same compassion for the victims of an earthquake in China as for someone suffering closer to home. Almost two hundred and fifty years after Smith raised this challenge, images from the earthquake in China's Sichuan province in May 2008 were flashed around the globe, prompting an outpouring of offers to help. It is not just sympathy that today flows across borders. As the financial crisis that followed that autumn showed, economic decisions made in Beijing have a huge impact in New York and Washington. Globalization is with us. Our global governance systems need to catch up.

Even before the economic crisis, the global institutions were showing signs of age. Kofi Annan's attempts to streamline the Byzantine bureaucracy of the United Nations had largely failed, despite the need being blindingly obvious. The IMF was drifting into irrelevance, as was the World Bank, which was struggling to find countries willing to borrow its money. It is tempting to think that we might be better off without these creaking organizations that force us to strike often unsatisfactory deals with countries whose ethics offend us. Yet, if isolationism was a mistake that America made in the 1920s, in the globalized world of the twenty-first century it would surely be a catastrophic blunder. The only real choice available to us is whether to continue to muddle along, or to remake the system so that it works. And that should be no choice at all.

Today there is no alternative economic model, such as communism, that threatens to replace capitalism. But there are plenty of fractured, populist political movements that challenge the status quo, from Islamist extremism to the antiglobalization protestors, as well as politically incoherent terrorist groups that threaten the legitimacy of governments, from drug gangs in Mexico to the brutal Lord's Resistance Army in Uganda. All of these groups, despite their diversity, benefit from the failure of global capitalism to offer prosperity to all, and, together, they make that task more difficult.

The world's leaders should see the current crisis as an opportunity to build a system of global governance that works, by creating a stable, effective system of oversight and a level playing field for global finance and trade. As it faces up to these challenges, and above all climate change, the world faces a classic problem of collective action.

To stand a realistic chance of keeping the average increase in the global temperature below the 2-degree-Celsius rise that experts fear could trigger serious consequences, the countries of the world must together cut emissions of carbon dioxide by half at least by 2050, with significant progress before then. Otherwise there may be a climatic disaster that would make the world as a whole one-fifth poorer, according to some estimates. (That would be the equivalent of a permanent global Great Depression.) There would also be massive geopolitical instability as countries adjusted to the physical consequences—rising sea levels and the like.

The central problem regarding climate change is agreeing who should bear the cost of stopping it. The demand for energy in poorer countries such as China is expected to treble by 2030, and these nations are already major polluters—China even overtook the United States as the world's biggest emitter of greenhouse gases in 2007. Yet when it is suggested that they should grow more slowly, or invest heavily in cleaner energy technologies, developing countries retort that it is nearly two centuries of industrial development in the rich world that has gotten us to where we are today and that each American, for example, pumps out far more carbon dioxide than the average Ugandan or Korean. Surely those who are already rich should pay the most? With some justification, developing countries argue that asking them to cut their emissions now amounts to pulling up the drawbridge on their development. Getting them to agree to shackle their economic growth in the middle of an economic crisis that is causing factories to close and jobs to be lost would be a tough sell.

Instead of trying to get one group of countries (rich or poor) to pay the bulk of the cost, a global deal on climate change will require an unprecedented amount of give and take. It will stand or fall on the actions of two countries, above all: the United States and China, as the biggest sources of greenhouse gases. By putting other important issues on the agenda, including a global reserve currency, reform of the IMF and the UN Security Council, and trade liberalization, it may be possible to negotiate a "big bang" global deal for prosperity that allows national governments to make the compromises necessary to tackle climate change.

That will require political leaders of vision that is all too often lacking, with a willingness to make short-term sacrifices in order to build a better world. In the past, it has taken the aftermath of war to provide the impetus for such idealism—from the formation of the League of Nations and the United Nations, to the European Union. Hopefully, this time, war will not be necessary. Yet this idealism will not be required of politicians alone.

The institutions and individuals that make up capitalism also bear a responsibility to work better for the benefit of all, by focusing on long-term success rather than hyping short-term profits. It is a sign of how far capitalism has fallen that it took Wen, the premier of a country still nominally Communist and certainly no democracy, to remind the bosses of the world's biggest companies gathered in Davos that business should be based on ethical values. Capitalism must also heal itself.

8

THE AGE OF PHILANTHROCAPITALISM

Capitalism must rediscover its soul

They did not actually say that "greed is not good," but the oath taken in June 2009 by more than four hundred students graduating from Harvard Business School amounted to much the same thing. At an unofficial ceremony the day before they received their MBAs, the students promised they would, among other things, "serve the greater good," "act with the utmost integrity," and guard against "decisions and behavior that advance my own narrow ambitions, but harm the enterprise and the societies it serves."

You may snigger. Yet with around half of that year's graduating class taking the pledge, Max Anderson, an MBA student himself, saw it as a triumph for a campaign that he had launched only a month before. He had hoped to get a hundred of his classmates to sign up at best. The economic crisis seems to have been behind the rush. Students wanted to distance themselves from earlier generations of MBAs, whose wonky moral compasses were seen to have contributed to the turmoil, especially on Wall Street, the biggest employer of Harvard MBAs in recent years.

In the aftermath of the collapse of the financial system in

September 2008, the populist line was that the mess was the result of greed gone wild, that everyone on Wall Street had been behaving like supercharged Gordon Gekkos, driven by the belief that "greed is good." As Michael Moore, the polemical left-wing documentary maker, put it, there is "this incredible flaw in capitalism, the greed flaw. The thing that says that the rich man will sell you the rope to hang himself with if he thinks he can make a buck off it." Enjoying the moment, he added wishfully, "Well, I'm the rope."

Wall Street helpfully provided plenty of circumstantial evidence to support this populist analysis, including a couple of villains straight out of central casting. The arrest of Wall Street grandee Bernie Madoff in December 2008 after he confessed to presiding over a maybe $60 billion Ponzi scheme was the most shocking example, followed soon after by the arrest on fraud charges of another billionaire money manager, the mustachioed charlatan Sir Allen Stanford.

Certainly, bubbles are times when dishonest behavior in the markets increases sharply, as John Kenneth Galbraith noted in his classic book *The Great Crash of 1929*. At any given time, he explained, "there is an inventory of undiscovered embezzlement in—or more precisely not in—the country's businesses and banks. This inventory—it should perhaps be called the bezzle—amounts at any one time to millions of dollars . . . In good times people are relaxed, trusting and money is plentiful. But even though money is plentiful, there are always many people who need more. Under these circumstances the rate of embezzlement grows, the rate of discovery falls off, and the bezzle increases rapidly."

Equally, Galbraith argues, in the aftermath of a crash, the morality of the business world tends to improve. In tougher economic times, "money is watched with a narrow, suspicious eye. The man who handles it is assumed to be dishonest until he proves himself otherwise. Audits are penetrating and meticulous. Commercial morality is enormously improved. The bezzle shrinks."

The public outrage in the current crisis was not limited to cases of out-and-out fraud. Banker-bashers had a field day over the determination of executives at financial services firms to cling to their multimillion-dollar bonuses even though their firms remained in business only because the taxpayer had come to the rescue. This added to earlier fury directed at those failed executives who, having led their firm to the brink of disaster, walked away with lavish "golden parachute" redundancy packages. Stanley O'Neal, who was ousted as boss of Merrill Lynch in the early stages of the credit crunch in September 2007, for example, was widely derided for his exit package valued at $161.5 million. Later, his successor, John Thain, who was forced to sell Merrill Lynch to Bank of America on the same weekend that Lehman Brothers went bust, became a symbol of executive excess when it was revealed that he had spent $1.2 million of the investment bank's money doing up his office. This included a wastepaper basket costing $1,400.

In Britain, most public rage was directed at the £700,000 ($1.2 million) annual pension pocketed by Sir Fred Goodwin, who had run the Royal Bank of Scotland for a decade. Ministers in the British government, who by then owned the failed RBS, complained that the decision was not in their hands, but in March 2009 disgruntled taxpayers took revenge on Sir Fred by smashing the windows of his Edinburgh home. "We are angry that rich people, like him, are paying themselves a huge amount of money, and living in luxury, while ordinary people are made unemployed, destitute, and homeless," said a group that claimed responsibility, echoing the wider public mood. "Bank bosses should be jailed. This is just the beginning," they warned. (In reaction to this outcry, Sir Fred eventually agreed to a reduction in his pension.)

Yet blaming everything on executive avarice is way too easy, even though greed certainly played a part in the recent bubble and crash, just as it did in every previous one. The current crisis of capitalism is in part a morality tale, but it is not a simple one. And it owes at least as much to failures of design, especially too much reliance on short-term measures of success, as it does to ethical lapses.

An obsession in the business world with short-term profits clearly helped to inflate the recent bubble. Increasingly, employees throughout the system were paid to maximize short-term financial returns, such as ever-expanding quarterly earnings and rising share prices. There were no rewards for asking tough questions about whether what was good in the short term was also good in the long run. Even regulators kept quiet.

Gradually, a culture known as IBGYBG grew up in many businesses—especially in the financial industry, which was largely based on one-off transactions rather than long-term relationships. In this culture, employees excused themselves from thinking about the long run by saying that by the time it becomes clear whether or not a transaction was any good, "I'll be gone, you'll be gone." This was pervasive throughout Wall Street, in mortgage lenders, and even in accounting firms and ratings agencies, where much of the professional reputation of a company depended on its integrity over the long term. Alas, all too often this integrity was sacrificed to make a quick buck.

One part of the solution to this crisis, to promote long-termism, is the revival of professionalism—or, in the case of management, to become a profession for the first time. The Harvard MBA oath may be part of that process.

Admittedly, this is hardly the first time that this call has been made. In 1912 the great American progressive lawyer Louis Brandeis gave a speech on "business as a profession," in which he expressed the hope that an ethical, professional approach would help the term "Big Business" to lose its "sinister meaning." As he concluded, optimistically, "Big business will mean professional-ized business, as distinguished from the occupation of petty traf-ficking or mere moneymaking. And as the profession of business develops, the great industrial and social problems expressed in the present social unrest will one by one find solution."

Two years later, Brandeis published a scathing attack on the financial industry, *Other People's Money—and How the Bankers Use It*. He would not have been surprised by the culture of IBGYBG that flourished on Wall Street in recent years.

If the move to greater professionalism is to mean any-thing, clearly compensation schemes should be fundamen-tally redesigned so they reward long-term performance, not short-term. Yet that alone will not be enough. After all, many of the biggest losers when Wall Street crashed were Wall Street exec-utives, such as Dick Fuld, who until Lehman Brothers went bust was a billionaire much admired around the world. He, like many others at the top of the financial services industry, had a big share-holding in his firm, which should have given him a powerful incentive to prioritize long-term over short-term performance. Moreover, it was not just Fuld: Lehman was generally reckoned to have one of the most sophisticated approaches to pay on Wall Street, focused on long-term performance rather than deals done. So while restructuring pay to reduce short-termism is an urgent priority, it will not do the trick on its own.

Rather than seeing Fuld as a man made reckless by financial greed, a more plausible account of his behavior is that some com-bination of overconfidence in his own abilities as chief executive and a sentimental refusal to sell the firm he loved blinded him to the reality of his situation. Intervening when a chief executive is blinded in this way is supposed to be the job of the board of direc-tors—yet Lehman's board stood by their man to the very end.

It is clear that the board was not up to the job. Apart from Fuld, few board members had any direct experience in the financial services industry, although the board did include a retired admiral, a theater producer, and, until 2006, Dina Merrill, an octogenarian actress whose other credits included a role in the film *Caddyshack II.* If this alone was not evidence of a lack of competence, the fact that according to filings with the SEC, the board's risk committee met only twice each year in 2006 and 2007 proved the point beyond a reasonable doubt. In March 2008, the Corporate Library, an organization focused on improving corporate governance, gave Lehman's board a D grade.

This raises an even more fundamental question: What on earth were Lehman's shareholders doing electing a board so manifestly ill-equipped to watch over their investment?

In theory, American public companies are a form of shareholder democracy, in that each share comes with a vote that can be cast in the election of the board of directors. In practice, these votes are largely worthless. It is hard for outsiders to nominate their own candidates for the board, as the incumbent board has no obligation to put these names on the ballots it sends to shareholders. This clearly needs to change, so that shareholder democracy actually means something. New laws are needed.

Yet meaningful voting rights will not change much unless the voters use them to get the right people and policies in place on Wall Street, and indeed throughout corporate America. Unfortunately, too often shareholders, especially the pension funds and mutual funds that invest the retirement savings of most of us, have been part of the problem. They have been at least as obsessed as corporate executives with short-term performance, due largely to a bonus-driven culture focused on rewarding fund managers by how their returns compare, quarter by quarter, year by year, with market benchmarks and their peers. Few of them seem even to think about whether corporate executives are incentivized to pursue long-term shareholder value creation rather than short-term profit maximization. Indeed, insofar as share prices rise in response to increases in short-term profits, fund managers with bonuses skewed to short-term performance may well encourage executive compensation schemes that incentivize short-term profit maximization.

If capitalism is to emerge from the current crisis in better shape than before, it must be refocused on the longer term. That will require new regulations and business strategies that do not hurt long-term profits by overemphasizing short-term profits. More fundamentally, and this is where the oath-taking Harvard MBAs are on to something really important, it will need a deeper understanding, especially among business leaders, that capitalism does not exist in a vacuum. As well as generating profits, capitalism needs to give back, including by being part of the solution to society's most pressing social and environmental problems.

The time has come for business leaders to stop offering up as an excuse Milton Friedman's famous argument that "the social responsibility of business is to maximize its profits." That claim may make some sense when it is used against ill-considered government plans to impose social responsibilities on businesses (a renewed danger in these times of rapidly expanding government), but it does not justify an obsession with the short term and a myopic perspective on the role of business in society.

Business would not be business without the pursuit of profit. Yet the strategies needed for maximizing long-term profits are likely to be quite different from those that can maximize short-term profits. A company asking, "What do we need to do to succeed in ten or twenty years?" must also ask, "What sort of society will shape our customers in ten or twenty years?" The answer to the latter is, hopefully, a richer society, with a greater number of people concerned about the values of the firms from which they buy. This is likely to include everything from how they treat workers in their supply chain in poor countries to how they contribute to the fight against climate change. Rising incomes combined with the transparency brought by modern technology can only accelerate this trend, which is already gathering momentum— and, like it or not, businesspeople had better respond positively to it. (So, too, the trend for workers, such as those Harvard MBAs, to want employers that share their values: demonstrating those values will be ever more crucial as firms try to win the "war for talent.")

Is this just wishful thinking, the result of a temporary existential angst within capitalism brought on by the crisis, that is likely to prove short-lived as business returns to normal? There are grounds for optimism. Even before the crisis, business leaders such as Bill Gates were talking about "creative capitalism"—his concept of a "market system that eases the world's inequities."

Gates, who has pledged to give away most of his fortune to fight poverty and disease in the developing world, is one of the leaders of a movement we call philanthrocapitalism. Yet philanthrocapitalism is about more than personal or corporate giving; it is also about firms making profits by operating in ways that benefit humanity, "doing well by doing good." Some world-class firms, such as GE, Starbucks, Cisco, Nike, Pepsico, Virgin, and Wal-Mart, already show signs of understanding that it is in their enlightened interest to be leaders, not laggards, in embracing long-termism. A similar understanding is now needed in the investment firms that contributed so profoundly to the current crisis by failing to use their power as shareholders to encourage companies to focus on the long term.

Such a transformation of capitalism will require a new generation of business leaders who are willing to think long-term and take a broader view of what it means to be successful. The true test of the Harvard Class of 2009 is not what they were willing to pledge as they finished their studies but what they do once they have real business responsibilities. That is where their predecessors manifestly failed.

FIRST, DO NO HARM

"I will not accept the Nuremberg excuse," said former Federal Reserve chairman Paul Volcker in February 2009. He was recalling an e-mail he had sent to his grandson at the height of the financial crisis. One of the "saddest days of my life," he said, was when the grandson had told him that he wanted to be a financial engineer. In 2008, Volcker's daughter saw some disparaging remarks her father had made about financial engineers and forwarded them to her son, by now working in his dream job.

According to Volcker, "He sent me an e-mail, 'Grandpa, don't blame it on us! We were just following the orders we were getting from our bosses.'" That was when Volcker decided he had no choice but to send his e-mail. Comparing your grandson to a Nazi war criminal is pretty stern stuff, but that's families for you. Yet the point he made was absolutely right: being incentivized to do something does not remove your responsibility to ask whether that is the right thing for you to do.

That sense of responsibility to a set of values is the defining feature of a profession. The best-known example of this is the Hippocratic oath taken by doctors for centuries, normally paraphrased as "First, do no harm." The creation of a Hippocratic oath for business is an attempt to professionalize management. It was first proposed in 2003 by some young leaders at the World

Economic Forum, one of whom, Angel Cabrera, became president of Thunderbird, one of America's leading business schools, and challenged his students to come up with some suitable words.

Since 2006, MBA students have signed the following oath when they graduate from Thunderbird: "I promise I will strive to act with honesty and integrity. I will respect the rights and dignity of all people. I will strive to create sustainable prosperity worldwide. I will oppose all forms of corruption and exploitation, and I will take responsibility for my actions. As I hold true to these principles, it is my hope that I may enjoy an honorable reputation and peace of conscience. This pledge I make freely and upon my honor."

As Cabrera admits, "Most of the CEOs and top executives of the financial institutions that have failed are graduates from the finest business schools in the world. We cannot take credit for their success one day and then the next day pretend we are devoid of responsibility when we witness such widespread failure of leadership. Business schools have contributed to the perpetuation of a vision of business and management at times incomplete if not outright misleading. The excesses that now occupy the news, and the public mistrust in business leaders that has ensued, are in some ways a direct consequence of the values that still dominate the traditional business curriculum."

In 2008, an article in the *Harvard Business Review* by two Harvard Business School (HBS) professors proposed an oath with tougher language than Thunderbird's rather motherhood-and-apple-pie version. It was this that inspired the oath taken at HBS in 2009. It covers issues including selfishness ("I pledge that considerations of personal benefit will never supersede the interests of the enterprise I am entrusted to manage") and transparency ("I vow to represent my enterprise's performance accurately and transparently to all relevant parties"), and an overarching goal of serving "the public's interest by enhancing the value [their] enterprise creates for society."

"Unlike doctors and lawyers, managers don't need a formal education, let alone a license, to practice. Nor do they adhere to a universal and enforceable code of conduct," wrote the two professors, Rakesh Khurana and Nitin Nohria. Even if individual firms write and enforce corporate codes or value statements, "there's no universally accepted set of professional values backed up by a governing body with the power to censure managers who deviate from the code."

Yet, Khurana and Nohria pointed out, in 1908, when HBS was founded, it was inspired by the goal of making management a profession, like law and medicine. This ambition spread beyond Harvard. In 1925, at the newly created Stanford Business School, Wallace Donham, the second dean of HBS, gave a speech, "The Social Significance of Business," in which he declared that the "development, strengthening, and multiplication of socially minded business men is the central problem of business."

Donham feared that as scientific, technological, and material progress accelerated, the traditional sources of professional ethical leadership (such as the law and the clergy) would be unable to cope, and that it would fall to the "new profession of business" to save modern industrial civilization from itself.

As he put it, "The socializing of industry from within on a higher ethical plane, not socialism nor communism, not government operation nor the exercise of the police power, but rather the development from within the business group of effective social control of those mechanisms which have been placed in the hands of the race through all the recent extraordinary revolutionizing of material things, is greatly needed. The business group largely controls these mechanisms and is therefore in a strategic position to solve these problems. Our objective therefore, should be the multiplication of men who will handle their current business problems in socially constructive ways."

In his 1912 speech on "business as a profession," Louis Brandeis argued that "business should be, and to some extent already is, one of the professions." For Brandeis, there were three defining characteristics of a profession. "First. A profession is an occupation for which the necessary preliminary training is intellectual in character, involving knowledge and to some extent learning, as distinguished from mere skill. Second. It is an occupation which is pursued largely for others and not merely for one's self. Third. It is an occupation in which the amount of financial return is not the accepted measure of success."

There are some obvious reasons why management has failed to become a profession—mainly, the fact that there are significant differences between the requirements for success in management and in the older professions such as medicine and the law. In business, the success of iconoclasts such as Bill Gates might suggest that a lack of formal management training was a positive advantage. Medicine and law have far fewer examples of top practitioners succeeding without professional training—despite the popularity of some alternative healers and upstart legal heroes such as Erin Brockovich. In business, profit can go up for years even when a manager is overseeing activities that neither maximize the long-term value of the company nor aid society.

Yet, as the two Harvard professors point out, steps could be taken in the right direction, now that the need for greater professionalization has become clear. A start would be for management education to "adopt the more stringent knowledge and competency standards required by true professions," they argue. For instance, the Association to Advance Collegiate Schools of Business "could devise and administer an exam that all graduating MBAs would have to pass before they were licensed to practice." Managers could also be required to take refresher courses to retain their licenses. Management jobs could be classified according to the amount of professional training required, in order to allow the market to make clear the value of such training. (Even so, it is hard to imagine the traditional entrepreneur educated at the University of Life going out of fashion.)

The irony in all this is that, in many ways, business has embraced high standards of behavior more thoroughly than any other part of society. Thanks to a combination of the need to recruit and retain the best talent, and the litigation risk of failing to comply with increasingly demanding laws, the leading companies, at least, are often extremely enlightened on issues such as removing gender, race, and sexuality biases from recruitment and promotion decisions and cracking down on sexual harassment. Their public statements tend to be far more truthful than, say, those that ever emanate from a typical politician.

But admirable as this is, it falls far short of professionalization. Debating what should be in a so-called Hippocratic oath for business would offer a way to reach a general agreement in the business world on what constitutes professional standards of behavior. If they are wise, today's business leaders and educators will see it is in their enlightened self-interest to take the goal of professionalization seriously, and thus start to regain society's trust.

Nobody should underestimate the difficulty of being professional in today's business world. Even established professions that were supposed to uphold high professional standards let their standards slip during the bubble years. These entities include auditors, law firms, and ratings agencies. The pursuit of short-term profits has done serious damage to reputations for professionalism that took many decades to build. Accounting firms doing consulting work for audit clients created a lucrative but deadly conflict of interest. Ultimately, it reduced the quality of audited corporate accounts and exposed audit firms to legal risk that, in the aftermath of Enron's collapse, led to Arthur Andersen going out of business. In the end, regulation was introduced to prevent auditors from selling consulting services to clients.

Perhaps a similar response will be needed to address the conflict of interest at ratings agencies, such as Standard & Poor's and Moody's, which are paid by those whose bonds they rate. During the frenzy of issuance of subprime mortgage securities during the bubble years, ratings agencies processed so many deals that it seems inconceivable that traditional professional standards could have been maintained. One calculation suggests that at the peak of the bubble, each agency employee had to rate a security every 90 minutes—so it's no wonder they did such a poor job.

The failings of these firms highlight the need for financial incentives that encourage professionalism. This mission to professionalize management is unlikely to succeed unless it is accompanied by a dramatic transformation in how executives are paid.

YOU GET WHAT YOU PAY FOR

In March 2009, the news that twenty executives at AIG, an insurer that barely six months earlier the government had saved from going bust, had been paid combined bonuses of $165 million prompted outrage in America—especially as these executives worked for the financial products unit that had run up billions of dollars in losses. President Obama instructed his treasury secretary, Tim Geithner, to find a way to stop them from being paid, saying, "This isn't just a matter of dollars and cents. It's about our fundamental values." Eventually, most of the executives were shamed into returning the money, though one resigned in protest via a letter to the *New York Times*, complaining of "untrue and unfair accusations from certain members of Congress" and pledging to give the entire bonus to charity.

Obama's attack on AIG executives was, perhaps, understandable, given the public outrage. But it highlighted a serious problem: how people were paid in the financial industry played a huge part in the short-termism that brought the industry, and with it the economy, to its knees. A revolution is needed in how people are paid in finance. Yet getting this right will need careful thought.

Capitalism works because it taps into the widespread desire to become wealthier. However popular politically, restricting the ability of people in business and finance to earn way above the average would be a huge mistake, discouraging wealth creation and creating an incentive to waste resources finding ways to get around the restrictions. The problem is people getting rich for doing things that are ultimately wealth-destroying. This has occurred because of a compensation system that rewards short-term profits even when these arise from doing things that harm long-term profitability. The financial crisis has destroyed—or ought to have destroyed—this system. This is true of bonuses based on deals done, irrespective of whether those deals ultimately turn out to be good. And it is true of efforts to tie executive compensation to share performance, especially through share options, which failed to take into account the incentives that these gave executives to manipulate their firm's share price.

When Geithner outlined a series of proposed reforms in June 2009, he said that, contrary to some expectations, the government would not impose fierce restrictions such as caps on pay. Nor would it meddle in the detail of compensation packages. This was wise. In 1993, the previous time a president had tried to curb fat-cat salaries, Bill Clinton signed a law restricting the tax deductibility of executive pay to $1 million. This merely prompted a burst of creativity. Perks were devised that got around the cap, and there was a boom in paying executives with shares and options that, thanks to the bull stock market of the 1990s, made everybody far wealthier than they would have been using the old pay formulas.

Instead, Geithner said, the government wanted companies to adopt a series of broad principles on pay, and it intended to make it easier for shareholders to ensure that they did so, by voting on a "say on pay" resolution. (Experience in Europe, where these ballots are common, has shown that such resolutions encourage boards to consult more actively with shareholders on pay issues ahead of formal polls.) Firms that had been bailed out by the government would face stiffer restrictions on bonuses and other forms of pay, however. Some were required to submit senior managers' compensation for review by a newly appointed government official known as the "special master," who, inevitably, was soon nicknamed the "pay czar."

Looking more broadly, Geithner urged all companies to take a fresh look at the way they reward staff. Among other things, Geithner said, they would do well to avoid plans that offer big rewards for short-term risk taking. He called for a reconsideration of the golden parachutes for executives that can produce payouts that would make Croesus blush, such as that given Merrill Lynch's Stanley O'Neal, ousted for poor performance. He also exhorted firms to be more open with investors about the logic behind their decisions on pay.

Some explanation is certainly needed, and not just in financial services. How executives of public companies are paid is one of the worst flaws in the capitalist system. Pay levels have soared, in absolute and relative terms. The median American chief executive earned 30 times what the average worker did in the 1970s. By 2007, the ratio was closer to 200 times, or more. This increase has borne little relationship to long-term performance. Many executives have made a mint even though their firms' track records have been lousy.

One reason is that many bosses have packed their board's remuneration committee with people who are friendly to their cause—chief executives at other firms, for instance, who might offer a board seat in return. Legendary former GE boss Jack Welch has advised fellow chief executives to ensure that the compensation committee is "chaired by someone older and richer than you, who is not threatened by the idea of your getting rich too." Under no circumstances should the committee be chaired by "anyone from the public sector or a professor."

To address this issue, the Obama administration said it would introduce legislation to give the SEC powers to ensure that compensation committees are truly independent of management. It also intended to require the SEC to ensure that consultants who advise such committees on pay are independent as well. Not that independence is the only worry. A bigger problem is that the incentives for pay consultants encourage them to propose above-average pay at every firm they work for. Every board wants to believe it has hired someone of above-average ability to run the firm, and is unlikely to keep on a consultant whose recommendation suggests otherwise. In a world where everyone is being awarded an above-average package, the average tends to rise fast.

Ideally, pay should be tailored individually to the long-term needs of each firm. Sometimes—as on the trading floor of a Wall Street firm—short-term performance should be generously rewarded, provided those in charge of the firm understand the risks to which this can expose their firm and take steps to manage it.

Many financial firms would do well, however, to increase the pay of risk managers relative to that of risk takers. Linking executive compensation to the performance of their firm's shares may make sense, provided this is long-term performance. Schemes that award shares but do not allow the executive to cash in most of these shares until a year or more after he or she has left the firm have particular appeal. So do arrangements that allow firms to "claw back" bonuses if they later turn out to have been awarded for deals that proved mistaken.

The Obama administration was right to show restraint in the face of strong populist temptations. Reforming how people are paid, especially at the top, is an urgent priority for capitalism, but it is not something government is likely to do well. This is ultimately a matter for shareholders, who have lost substantial sums of money due to the current arrangements. Government should limit itself to ensuring that shareholders do have a say on pay, and to encouraging them to use that power.

POWER TO THE SHAREHOLDER

"The credit crisis we find ourselves in is a direct manifestation of board members' lack of oversight. Alarm bells should have gone off in boardrooms as crisis loomed, but many boards looked the other way," thundered Carl Icahn in October 2008. "Our economy has floundered for nearly two years because boards allowed their companies to make vast leveraged investments into faltering mortgage-backed securities. These investments vaporized trillions of dollars in shareholder value and left the banking industry in crisis. Boards gave permission to CEOs to take these risks, which oftentimes they misunderstood, which is like giving the fox permission to guard the henhouse."

Icahn, a legendary Wall Street investor now in his seventies, has been complaining about the lousy governance of corporate America for years, caring not a jot about how unpopular this made him. (As he likes to joke, "In this business, if you want a friend, get a dog"—a remark later "stolen" by Gordon Gekko in the movie *Wall Street*.)

Icahn used to be known as a "corporate raider" or a "green-mailer" (who would buy shares in a company and criticize management, allegedly so they would pay over the odds for those shares to be rid of him). Now he presents himself as an activist for better corporate governance. His comments in October 2008 marked the launch of United Shareholders of America, a "voice for large and small shareholders," as he described the new organization. "We must have a strong voice in Washington to combat the pro-management forces. United Shareholders of America will aim to push back against board entrenchment and make it easier for shareholders to promote change in companies they own."

This seems an obvious campaign, long overdue. The governance of American companies is built on the democratic principle of one share, one vote—much like in Britain, Australia, and a growing number of countries that are gradually embracing the "Anglo-Saxon model" of capitalism. And yet in practice one vote can do very little, even when it is on the side of an overwhelming majority of the votes cast—particularly in America. As Bob Monks, another veteran shareholder activist, albeit more of a patrician than Icahn, puts it, "The American shareholder cannot nominate directors, he cannot remove them, he cannot—except at the arbitrary pleasure of the SEC—communicate advice to them. 'Democracy' is a cruelly misleading word to describe the situation of the American shareholder."

To be precise, a shareholder can nominate directors, but to do so it has to hand out a separate proxy paper, containing only its candidates, and secure more votes than the official slate of board candidates on the proxy distributed by the board. This is costly, because of both the distribution of the proxy and the campaigning for candidates. By contrast, official nominees' campaigns can be paid for out of corporate funds. That is why there are so few contested board elections. That explains why boards tend to be stuffed with the cronies of the chief executive, who one way or another gets the people he or she wants nominated. A study by Lucian Bebchuk of Harvard Law School found that during 1996–2004, incumbent directors faced rival slates from candidates seeking to run the firm as a stand-alone entity on only 117 occasions at companies with a stock market value of more than $200 million, only two of which contests were successful.

Nor is it easy for shareholders to remove an official nominee for the board by casting their votes against him or her. Under today's rules, only votes in favor count; votes against or withheld are ignored. Under this "plurality" system, a single supporting vote may get a director elected. This system came under scrutiny in 2004 when 45 percent of the votes cast by Disney shareholders did not support the reelection to the board of the entertainment firm's then boss, Michael Eisner. Those who favor greater shareholder power can take some comfort from the fact that this marked the beginning of the end for Eisner at Disney—though he and his board would have been fully within their rights to ignore this almost unprecedented shareholder rebellion. The introduction of majority voting is long overdue.

Shareholders can also propose motions for debate at a company's annual meeting. Typically, however, the board is free to ignore these, even if shareholders vote overwhelmingly for them. Most shareholder resolutions on the proxy are "precatory"—that is, advisory only. Boards have a long record of ignoring such advice. For example, points out Bebchuk, in 1997–2003, 131 resolutions to abolish staggered boards (in which only a minority of directors face reelection each year) received a majority of the shareholder votes cast. By late 2004, less than a third of those resolutions had been acted on.

Boards also have considerable discretion over which resolutions to allow on the proxy. Shareholder resolutions are not supposed to interfere with a board's autonomy to make ordinary business decisions.

The inadequacy of shareholder rights in practice is matched by the lack of interest of most shareholders in exercising them. Typically, the few shareholders willing to vote against management are combative investors such as Icahn and the small band of younger activist hedge funders he has inspired, or politically motivated shareholders, such as union pension funds, which often propose resolutions related to their campaigns. There is a small, but growing, group of "ethical investors" that is trying to challenge management to do better, but typically they have expressed their ethical concern by refusing to buy shares in companies whose practices they disapprove of, rather than actively trying to change them. This is starting to change, however, as they see the potential for greater shareholder activism.

It is the silent majority of shareholders that has failed to hold management to account—insofar as the system allows it. These shareholders deserve much of the blame for the short-termism of corporate America and of the financial system in particular. This is especially true of pension funds and mutual funds, which supposedly have a responsibility to vote carefully. Alas, these institutions tend to pay their own staff in ways that encourage short-termism. For instance, bonuses for fund managers are often determined according to results relative to an industry benchmark in a given year, which tends to encourage short-term herding behavior rather than independent, long-term investing.

In his 2006 book, *The Battle for the Soul of Capitalism,* one of America's most respected mutual fund bosses, John Bogle, founder of index-fund pioneer Vanguard, argued that "many of these institutions, which now own two-thirds of the shares of corporate America, are fundamentally failing in their fiduciary duty." The crisis has proved him right.

It is tempting to regard the shareholder democracy model of governance for public firms as a lost cause. The question is, can a better alternative be found? Arguably, Wall Street used to have one: the partnership. Firms such as Goldman Sachs kept pay related to performance through peer review. They were far less likely to make decisions for short-term gain when they were run by partners whose wealth was largely illiquid and depended on their firm doing well consistently year after year. Not for nothing was Goldman's unofficial motto "Long-term Greedy." Strikingly, in this crisis, privately owned financial firms avoided the disastrous fate of some public firms. So, too, did mutuals and co-operatives: two forms of ownership that had fallen out of fashion, but may now come back.

After Goldman's near-death experience during the crisis of 2008, many within the firm debated whether it should return to the partnership status it gave up in an IPO in 1999. In the end, however, the advantages of being a public company—particularly the ability to raise large amounts of capital and the advantages of liquid shares as a currency for doing deals and rewarding staff— were judged too good to give up, at least for the immediate future.

Certainly, smaller partnerships and "boutiques" are likely to be more common in some areas of financial services as talented bankers opt out of big firms struggling to deal with the toxic aftermath of the crisis. Hedge funds and private-equity firms had been the last sector of the financial services industry in which partnerships were still thriving even before the crisis—though there, too, the temptations to go public were increasing. Both Fortress, a hedge fund company, and Blackstone, a private-equity firm, did IPOs shortly before the bubble burst.

Ironically, private equity had been touted as an answer to the corporate governance crisis of public companies. Buying up firms traded on stock markets and running them privately gave the new owners the ability to tailor remuneration to the long-term goals of the shareholders, and to avoid the constant public scrutiny of quarterly performance that does so much to make managers take short-termist decisions, the argument went. As one private-equity legend, Henry Kravis, cofounder of Kohlberg, Kravis and Roberts (KKR), put it in a speech in 2004, "If you examine all the major corporate scandals of the past 25 years, none of them occurred where a private-equity firm was involved." Private-equity firms, he said, are "vigilant in our role as owners, and we protect shareholder value."

The crisis did serious damage to private-equity firms, however, as it turned out that many of their deals were based on cheap credit, and on the expectation that such credit would be readily available for years to come. Investors in private equity will certainly have lost a ton of money during 2007–08, which means that there is no longer any serious prospect of private equity replacing the public stock market. (At the same time, the discipline that the partnership model was supposed to bring broke down in some private-equity firms and hedge funds. Typically they charged an annual management fee of 2 percent of the money in their portfolio. The possibility of banking these fees, regardless of performance, seems to have encouraged many of them to try to grow assets under management as fast as possible, regardless of their ability to put the money raised to profitable use.)

Class-action lawyers who pursue lawsuits on behalf of shareholders are unlikely to be the solution to the failure of shareholder democracy, either. These lawsuits are typically brought after a fall in a firm's share price, which the lawyer would allege was due to wrongful behavior by managers. The market crisis prompted a surge in class-action lawsuits against financial firms in 2008: 210 such lawsuits were brought, alleging losses of

$856 billion, due mainly to failure to report toxic assets, according to researchers at Stanford University Law School.

Whether shareholders benefit from this kind of action is unclear, as it is their own money that is paid out to them when they win—minus the legal fees, of course. In recent years, some lawyers have demanded corporate-governance improvements as well as money from firms, but this has yet to generate much change.

All of which means that Icahn is right: shareholders do need to find their voice—and the government should grant them the power to have that voice listened to by the management of the firms they own. True, Icahn is not the ideal man to mobilize the shareholders of America to demand a long-term focus from business. But this is a huge opportunity for someone younger, with an ability to see the bigger picture. Indeed, the puzzle is, given how much is at stake for us all, that there has not been a serious effort to mobilize a mass movement of the ultimate shareholders—all of us, through our retirement savings—to demand much better from those fiduciaries we entrust with our money.

Perhaps it is only a matter of time. After all, workers and consumers are increasingly demanding a longer-term vision from business, and they are starting to get it from business leaders who themselves increasingly want to change. If those who ultimately own companies demand that change as well, they—we—may turn out to be pushing at an open door.

DOING WELL BY DOING GOOD

"The capitalist system now is a half-done system. It needs to be completed," said Muhammad Yunus. The Bangladeshi economist, who was awarded the Nobel Peace Prize in 2006 for his work in relieving poverty through his Grameen microfinance bank, was addressing a roomful of movers and shakers in the business world at the World Economic Forum in Davos in January 2009.

The mood in the Swiss mountains had been unusually somber all week, as the great and good considered what to do about the collapse of the global economic system over which they presided. The unofficial theme for 2009's gathering was "How to Reboot the System." All were desperately seeking a big idea to lead them out of the mess. Completing capitalism could be it.

There were few bigger economic messes than Bangladesh when Yunus launched Grameen in the early 1970s after a bloody fight to win independence from Pakistan. Yet he managed to harness the tools of capitalism to the drive for a better world to lift millions of people out of poverty. Speaking alongside Yunus were two men who shared his desire for a capitalism that cares, what we call "philanthrocapitalism": the most successful capitalist of his age, Bill Gates, and the buccaneering British entrepreneur Sir Richard Branson. In different ways, all three men understood that capitalism does not exist in a vacuum and that it needs to give back by being part of the solution to society's biggest problems. Their motivation is not sentimental altruism. They understand that if capitalism is to emerge from this crisis in better shape than it was before, it must be refocused on the longer term. That will require new business strategies that do not compromise long-term profits by overemphasising short-term profits.

"It's not rocket science," explains Ron Grzywinski, founder of ShoreBank, a financial institution with some of the greatest exposure to, and lowest default rates on, the subprime-mortgage market that brought down much larger lenders during the crisis of 2008. The secret, he says—which is no secret at all—was to "do it the old-fashioned way." As he explains, "We meet with the borrower, and it's old-fashioned lending. Who is the borrower? What kind of down payment do they have? Where's the money coming from? How real is the value of the house? Can they make these payments? All that kind of stuff. We do verification of value and of income. We lend in the markets that we know."

While ShoreBank was not untouched by the recession, if mainstream banks had done their sub-prime mortgage lending as effectively as it did, they would not have gotten into such a mess. Many in the banking industry are quick to blame America's Community Reinvestment Act for encouraging irresponsible lending in poor communities. Yet Grzywinski had proposed the idea and in 1977 was the only banker to testify before Congress to urge passage of the law, which requires banks to make a certain amount of loans in the places where they operate. He built his successful bank by lending responsibly in those communities.

In 2007, ShoreBank even launched a Rescue Loan Program in Chicago, to help people who had mortgages with adjustable interest rates. There had been massive defaults on these adjustable-rate mortgages (ARMs), which were often granted without asking basic questions about income, employment, credit history, and so on. Yet it turned out that many of these borrowers would in fact have qualified for traditional fixed-rate mortgages, which would have served them much better, according to Grzywinski.

Grzywinski was speaking in March 2009 at the launch of the new Global Alliance for Banking on Values. ShoreBank, which was founded in Chicago to serve local customers neglected by the mainstream financial sector, was one of the leaders of the alliance. It was created as a bank with a mission: to demonstrate that a regulated bank could be instrumental in revitalizing the communities being avoided by other financial institutions. It added an environmental focus, in the belief that "communities cannot achieve true prosperity without also attaining environmental well-being."

Alongside ShoreBank, the other leaders of the new alliance

were Triodos Bank, which opened in 1980 as Europe's first bank explicitly designed to be sustainable, and BRAC (Bangladesh Rural Advancement Committee) Bank, which like Muhammad Yunus's Grameen Bank was created in Bangladesh in the aftermath of the Bangladeshi Liberation War of 1971 and is now probably the world's largest microfinance institution. These institutions, which had long been treated as, at best, a sideshow in the world of finance, were showing a newfound confidence in a more values-driven kind of capitalism. "We will lead the debate on the banking models we think could inspire profound changes in the mainstream financial industry," promised Mary Houghton, Shore-Bank's president.

Bill Gates is one of the leading proponents of the idea that capitalism can and should do good; it is part of what he calls "creative capitalism." He stepped down from the leadership of Microsoft in mid-2008 to become a full-time philanthropist, giving away not only his own fortune but also that of the second-richest man in the world, Warren Buffett. Although they are together giving away $4 billion a year, even this amount of money is small compared with the budgets of governments and big business. Yet Gates believes that by deploying the same talents that enabled him to succeed in the for-profit world to this giving, he can achieve an outsized impact. For example, by leveraging his money through creative partnerships with business, governments, and nonprofits, Gates is trying to end deaths from malaria, which currently kills over 1 million people a year in poor countries. The coalition spans News Corp, Exxon Mobil, the World Bank, the nonprofit Malaria No More, the British government, Pastor Rick Warren, Bono, and the National Basketball Association, among others.

On the panel on philanthrocapitalism in Davos, Yunus created a minor stir by accusing his fellow panelist of becoming a philanthropist to escape from the "one-dimensional" profit-driven person that business had required him to be. "I am as bad or as good as I ever was," retorted Gates. While giving by rich individuals is part of the philanthrocapitalism story, some of the most exciting changes taking place concern the ways in which for-profit businesses are embracing a new kind of capitalism that gives back to society and cares for the environment.

This is, in some ways, the hallmark of the third panelist, Sir Richard Branson. This colorful entrepreneur is nowhere near as generous as Gates in giving his money away. But he has dedicated the future profits of his Virgin airline to finding new ways to power planes without ruining the environment. Some chide Branson for meanness, since he is investing his cash rather than donating it. Yet this is the type of long-term thinking in business that has been in too-short supply, especially in the financial sector. By investing in speculative new green-energy technologies, Sir Richard may have to sacrifice financial returns, in the short term at least. Yet there has been a growing interest in the idea that, at least in some circumstances, profit should not be the only measure of the success of an investment.

A few weeks after Lehman Brothers went bust, several hundred people gathered in San Francisco for SoCap08 (Social Capital Markets 08), the first annual conference dedicated to the challenge of building capital markets that invest in social good. "There was a surge in registrations after Lehman collapsed," said Kevin Jones of the carefully named Good Capital, who organized the event. "Some of them had worked on Wall Street and thought they could find a job that used their skills and made them feel more useful. Others simply wanted to see if there was a better way of doing capitalism."

The question that dominated the conference was how to measure social impact and its relationship to profit. Jed Emerson, one of the speakers at SoCap, has spent much of his career exploring these questions from various perspectives. He developed a theory of "blended value," a "triple-bottom-line" approach in which firms are judged by their social and environmental impact as well as their profits, while working as an academic at Harvard. He later worked for Generation Investment Management, an investment firm created by former U.S. vice president Al Gore and David Blood, formerly of Goldman Sachs, which buys shares in companies with good environmental strategies on the basis that this will generate the highest financial returns. More recently, he has focused on how to promote blended value in the financial industry, including by examining the circumstances in which the short-selling of shares can be a force for social good and how to create environmentally sustainable hedge funds.

"Traditionally, we have thought of value as being either economic (and created by for-profit companies) or social (and created by nonprofit or non-governmental organizations)," says Emerson. "What the Blended Value Proposition states is that all organizations, whether for-profit or not, create value that consists of economic, social and environmental value components—and that investors (whether market-rate, charitable or some mix of the two) simultaneously generate all three forms of value through providing capital to organizations. The outcome of all this activity is value creation and that value is itself non-divisible and, therefore, a blend of these three elements."

There is certainly a long way to go before measurements of social and environmental impact are developed that are anywhere near as rigorous as those for financial returns and profit. However, in recent years, companies have provided a growing amount of data in these areas, as a result of public demand and regulation. Without wishing to impose massive data-gathering costs on firms, investors and regulators should make it a high priority to identify the best measures of impact and require firms to publish relevant data. That would allow investors to analyze rigorously what the relationship is between social and environmental impact and financial return, to figure out in an informed way how much they care about that impact, and thus how much they want to incentivize firms to deliver it.

There is, of course, a risk that thinking about return on investment in terms other than financial may result in a mushy, stakeholder capitalism in which money is invested poorly and social returns are used as an excuse for bad decisions. However, for some of the participants at SoCap, the really exciting challenge of ideas such as "blended value" is that they may help them spot the win-win investments that offer both financial and social returns.

Even before the economic crisis, a growing number of companies were starting to take seriously the need to put values at the heart of their business model. These included some of the best-known and most profitable firms in the world. Like philanthropy, this is something that needs to be central to the new form of capitalism that will emerge from the crisis. The mantra for businesses in the age of philanthrocapitalism should be "doing well by doing good." Many companies are missing out on substantial long-term profit opportunities because they are too focused on short-term profits and not enough on figuring out how to help society make progress.

The best example of how a company can transform itself by taking seriously the opportunity to do well by doing good is Wal-Mart, the giant American retailer and, at one time, one of the most unpopular companies in America. After the corporation had played a valuable role in helping the victims of Hurricane Katrina in 2005, using its logistics expertise to ship food and water quickly to the area, the firm's then chief executive, Lee Scott, had what he calls his "lightbulb moment."

As he recalled in a speech, "Katrina asked this critical question. What would it take for Wal-Mart to be that company, at our best, all the time? What if we used our size and resources to make this country and this earth an even better place for all of us: our customers, associates, our children, and generations unborn? What would that mean? Could we do it? Is this consistent with our business model?" These are questions that every boss should ask about his or her firm, all the more urgently in the aftermath of the financial equivalent of Katrina.

Under Scott's leadership, Wal-Mart Stores, Inc., decided that the answer to his question was to embrace greenery. It launched a host of eco-friendly products, ranging from low-energy light-bulbs to sustainably harvested fish, taking the previous niche of ethical consumerism to the sort of mass-market consumer who values the "every day low prices" at Walmart stores.

Walmart certainly remains the subject of criticism over its opposition to unionization and the quality of its employee health-care program. Yet it has won over veterans of the green consumerism movement. In 2008, Jeffrey Hollender, boss of the eco-friendly household products firm Seventh Generation, said that after three years of conversations with the company and especially chief executive Scott, he had decided to reverse his ban on letting Seventh Generation products be sold at Walmart stores. The firm still has a massive negative environmental footprint, he acknowledged, but it is "now moving on the right trajectory." In July 2009 the discount giant took another step in the right direction by launching an index to rank the social and environmental sustainability of its products. Walmart says it will use this information about its suppliers to decide which products end up on its thousands of miles of shelves as part of its plan to get to zero waste and to shift to 100 percent renewable energy.

Climate change is perhaps the most tangible threat to our

future prosperity, which is perhaps why it is the fastest-growing issue for corporate do-gooding. In 2005, HSBC (Hong Kong and Shanghai Banking Corporation) became the first big bank to announce that it was carbon-neutral. Along with other financial institutions, including Swiss Re, a reinsurer, and Goldman Sachs, an investment bank, it is waging war on climate-warming gases (of which carbon dioxide is the main culprit). HSBC's decision to become carbon-neutral is part of a plan to develop a carbon-finance business, for both retail consumers and corporate clients. "We believe it is a major business opportunity for us, not a hobby or corporate social responsibility," said Francis Sullivan, who oversaw this move at HSBC.

In 2008, a report by CERES, a nonprofit that campaigns for environmental reporting, noted that Citigroup had pledged $50 billion to invest in green initiatives over ten years, including $31 billion for clean technologies. Bank of America had made a $20 billion commitment. (The extent to which either commitment survived the financial crisis remains unclear.) Alone among big banks, it has also said it will put a price on carbon dioxide (of between $20 and $40 per ton) when scrutinizing loan requests from industry. Citi, JPMorgan Chase, and Morgan Stanley had also unveiled a set of "carbon principles" designed to tighten financing terms for polluting power plants. This may be a good start, but there is a lot further for them to go.

Even some of the toughest investors in the business are seeing the light. The private-equity firm KKR was famously branded "the Barbarians at the Gate" twenty years ago in a book of that name about the firm's hostile takeover of RJR Nabisco. Now KKR is embracing un-Barbarian environmentalism, in a new partnership with the nongovernmental organization Environmental Defense Fund (EDF). The alliance is the result of the acquisition in 2007 of a Texas-based electricity firm, TXU, by KKR and TPG, another private-equity firm. TXU wanted to build eleven new "dirty" coal-fired power stations, which EDF and other green campaigners fiercely opposed. As part of the acquisition, KKR and TPG agreed to cancel those plans and look for greener alternatives. EDF helped convince the media that this promise was sincere.

Since then, KKR has expanded this relationship into a formal alliance that will ultimately include all the firms in its portfolio. EDF has been one of the leaders among nonprofits in its willingness to work with companies since it helped McDonald's introduce eco-friendlier packaging in the 1980s. To avoid conflicts of interest, it never accepts money from companies, relying instead on funding from supporters. The attraction of the green agenda to KKR is primarily financial, cutting costs, though it also says that leading firms nowadays must play a positive role in causes such as this. And not just on the environment. Although KKR has been attacked over its employment practices by the influential SEIU (Service Employees International Union), it is working to develop what it says are constructive, innovative solutions to labor problems (including sharing with workers gains that result from restructuring), in partnership with former Democratic senator Dick Gephardt. Barbarians no more?

It is true that much of what has gone under the banner of corporate social responsibility has been superficial public relations, deployed cynically in a classic example of "putting lipstick on a pig." Moreover, some corporate activities to influence society have been of the worst kind—lobbying behind the scenes to win a prized contract or tilting the playing field in favor of one firm over the interests of another, and often of the customer. Equally, there will always be limits to what a company can do to improve society, given its fundamental need to be profitable and to keep its shareholders happy.

On the other hand, over the years many firms have harmed

themselves, and society, by ignoring their long-term interest in improving the state of the world, or at least that bit of it where they operate. As Klaus Schwab, the founder of the World Economic Forum, has argued, too often there is "corporate attention deficit disorder, whereby companies lose focus on the big picture."

Financial firms, in particular, should look to aspects of their business where understanding society would help them make better decisions. For instance, even if the biggest banks did not share ShoreBank's conservative aversion to financial innovations such as securitized adjustable-rate mortgages, had they understood the subprime customer as well as ShoreBank did, they surely would not have gotten into such a mess.

The economic crisis should be a wake-up call to business to refocus. The experience of mission-driven businesses such as ShoreBank, of big traditional multinationals like Wal-Mart that have had their lightbulb moment, and even of hard-nosed investors like KKR shows that there are potentially huge win-wins to be had by putting corporate citizenship at the heart of corporate strategy. It is in most companies' long-term enlightened self-interest. If that wins them plaudits because they are responding to what consumers and, hopefully, shareholders want, then surely that is a success for a more humane capitalism.

A century ago, the Scottish-American tycoon Andrew Carnegie published his "Gospel of Wealth," which called on the rich to give their money away as a palliative for the consequences of capitalism. Many at the time thought he was trying to ease his conscience and burnish his reputation, having made his money by crushing the competition and the unions. The threats to capitalism when Carnegie was writing, communism and socialism, have evaporated, but today the reputations of business and the wealthy certainly need a polish.

Yet philanthrocapitalism is a very different movement. While many in the financial sector stand condemned of blinkered short-termism, other business leaders are already thinking long-term and building models for a better kind of capitalism. Their differences—especially in their scale and their use of philanthropic and state funds as well as the capital markets—certainly limit how much behemoths such as Citigroup can learn from their smaller sustainable counterparts like ShoreBank. Yet they can unquestionably learn something. A few years ago Citigroup started to invest in microfinance, not merely as a philanthropic activity but as a potential source of profits. Admittedly, this was a tiny initiative compared with Citi's American consumer lending—though, given the generally low losses sustained on microfinance, had Citi switched more resources away from American borrowers into overseas microfinance activities, perhaps it would have come through the economic crisis in better shape.

Today it is easy to be cynical about capitalism. Nevertheless, over the past decade, for every blinkered banker chasing short-term profit, there has probably been a social entrepreneur, an ethical investor, or a philanthropist trying to find a more sustainable way of making money. If business leaders, shareholders, and consumers want a better capitalism, now may be the best time to remake the system.

9

WE ARE THE CHANGE

Making the right choices means
increasing the wisdom of crowds

The biggest risk is that, you know, we don't have the political will," warned Federal Reserve chairman Ben Bernanke in an interview for CBS television's flagship *60 Minutes* news program in March 2009. Bernanke does not give a lot of interviews. Fed chairmen prefer to make delphic statements. So why did he take this rare opportunity to talk about politics rather than the monetary economics that has been his lifetime's vocation? His aim, it seems, was to throw his weight behind the Obama administration's effort to get Congress to pass a huge economic stimulus package—a tough challenge, which, he said, was "going to take some support."

Finding the road from ruin to prosperity will require new thinking from economists and business. Yet the lesson of history is that it will also demand political vision. Perhaps the biggest threat to the economies of America and the world by the middle of 2009, as the initial panic eased, was that governments would not be willing to take the bold decisions necessary. Economists feared that while half measures might be enough to avoid a complete meltdown, they could also result in economic stagnation, as they had done in Japan in the 1990s.

When Japan's asset price bubble burst in 1990, its government shied away from tackling the problem head-on. Fearing a taxpayer revolt, rather than pumping in money to clean up the banks' balance sheets, the Ministry of Finance left the banks to clean up their own toxic assets. When this did not work, the government simply nibbled at the problem, trying to keep the costs down. Yet even this limited effort provoked a fierce political backlash as opposition parties called for the finance minister's resignation and staged a sit-in at parliament.

The problem was not just politicians. According to one poll, 87 percent of Japanese voters disapproved of the government's action. Unsurprisingly, further initiatives were postponed and the problems of the economy were allowed to fester. It was only reluctantly that the government sold what was renamed Shinsei Bank out of bankruptcy to foreign investors in 2000. The government soon rued its decision when Shinsei broke the traditional face-saving etiquette of Japanese business by refusing to forgive loans to Sogo, a venerable retail chain. At every stage in this economic disaster, politicians, urged on by the majority of the public, opted for denial.

As economists and policymakers in America gazed across the Pacific, they shook their heads sadly at the way Japan's business and political culture had produced so botched an economic rescue plan. "The Japanese had purposely accepted hugely expensive economic stagnation to avoid a massive loss of face for many companies and individuals," reflected Bernanke's predecessor, Alan Greenspan, in his memoirs. Surely it could not happen in America? Well, think again.

Bad politics lay behind many of the failures to tackle the flaws in the U.S. financial sector before the bubble burst; and in some cases, such as Congress's cheerleading for mortgage lending, bad politics added flaws. Bad politics cowed the government into letting Lehman Brothers fail and worsened the market panic that resulted when Congress rejected the first version of the bank rescue plan. Bad politics constrained the stimulus package; ruled out the quickest, cleanest way of sorting out the banks, nationalization; and was the biggest obstacle to the fundamental regulatory reform that the crisis showed to be long overdue.

There is less scoffing at Japan now, with so many of its government's failings having been repeated in America. Indeed, this was not the first time politics had led America astray. In a remarkably honest piece in *The Economist*, reflecting on the policy errors that tipped the U.S. economy back into recession in 1937, just as it appeared to be recovering from the Great Depression, Christina Romer, head of President Obama's Council of Economic Advisers, reflected: "As someone who has written somewhat critically of the short-sightedness of policymakers in the late 1930s, I feel new humility. I can see that the pressures they were under were probably enormous."

So what can be done about those pressures, to help our politicians make the right choices now and in the future? In the end, the answer must lie with the media that debate the policy options and the voters whom the politicians court, as well as with the politicians themselves. In short: when it comes to running the economy better, all of us need to raise our game.

The media, with a few exceptions, at times credulously pumped air into the bubble as it inflated in the early years of the new millennium; too many journalists did far too little rigorous scrutiny of what was driving the boom economy. Since the bubble burst, this has changed, perhaps too far, as the media have helped to lower confidence with their sometimes over-gloomy reporting. True, the celebrity economist has returned—Nobel Prize–winning economist and *New York Times* columnist Paul Krugman has actually started writing about economics, rather than his old obsession, railing against the transgressions of the Bush administration. Once-arcane economics jargon, such as "quantitative easing," is bandied about on the evening news. Yet it is too early to call this a renaissance of the financial media. News coverage is still too simplistic and oriented around blame and denial. The media need to think about their responsibilities and look at their practices.

Ultimately the public must accept its share of the blame. The citizens of America and other rich nations too easily allowed themselves to be seduced into thinking that they could live indefinitely on credit, thanks in some measure to the ever increasing value of their homes. Since the bubble burst, many people, not just subprime borrowers, have been discovering the error of their ways. In a world of increasingly complex personal finance decisions and with some tough economic policy choices to make, we can ill afford to be financially illiterate.

DROPPING THE BALL

Musing on the lessons of the Wall Street Crash of 1929, John Kenneth Galbraith observed that "throughout history, financial capacity and political perspicacity are inversely correlated"—people who are good at finance are bad at politics, and vice versa. History seems to have repeated itself in the run-up to the current crisis and in the aftermath. As the Great Moderation cruised along in the early days of this century, despite the dot-com crash, the problem was not that government was unaware that there were flaws in the system. It was that there was no political will to tackle them.

In the 1990s, Arthur Levitt, then chairman of the Securities and Exchange Commission, had tried to address a worrying conflict of interest in the audit profession by banning accounting firms from selling consulting services to audit clients. He was blocked by Congress. Around the same time, Congress also made clear its opposition to, and thus sabotaged, an attempt by the accounting regulator, the Financial Accounting Standards Board, to properly recognize in company accounts the cost of awarding share options to employees.

Similarly, the Bush administration, urged on by Fed chairman Greenspan, had made several attempts to rein in the giant mortgage agencies Freddie Mac and Fannie Mae, on the (prescient) grounds that they posed a serious threat to the stability of the financial system. These attempts, too, were blocked in Congress, thanks to the legendary lobbying clout of Fannie and Freddie.

For all his intellectualizing about irrational exuberance, Greenspan himself may have been influenced to be cautious as much by politics as by his belief in the efficient market hypothesis. In the early 1990s he had run into conflict with President George H.W. Bush, who, with an election looming, had wanted him to cut interest rates faster to lift the economy out of recession. Greenspan held firm and was blamed by many Republicans for Bush's defeat by Bill Clinton, whose catchphrase was "It's the economy, stupid." Greenspan's memoirs make clear that it was a scarring experience for the technocrat to be drawn into the highest-stakes game in politics.

Greenspan also learned that congressional and media adoration came from encouraging the markets, not holding them back. The political hostility he was subjected to in Congress when he talked about irrational exuberance in the stock market in 1996 may have stopped him from adopting an interest-rate policy designed to let the air out of a bubble. Even as respected a figure as Greenspan knew that his credibility hung on continuing the boom, and he believed that he did not have the political clout to survive the backlash.

Even as the storm clouds gathered, the government seems to have been frozen with fear of political hostility. The Treasury, for example, ducked a number of tough decisions because they were deemed politically unsellable. These included focusing on cutting interest rates for struggling homeowners to reduce housing foreclosures, even though the Treasury knew this would be less effective than subsidizing write-downs of mortgage principal. "Political constraints were an important factor in the reluctance at the Treasury to put forward proposals to address the credit crisis early in 2008," explained former Treasury insider Phillip Swagel in the first inside account published about the efforts to end the credit crunch and then save the banking system.

A recurring theme in Swagel's story was the extent to which the impotence of the technocrats in the face of political forces was the unacknowledged elephant in the room. Congress's refusal to pass the first draft of Treasury Secretary Hank Paulson's banking rescue package was the most visible example of politicians choosing either cheap, bash-a-banker populism or spouting intransigent free-market dogma about moral hazard straight out of the Andrew Mellon textbook on how to cause a depression.

Despite its profession of bipartisanship, the Obama administration did not create a consensus for decisive action to clean up the banks. By contrast, when Sweden was hit by a financial crisis in the 1990s, the government took over two banks and issued a blanket guarantee of bank liabilities even though the governing coalition did not have a majority in Parliament. The Swedish government first ensured it had the support of the opposition party from which it had inherited the crisis (sound familiar?) and then obtained authority from Parliament for unlimited funds, so it did not have to return for more money later. This was not an easy option. According to Bo Lundgren, the finance minister at the time, Swedish voters would have rejected the bailout had it been put to a referendum.

Yet this sort of vision was lacking from U.S. politicians who, out of hand, dismissed the possibility of public ownership of America's banks. President Obama argued against Swedish-style nationalization on the grounds that America has too many banks, despite the fact that the number of systemically important banks that needed to be rescued could have been counted on the fingers of one hand, maybe two. The real problem was that even temporary public ownership was deemed incompatible with American capitalism. Admittedly, such dogma was not a problem for Sweden's big-government enthusiasts, yet it was still dogma. A crisis is the time to reject rather than embrace such orthodoxies.

Rather than trying to win support for new thinking to deal with the banks, the president then jumped on the banker-bashing bandwagon. For someone famously calm, like Obama, to say he felt "anger" about the bonuses being paid to AIG executives, surely this was an important issue? It was not. True, throwing blame around is maybe a necessary part of the public catharsis after a crisis. In an echo of the parliamentarian who wanted the directors of the South Sea Company drowned in sacks, a senior Republican, Charles Grassley, suggested that AIG executives should apologize Japanese-style, first bowing and then perhaps committing suicide. For the president to join in this minor, distracting debate was a mistake and risked superficial and damaging government intervention in the pay of financial-sector executives.

President Obama did, however, show leadership in pushing for a large economic stimulus package. This debate, too, was sucked back into dogma, as fiscal conservatives bristled at the consequences for the public debt, denying the possibility of the economic meltdown that could result from a failure to pump money into the economy. Free marketeers then reverted to orthodoxy in calling for the stimulus to come through tax cuts rather than government expenditure, even though the growing evidence of a liquidity trap suggested that much of this money would be saved rather than spent, rendering it ineffective. As, hopefully, the crisis eases and the economy recovers, the temptation to throw out the fiscal anchors too early will be enormous. FDR's government succumbed to that temptation in 1937 when it introduced social security taxes, causing a sharp fiscal contraction that stalled the recovery. We should not make the same mistake.

Politicians also showed a lack of vision and of will in the spring of 2009 when they started to take on the long-term reform challenges. One big failure of regulation in the run-up to the crisis was the fragmentation of responsibility between the SEC, the Commodity Futures Trading Commission (CFTC), and other regulators, so that no one in authority saw the whole picture of how risks were building up across the financial sector. When the administration's reform proposals were published in the middle of 2009, however, the much discussed idea of merging America's many financial regulatory agencies into a superregulator was off the agenda. Powerful congressional committees did not want to be stripped of their oversight powers, notably the agriculture committee that controlled the CFTC.

Each of these issues is difficult and complex. One danger is that rather than engaging in the difficult battle of ideas, politicians revert back to old orthodoxies. This is a recurring theme in politics, from the Hoover administration's do-nothing response to the Wall Street Crash of 1929 back to President Andrew Jackson's decision in 1833 that effectively closed down the nascent central bank to satisfy his states' rights agenda (condemning Americans to a wobbly, panic-prone banking system for the rest of that century). The other danger is that politicians simply play for short-term gain, as President William H. Taft did by excoriating his predecessor, Theodore Roosevelt, for agreeing to the merger of TC&I with U.S. Steel in 1907, a merger that was, in fact, a courageous decision that helped save the American economy from meltdown.

Some political decisions, however, may owe less to mistakes of principle than to the lobbying power of special interests. One of the most powerful legislators charged with cleaning up the financial sector in 2009 was Christopher Dodd, the chair of the Senate Banking Committee. An unsuccessful contender for the Democratic presidential nomination in 2008, Dodd had received more than $13 million in campaign contributions from the financial sector, including $104,000 from AIG. (Even Barack Obama received $130,000 from AIG in 2008, while still a senator.) Dodd (but not Obama) was also one of the congressional "Friends of Angelo" who received favorable mortgages from Angelo Mozilo's Countrywide.

In part the problem rests with individual members of Congress and the interests they serve, but there is a wider challenge to the media and the general public. To take one example, when the stimulus package was under discussion in early 2009, according to research by the nonprofit Media Matters, of fifty-nine news items that discussed the stimulus on the mainstream news channels ABC, CBS, and NBC, only three of those broadcasts discussed whether the package was big enough, even though this was a crucial question raised by many leading economists. Then again, arguing for more deficit spending is always going to be a tough sell to the American public. According to a *Wall Street Journal* poll published in June 2009, 58 percent of respondents wanted the government to focus on keeping the budget deficit down, even if that would slow the recovery.

The media and the general public must also accept responsibility for the boom that ended so catastrophically. While it is easy to blame unscrupulous mortgage lenders for the housing boom, or affirmative action programs that demanded that loans go to poorer borrowers, this was a nationwide, indeed international, bubble that caught up rich and poor alike.

Perhaps the way in which the media were most culpable in promoting a bubble mentality among consumers was the way they filled the airwaves with uncritically bullish shows about getting rich in real estate, such as *Trading Spaces, House Hunters, Sell This House,* and *My House Is Worth What?* While these shows may make great viewing, program makers could have done more to incorporate into them some fairly frequent reality checks. But even in the more sophisticated financial media market, reporting seems often to have been too credulous and too optimistic.

The public, of course, lapped this up and borrowed, borrowed, borrowed to spend, spend, spend to such an extent that by 2005, in net terms, there was no household saving. Poor households alone could not have gotten the country into that fix—everybody had taken on too much credit. Too late, after the crash, American households began to run down their debts and crank up their saving, which sucked demand out of the economy, making the slowdown even worse. This is what Keynes described as the paradox of thrift. The potentially disastrous consequences for the economy could only be averted by government-led economic stimulus. Yet, perhaps, had the public been more financially literate, it might not have dug itself into such a deep hole—or there might have been a better debate about what needed to be done to dig itself out again.

THE PRO-CYCLICAL MEDIA

"I understand you want to make finance entertaining, but it is not a fucking game," says Jon Stewart, the host of *The Daily Show,* to

James Cramer, host of the *Mad Money* show on business channel CNBC. The "Stewart-Cramer Smackdown," as it was soon known, in March 2009 was watched by millions of people around the world on television and shared via the Internet. Never mind that *The Daily Show* is billed as satirical, and Stewart is a comedian, the show has turned out to be one of the primary sources of news for Americans under the age of forty.

Cramer had the distinction of being the most famous face of CNBC, which had become both lucrative and influential since its launch in 1989, as it rode the bull market. Cramer was the obsessive trader, always ready with a tip for the next hot stock, delivered no-holds-barred via camera angles designed to make him seem right in the viewer's face and, well, maybe a little crazy. Nonetheless, his tips were taken as lore by many, a faith encouraged by CNBC's slogan for the show, "In Cramer We Trust."

Stewart's critique of CNBC was that Cramer and his colleagues knew that there was a bubble going on but continued to act as its cheerleaders on-air. As he put it to Cramer: "Listen, you knew what the banks were doing, yet were touting it for months and months, the entire network was." Stewart made Cramer squirm, running video clips of a private meeting in which the CNBC host explained how hedge funds could manipulate the stock market, apparently endorsing the practice enthusiastically.

In his pioneering early study of American democracy, Alexis de Tocqueville wrote that "nothing but a newspaper can drop the same thought into a thousand minds at the same moment." Today the media can put the same thought into millions of minds at the same moment, and thus influence the mood of the crowd—for good or ill. There is a huge potential for inaccurate or misleading financial reporting to do damage. The immediate impact that new information has on the markets can make erroneous financial reporting far costlier than in most other news. Alas, recent years have produced plenty of evidence that this is a genuine problem, and that the media need to raise their game if they are to avoid exacerbating future bubbles and crashes.

Information is power—and in financial markets, that power is primarily the ability to make money. Having better access to information than your rivals is a crucial way to get an edge as an investor, which is why in the earliest days of financial markets, investors gathered together to share facts and gossip in coffee shops, such as Edward Lloyd's in London (where the insurance market for shipping was born around 1688), or under the buttonwood tree on Wall Street (where in 1792 the New York Stock Exchange was formed).

Over time, distributing accurate information about prices became one of the key roles of a financial exchange, a task that was made considerably easier by successive waves of technological innovation, from the telegraph-based ticker tape to the television and, most recently, the Internet. Yet much valuable information continues to be transmitted informally, sometimes still in coffeehouses and other watering holes. Despite the promise that technology can make all communication virtual, thereby freeing investors to spend their days on the beach trading via a laptop, in reality they and the journalists who report on their activities continue to cluster together in financial centers, from New York to London to Dubai.

From the early days of capitalism, the media have played a key role in distributing financial information—and, too often, misinformation. At the time of the South Sea Bubble, for example, pamphleteers were paid to tout shares in all manner of dodgy companies, helping to inflate prices. Likewise, in the aftermath of many other bubbles, including Tulipmania, pamphleteers controlled by opponents of the investor class have spread (often invented) stories of abuses of ordinary investors by powerful market insiders.

In a rare study by leading academic economists of the role of the media in financial markets, "The Media and the Bubble," Alexander Dyck of Harvard Business School and Luigi Zingales of Chicago Business School argue that the media have an inherent bias to bullishness. The media tend to operate in a pro-cyclical way, they argue, helping to inflate bubbles on the way up, but sometimes making matters worse on the way down.

The bullish bias, they argue, comes from an implicit "quid pro quo relationship between companies and journalists," arising from the need for journalists to cultivate informed sources. In a bubble, bad news tends to be disproportionately damaging for a company's share price, as it stands out more obviously from the generally rising tide of good news. Companies' incentives to "spin news positively and to aggressively challenge bad news are therefore greatest during a bubble."

The behavioral economist Robert Shiller argues in his book *Irrational Exuberance* that the media fuel bubbles. Shiller, however, thinks that the problem is largely the media's ignorance: "Driven as their authors are by competition for readers, listeners, and viewers, media accounts tend to be superficial and thus to encourage basic misconceptions about the market."

Firms have become increasingly effective at controlling information about themselves, which arguably can make journalists overly reliant on well-connected inside sources, who on balance may have a strong interest in putting a positive spin on the firm. As Chrystia Freeland, American editor of the *Financial Times*, told a conference at Columbia University in 2008, "One thing this crisis should remind all journalists about is our duty not to be seduced by the trappings of wealth and power, to be skeptical. . . . That can be hard if you're a reporter, if all the people you've talked to are powerful, and seem to have succeeded in their bets, and agree with each other."

More sinister pressures can also be brought to bear. When the *Boston Post* tried to expose Charles Ponzi in 1920, it was only its persistence after losing one libel case that led it to finally expose the fraudster. The paper finally blew Ponzi's racket when it commissioned the pioneering financial journalist Clarence Barron (founder of *Barron's* magazine) to produce an analysis that showed that Ponzi's business was an empty shell. Legal action is still a weapon that the wealthy use to intimidate the media. Lionel Barber, editor of the *Financial Times,* says he has kept a record of all the libel suits that have been threatened by "well-heeled Russian oligarchs with City law firms being paid huge amounts of money trying to intimidate" his newspaper and other publications.

Some firms try to use their advertising budget to keep the media in line. The dependence of much of the media on corporate advertisers creates a massive conflict of interest that needs constant vigilant management. A notable example of the pressure and how it can be resisted occurred early in 2002, when *The Economist* published an article raising questions about the accounts of insurance giant AIG and suggesting that its shares were significantly overvalued. Among other things, the article noted the firm's "sophisticated but opaque forms of financial engineering," that it was a "large and growing participant in complex derivatives markets," and that "any cracks in the confidence that AIG knows what it is doing in derivatives would be highly damaging" (observations that were more than borne out six years later, in September 2008, when the insurer was rescued from impending bankruptcy by the American government).

The firm responded within hours by demanding that a research company cited in the article issue a public retraction of its comments about AIG, or face being driven out of business; getting a former British government minister to protest to the editor in chief of the magazine; and demanding a meeting, at which top executives of the firm, flown by private jet from New York to London, called for the journalist who wrote the story to be fired. At the time, AIG was one of the biggest advertisers in *The Economist*, and when the editor in chief refused to apologize or retract the story, it canceled advertising believed to be worth $1 million a year. This became something of a badge of honor for journalists at *The Economist*, who were encouraged by this vigorous demonstration of the ability of its editorial process to withstand commercial intimidation. Nor, it should be said, was there any suggestion from the "business side" of *The Economist* that the matter should have been handled any differently. Strikingly, however, the story was largely ignored by other media outlets, many of which continued to receive AIG's advertising dollars.

Other potential sources of distortion in financial journalism are the analysts working for investment banks, who evaluate companies and offer recommendations on whether to buy their shares. Financial analysts have become a prime source of information for journalists. While they are expert, and usually more available to talk, they have a well-known bullish bias. In 1999, during the dot-com bubble, Arthur Levitt, then chairman of the SEC, noted that only 1.4 percent of analyst recommendations were to "sell" a particular share, while 68 percent advised "buy," whereas in the early 1980s, the ratio was roughly one to one. There were "too many analysts who—whether they realize it or not—may be just a bit too eager to report that what looks like a frog is really a prince," he concluded. Yet "sometimes a frog is just a frog."

After the dot-com bubble burst, when *Barron's* magazine produced its damning independent analysis of the parlous financial situation of most of the new companies, efforts were made to address analyst biases and to better manage the conflicts of interest that may have tainted their recommendations. Wall Street's leading offenders paid substantial fines and agreed to reforms, including, for a limited period, making available to clients rec-ommendations by independent analysts alongside their own. These reforms were never implemented with much rigor (and in the end, some proved not all that popular with clients), and there remained a strong bias toward recommending "buy," which may well have influenced the journalists who turned to these analysts for advice.

In general, fuller disclosure by firms would help improve the quality of financial journalism. One area in particular need of reform is accounting, where the old efficient-market belief that disclosure in a footnote is as good as disclosure in the body of the accounts has surely been discredited. As Dyck and Zingales note, "The presence of the information in the public domain is not suf-ficient; the cost of gathering is also very important."

Footnotes and other complex disclosures increase the diffi-culty and thus the time required of the journalist to understand what the numbers really mean. "The higher this cost, the bigger will be the incentive for a journalist to skip this cost and rely on direct company sources." Yet if improving the intelligibility of financial information is one part of the solution, the other is increasing the financial literacy both of journalists and of the pub-lic that consumes their journalism. Even the specialist business media could do with better training for their editors and reporters, especially about new innovations, financial and otherwise.

If ignorance was a factor in the media's excessive bullishness before the crash, it may equally have been a problem afterward. "Call someone for heaven's sake!" screamed a wild-eyed James Cramer at his CNBC colleague. "This is a different kind of market, and the Fed is asleep," he said, calling the situation "Armageddon" and claiming that Ben Bernanke, the chairman of the Federal Reserve, had "no idea how bad it is out there, no idea."

Jon Stewart's attack on Cramer was that he had pumped up

the bubble that burst in 2008. Yet, to be fair to Cramer, he had never been the relentless cheerleader for the market that Stewart claimed—his Armageddon moment had taken place much earlier, as the credit markets froze in 2007.

He had also been a critic of dot-coms, companies that he had dismissed as "Fraud-U-Net" stocks, before that previous bubble burst in 2000. Indeed, Cramer had been mired in controversy before, when, in December 1998, he had said on-air that he was shorting a dot-com called WavePhore, whose chief executive he interviewed later that day. WavePhore's share price promptly plunged, presumably because Cramer's viewers followed their leader and started to sell. The Securities and Exchange Commission began an investigation, prompting CNBC to suspend Cramer—despite his insistence that he had misspoken, and did not in fact short the company through the hedge fund he then ran. In the end, this came to nothing.

Ironically, Cramer was criticized for his 2007 personal meltdown (along with the credit markets) as much as for pumping up the bubble. Indeed, the media as a whole have been accused of making the post-bubble downturn much worse than it needed to be by spreading misinformation and fomenting panic in the markets. Another CNBC colleague of Cramer's, David "the Brain" Faber, was criticized for repeating on-air anonymous tips that Bear Stearns had been denied financing by a counterparty, shortly before the investment bank had to be rescued and sold to JP Morgan. This was in the course of an interview with the chief executive of Bear Stearns and is widely reckoned to have undermined in the market his claims that all was well with the bank. (Privately, some of Faber's colleagues say he should not have mentioned such claims on-air without proper attribution.)

According to an opinion poll in December 2008 by the

Opinion Research Corporation, 77 percent of Americans believed that the U.S. media were making the economic situation worse by projecting fear into people's minds. The majority of those surveyed felt that the financial press, by focusing on and embellishing negative news, had damaged consumer confidence and dampened investment, making a difficult situation much worse.

In the Depression era, "there was something positive in every headline in the [New York] Times. The paper didn't want to be held responsible," according to its veteran economics commentator, Floyd Norris. "Not shouting 'fire' is worried about in every newspaper office, sometimes too much." So what has changed since the 1930s? Why do the media seem more prone to spread panic?

"The financial crisis—a complex and multilayered story— proved a difficult one for the media to track," reported the influential Pew Project for Excellence in Journalism. "Even though coverage intensified somewhat in early 2008, the press again drifted away from the economic story in the days just before the big September collapse. But after Lehman Brothers failed, coverage exploded, filling about a quarter of the news hole (26%) during the last three months of the year. The roller-coaster trajectory of coverage in 2008 reflected press problems in anticipating the meltdown and its proclivity to frantically 'flood the zone' once the dimensions of the crisis became obvious."

Is there any way to solve the media's bias toward pro-cyclical reporting? In banking, one proposed solution to the pro-cyclical bias of lenders is to have countercyclical capital requirements, whereby as bullish sentiment rises, banks must increase the amount of capital they hold in reserve as a proportion of the value of the loans they have made. Could there be similar countercyclical reporting requirements for the media?

Of course, it would be both impractical and wrong to insist that newspapers and other media outlets increase the proportion of skeptical stories in their reporting mix as the public's mood grows more exuberant. But there may be a case for the financial authorities—perhaps the Federal Reserve—to monitor and report on the mood of the media, so that editors are reminded that they might be getting caught up in irrational exuberance or pessimism, and the public are reminded to apply appropriate skepticism to what they read. Indeed, there is already an indirect measure of media sentiment that could play this role: the R-word index.

Devised by *The Economist*, for America this tracks how many stories in the *New York Times* and the *Washington Post* include the word "recession." It varies enormously, dipping as low as 100 a month in early 1990 and soaring to over 1,200 in 2001. Sometimes changes in the R-word index have been a leading indicator of changes in economic activity—most notably signaling the start of recessions in 1981, 1990, 2001, and 2008. But sometimes the index says more about the state of mind of the media, which, for example, continued to rant about recession for a year after it officially ended in March 1991. This guide to media gloom should probably be coupled with a bullishness indicator, though what word best captures irrational exuberance in the media remains to be seen. (Perhaps the number of bullish stock tips published in newspapers would do it?)

The failure of the media during the crisis also speaks to the wider problems of the industry. Traditional print and broadcast media are yielding an ever greater share of the market to new forms of digital media where speed is often more important than accuracy. There is a huge leadership challenge for the industry to maintain the skills and ethics of sound journalism. This will not be easy.

In the markets, time really is money—and competition has only intensified the pressure on media outlets to be first with the news. Journalists who can come up with a fresh angle are increasingly in demand, as traditional financial reporting has been commoditized. At the same time, there has been a growing reluctance to sit on a story any longer than necessary—which can put extreme pressure on the fact-checking process.

In the 1980s, the digital revolution opened the door to multiple delivery channels—broadcast, narrowcast, online, and wireless—around the clock, seven days a week. The proliferation of online publications, including blogs and bulletin boards, has been a new source of fierce competition for traditional media. As the BBC's business editor Robert Peston explained to a committee of British parliamentarians early in 2009, "Quite a lot of the information that gets disseminated which affects share prices gets disseminated outside of the established media. For example, when it came to rumours that were driving the share prices of a number of these banks, that was information that was going from the internal Bloomberg, the e-mail system, for example, from hedge fund to trader, from trader to investment manager."

It might be hoped that the thoroughness of their fact-checking, and thus the authority of their reporting, would give established media a competitive edge over their upstart rivals. However, there is a danger that this opportunity will be outweighed by competitive pressure to be first with the news—a goal that increases the risk of inadequate thought or fact-checking.

Strikingly, in March 2009 the *Wall Street Journal,* which has traditionally been regarded as the most thorough fact-checker in the business, instructed journalists to increase their focus on being first with news. In an internal memo, the editor in chief, Robert Thomson, said that, given the "revenue reality, henceforth all *Journal* reporters will be judged, in significant part, by whether they break news for the newswires." In a later memo, Thomson clarified that the premium on accuracy "cannot be overstated," yet he set out a compromise of accepting writing that is merely "workmanlike—'trade speed for polish'" in order to break a scoop. Alas, it is easy to imagine that polish will not be all that is traded by journalists under pressure to be first to break a story.

It may be the case that our psychological biases toward the quick, the vivid, and the familiar mean that objective reporting that challenges conventional wisdoms will struggle to compete with more populist media. If this is the case, the values of responsible journalism may have to be protected by a new business model for the media that treats informed debate as a public good, run as a not-for-profit.

This is already beginning to happen. The global debate on climate change was shifted dramatically by Al Gore's *An Inconvenient Truth*, a film that was not a guaranteed financial success and was funded by the billionaire philanthropist Jeff Skoll. Private-equity billionaire Pete Peterson has, more recently, donated a large chunk of his fortune to raising the public debate about the budget deficit, using innovative techniques such as computer games to help college students understand debt. Many will worry about the influence of rich "plutocrats" controlling the media to influence public opinion. (Ironically, one of the most notable first attempts to create such a philanthropic model for the media, a nonprofit investigative reporting organization called ProPublica, was endowed by Herbert and Marion Sandler, a couple who made their fortune from one of the leading pushers of subprime mortgages, Golden West Financial.) There certainly needs to be transparency about who is funding the media. In a pluralistic society the media have a crucial role to play in ensuring a diversity of opinions, and if philanthropy is needed to maintain this, so be it.

In the end, however, citizens cannot shift responsibility for their decisions onto the media. They need to seek out the facts and think seriously about the issues as much as the media do.

When it comes to our own finances and the economic health of the nation . . . well, to borrow from Jon Stewart, we need to recognize that it is "not a fucking game."

"I DON'T KNOW MUCH ABOUT MONEY, BUT . . ."

"Everybody wants it. Nobody understands it. Money is the great taboo. People just won't talk about it. And that is what leads you to subprime. Take the greed and the financial misrepresentation out of it, and the root of this crisis is massive levels of financial illiteracy."

For years John Bryant has been telling anyone who will listen about the problems caused by widespread ignorance of finance. In 1992, in the aftermath of the Los Angeles riots, he founded Operation HOPE, a nonprofit organization, to give poor people in the worst-hit parts of the city "a hand up, not a handout" through a mixture of financial education, advice, and basic banking. Among other things, Operation HOPE offers mortgage advice to homebuyers and runs "Banking on Our Future," a national personal-finance course of five hour-long sessions that has already been taken by hundreds of thousands of young people, most of them high-school students.

That many poor people do not have a bank account (more than 40 million people in America alone) and that few of them understand why this puts them at a disadvantage is at the heart of "the civil rights issue of the 21st century," says Bryant. He calls the attempt to help people help themselves out of poverty through financial literacy and economic opportunity the "silver rights movement."

There is a mountain of evidence that the public—and not just its poorest members—has not become significantly better at understanding finance than it was in 1929, when receiving stock tips from a shoeshine boy supposedly prompted Joseph Kennedy to get out of the stock market.

Financial illiteracy is not limited to subprime mortgage borrowers; it is pervasive in all age groups, income brackets, and countries. (That said, not all subprime borrowing was financially illiterate. For someone with no assets being offered a chance to participate in a rising housing market, it may sometimes have been a rational gamble. This was particularly the case in states such as California, where the law allowed borrowers to walk away from a mortgage without any legal liability. Thus they made money when the price went up, and if it fell, there was little downside.)

Perhaps the most tangible evidence of this is the failure of Americans to save adequately or prepare sensibly for retirement. In 2005, America's average personal savings rate turned negative for the first time since 1933, in the depths of the Great Depression. This time the willingness of so many Americans to spend more than their annual income apparently was due to irrational exuberance, not necessity, as they seemed to believe that spending money generated by the rising value of their homes would make up for their lack of savings. (Although one of the most striking reactions of American consumers in 2008 to the crisis was an abrupt halt to spending and an increase in the savings rate, this increase was to levels that were still far below what most economists think prudent. Moreover, it would need to be a permanent shift to count as a genuine improvement in financial literacy— and nobody believes that American consumers have yet abandoned forever their love of credit-card-fueled shopping.)

The financial-literacy problem is more pressing than ever because governments and businesses have pushed more of the responsibility for financial well-being onto individuals, whether by encouraging homeownership or by promoting personally managed retirement accounts rather than defined-benefit pensions.

The education system deserves much of the blame. Americans still leave school not knowing much about money. A sample of high-school students aged seventeen or eighteen gave correct answers to barely half of a set of questions about personal finance and economics posed in 2006 by researchers at the State University of New York at Buffalo. Less than one-quarter knew that income tax could be levied on interest earned in a savings account. Three-fifths did not know the difference between a company pension, Social Security, and a 401(k) savings account.

For Bryant, the key is to engage the emotions, rather than teaching financial literacy like a math class. Even the phrase "financial literacy" can be a turnoff. Bryant prefers to talk about "learning the language of money," challenging students by asking, "How do you expect to succeed in the most capitalist nation on earth if you don't speak the language?"

Providing role models in financial literacy is one way to engage the emotions. One of the most novel attempts to do this is by music producer and entrepreneur Russell Simmons, the "godfather of hip-hop." His philanthropy and social action group, the Hip-Hop Summit Action Network, now promotes financial literacy to the young fans who attend its events. Simmons describes this as "a bunch of rappers and Suze Orman" (a popular financial adviser), with stars such as Doug E. Fresh literally leading fans page by page through a textbook on financial literacy.

Promoting financial literacy would be easier if financial products were better designed and if the financial institutions that sell them did a better job of explaining them to customers. Better product design and financial education should work in tandem. (One reason why financial institutions do such a poor job at explanation may be that some of them hope to hide from customers the high cost and lack of suitability of their products. This is one reason why the Obama administration's decision to create a Consumer Financial Protection Agency may make sense, although it would be unfortunate if this encouraged consumers to feel that they did not need to do their own due diligence on banking products.)

One of the most interesting attempts to combine personal-finance teaching and superior products is taking place in New York City, championed by Mayor Michael Bloomberg, who made his fortune selling financial information. He created an Office of Financial Empowerment, which is trying to use the powers of government to promote both financial education and better design of financial products.

The city's regulatory powers mean that it can crack down on firms that exploit financial illiteracy, and educate the public at the same time. It found that many tax-preparation agencies offered "rapid refunds," which, as many consumers failed to realize, were in fact loans in anticipation of refunds. Its publicity blitz about these loans led to coverage on news programs in twenty-two states and Canada, allowing the city to promote the message that "anyone promising a tax refund within two days is selling a loan—don't do it."

One of the biggest problems may be the illiteracy of financial-services firms, which often fail to provide the products that poor consumers most want. That, at least, was the conclusion of a 2008 survey in two of New York City's poorer neighborhoods. Many people were using fringe financial products such as payday loans or money orders rather than the services of mainstream banks. Yet it turned out that these were frequently the best options available, because mainstream banks offered only a limited range of products in those communities, and charged high fees. In this case, the mainstream financial providers were not just cynically profiting from opacity, they seemed to be missing genuine market opportunities. Which only goes to show that consumers are sometimes only as literate as the products the financial-services industry chooses to sell them.

Bryant, who is now trying to persuade banks to see promoting financial literacy as a business opportunity, not as a cost, makes the same point more colorfully, noting that some of the first people to be hit by the subprime-mortgage crisis were the very brokers who had sold people inappropriate mortgages. Having drunk their own Kool-Aid, they found themselves with enormous debts and no job. "It takes less credentials to be a mortgage broker than a pimp on a street corner in Harlem," he says. "Because a pimp needs references."

TOWARD A COMPETENT ECONOMIC CITIZENRY

The early America–watcher de Tocqueville observed, optimistically, that "the greatness of America lies not in being more enlightened than any other nation, but rather in her ability to repair her faults." For America, and the rest of the capitalist world, this is a moment when we need to show that we can repair our faults. This is going to require serious reflection to work out what went wrong and how to put it right, avoiding the pitfalls of returning to old orthodoxies. This is a lot to ask.

The last time America faced such a catastrophe, the orthodoxies of economics had a destructive role, turning a recession into the Great Depression. Even as those policies failed, the political debate did little to escape from old ideas. It remains a great irony that the deficit spending of the New Deal era was a breach

of FDR's original balanced-budget electoral platform. This story
also shows, however, that political leaders can demonstrate vision
and break free from conventional wisdoms. Yet there were many
mistakes in the New Deal, as populist sentiment drove a culture
of blame that wrapped the U.S. economy in unnecessary and
damaging red tape. The retreat into economic nationalism and
protectionism in the 1930s was also an error that we should not
repeat.

"As a protection against financial illusion or insanity, memory
is far better than law," argued John Kenneth Galbraith in the 1975
foreword to *The Great Crash of 1929*. Maybe it was, when he wrote
those words. But memory can also play tricks. We all have a tendency to interpret the facts on the basis of information that is
freshest in our minds, what behavioral economists call the availability heuristic. Haunted by the Great Depression, Galbraith
warned of speculative bubbles, even in the tame markets of the
1950s and 1960s, and misdiagnosed the 1987 crash as the start of
another period of economic woe.

When, over time, the memory of the Great Depression faded,
people came to believe that crashes were a thing of the past and
that the boom would go on forever. Even when the facts changed,
people failed to learn from them. Could there be a better illustration of cognitive dissonance than the surge of money into
highly leveraged investments based on complex models even after
the collapse of LTCM?

The first reaction to the current crisis was rage. Jon Stewart's
smackdown of James Cramer was massively popular, as the public
relished the humiliation of someone regarded as one of the market's biggest cheerleaders. Blaming the financiers has always been
the populist reaction to financial crises. It may even be an important part of the healing process. The greater risk today is that once
the anger has passed, the public will move to a new, postcrash

heurisitic of pessimism, which leads them to be excessively cautious, both as spenders and as investors. With luck this psychological effect will be outweighed by Keynes's "animal spirits"— our natural tendency to be optimistic. But there is a danger that, with the crisis fresh in mind, the public mood will prompt governments to rush into heavy-handed regulation that does more harm than good, as arguably it did in the New Deal.

If good decisions are to be made in addressing the challenges the world faces—not just financial regulation but the global-governance challenges of monetary reform, trade liberalization, climate change, and so on—the media need to step up. This will not be achieved by government regulation of the media. The impetus for change must come from within the industry itself. If the financial sector is facing an ethics crisis, so too are the media. Chasing the most popular angle, whether it is that rising house prices will make you rich or that the financial world is coming to an end, may be good for short-term circulation, ratings, and profitability. But the owners and leaders of the media, as in other businesses, need to think longer-term about the consequences of their actions.

Public sentiment is a turbulent force. Modern societies have developed institutional mechanisms such as the rule of law and an independent judiciary to provide protection against the tyranny of the mob. There has been a growing recognition that some policy decisions are better made when insulated from the public mood, such as by giving control of interest rates to technocratic central bankers rather than elected officials.

But such protections can only go so far. Fiscal conservatives may wish to hand control of the public finances to an independent body that would ensure that the budget is always in balance. But any such rule would surely (and rightly) soon be swept away by circumstances of economic crisis like those that governments faced in the autumn of 2008.

In the end, the public's best protection against both folly and tyranny is to reform itself into a competent citizenry that can make sensible choices. This has long been understood in the political sphere. That is why society invests public money not just in the general education of citizens but also in the study of civics. That has not removed all the flaws from politics—but the situation would certainly be far worse without that investment in educating citizens. Today's world of complex financial choices that affect individual lives and the collective prosperity of society means that perhaps the most important challenge to come out of this latest crisis is the building of an economically competent citizenry.

10

CONCLUSION

The road ahead

A century and a half ago Karl Marx and Friedrich Engels's *Communist Manifesto* threatened that a "specter" was haunting capitalist Europe. That threat, communism, has gone away, but a new specter is haunting global capitalism: failure. Even in the boom times before the crash of 2008, there were grumbles that capitalism was not spreading the benefits evenly enough across the globe, or within individual societies. In the aftermath of the crash, many trillions of dollars created in the previous gilded era disappeared. Fundamental flaws have been revealed within capitalism itself.

People were angry and scared. So it came as no surprise that blame and denial dominated the initial public reaction. The crisis brought to a head old fears that America, and the economic and political values that it had long championed around the world, would not recover—indeed, that it had entered the process of terminal decline that has befallen every great power of the past.

This was not the first time that such doubts had been raised about America. Two decades earlier, in *The Rise and Fall of the Great Powers*, the historian Paul Kennedy predicted great things for the then surging economy of Japan and forecast American decline, despite the recent Cold War victory over the Soviet Union. Yet within a couple of years of those predictions, Japan's challenge to American dominance was shown to have been an illusion, created by the high point of an extraordinary boom that pushed Japanese asset prices to ridiculous levels. The Japanese model quickly turned from one of success to one of failure. Meanwhile, America's economy went from strength to strength, along with its global political dominance.

The difference this time around, say the most apocalyptic seers, is that America has gotten itself so deeply in debt to another nuclear power and the world's most populous country: China. This crisis, according to pessimists from the right as well as the left, will prove to be the moment when the Chinese model of authoritarian capitalism emerges as more productive and efficient than soft, complacent democratic capitalism. "The virus of authoritarian capitalism is slowly but surely spreading around the globe," warned one of these commentators, the Marxist philosopher Slavoj Žižek.

A different strand of doom is based on a revival of interest in the Kondratieff cycle. Popularized by the economist Joseph Schumpeter, based on an idea by the Soviet economist Nikolai Kondratieff, this says that capitalism goes through half-century-long cycles of technology-driven boom followed by bust. Perhaps the crisis of 2008 marked the beginning of a long economic downswing.

These arguments describe a world, as Marx did, in which we are the victims of inexorable historical forces. They tell us little about what went wrong and what we need to do next. Yes, this crisis is a turning point for capitalism, but the outcomes are not determined by some inevitable shifting of the tectonic plates of history. The crises of the past show that we have stared into the same abyss many times before, and it is our decision whether to fall in or not. As we set out on the road from ruin, it is the choices we make that will determine where we end up—depression, stagnation, or renewed prosperity.

This is not just an American crisis, it is a global crisis. China has discovered that the accumulation of foreign currency reserves does not make it economically invincible. Countries that had run trade surpluses turned out to be equally vulnerable, at least in the early stages of the crisis, since they were hit particularly hard by the collapse in export markets. For the same reason, export-dependent America suffered more than Europe in the Great Depression. However, unlike the United States then, China may have avoided a prolonged slump by boosting domestic demand to make up for the fall in foreign demand for its products. There is a shift in the balance of global economic power, but it is not just about China. America's economic position is also changing because of the rise of India, Brazil, and other emerging markets, as well as the successful launch of the euro and expansion of the European Union to include parts of the former Soviet empire.

No single rival is emerging to knock America off the top spot. No alternative economic model is challenging capitalism, for all its flaws, as the best way to meet the needs of the expanding global population. Yet things do need to change. The United States can remain powerful, but to do so it must learn to play as "the first among equals" rather than the undisputed hegemon. As Fareed Zakaria argues in his book *The Post-American World,* even if America cannot dictate to this new world, "it has not lost the ability to lead." One result of the crisis is that America can no longer set the global agenda, as it has done in the past, by insisting that its economic and political model is demonstrably better than the rest. In the future, American leadership will depend on its ability to remake capitalism in a way that is not only more productive but also sustainable, socially and environmentally. If it does not, models of capitalism developed in other countries may move to the front of the pack.

This is the dilemma facing America today: no other country is better placed to provide the leadership we need to get out of this crisis, yet to find the road from ruin America itself needs new ideas. Britain's decline from global supremacy in the mid-nineteenth century can be traced through a series of missed opportunities to realize that one of its great strengths, the gold standard, had started to become a liability. There were plenty of chances to abandon old orthodoxies and change course—from the Paris conference of 1878, to Churchill's decision to return to gold in 1925, to the overvaluation of the pound under the Bretton Woods system—but, again and again, Britain failed to make the right choices.

America can rise to meet today's challenges. This is no time to give in to pessimism, or to overlook the formidable strengths that the United States has as it seeks a way ahead. "There exists in human nature a strong propensity to depreciate the advantages, and to magnify the evils, of the present times," wrote Edward Gibbon in his classic *History of the Decline and Fall of the Roman Empire*. We should pay heed to that warning today.

Yet, equally, there is a real danger that America will choose denial. This is no time to simply reboot the system or attempt to restore the status quo ante. Serious problems have been revealed by the crisis that need to be put right.

STUMBLING ALONG

At least the initial response of governments around the world to the crisis of 2008 showed that they had learned some of the lessons of the past. Galvanized by the memory of the policy failures that led to the Great Depression, when the markets crashed in the autumn of 2008 the world's central banks moved quickly to cut interest rates. When it later became clear that this would not be enough to stop the global economy from entering a tailspin, they pumped cash into the system through so-called quantitative easing. Governments also did their bit to stimulate the economy with fiscal measures. At the G-20 summit in April 2009, the degree of coordination and agreement among the leaders of a rather diverse and unwieldy group of countries was, frankly, unprecedented in peacetime.

That said, the recovery was made much more difficult by confused thinking about what to do to rescue the failed financial system. This confusion had several causes. On one hand, free-market ideologues opposed all government intervention on the grounds that this would increase moral hazard. They wanted to let failed banks fail. This extreme free-market position found an unlikely ally in some of the more committed critics of financial capitalism. They felt that the financial system had never done much good for the economy and that its "masters of the universe" should be allowed to fail, so long as the savings of ordinary depositors were protected by the government.

Letting Lehman Brothers collapse may have been an easy way to please both of these camps. Yet it was a catastrophic error. In a world of complex, interlocking deals between large financial institutions—in which Lehman was a central player—sending the firm into a disorderly bankruptcy was the surest way to create maximum mayhem in the markets. It was only after they realized what a mess they had created that government leaders claimed they lacked the power to save Lehman Brothers—a claim that was utterly implausible.

Not much can be done about this now, except to learn the

lesson for next time. The middle of a crisis, when the financial system is on the brink of collapse, is not the time to be worrying about moral hazard. Governments should be concerned about moral hazard, but when the economy is functioning normally. That is when governments can put in place checks and balances and a contingency plan. That is the time to make sure that banks do not build up excessive risks that put the entire financial system in danger of failure. Forcing large banks and other financial institutions to maintain a "living will" backup plan for insolvency and requiring them to issue "contingent capital" that converts debt to equity at times of crisis are both good ideas. Not only would these proposals help concentrate managers' minds on the risks facing their institutions, they would also minimize the disruption if the worse came to the worst.

Free-market orthodoxy also hindered government efforts to clean up the mess after the financial system collapsed. Although temporary nationalization of failed banks had been proven to work in Scandinavia and, when it was eventually tried, in Japan, the "n" word was deemed unpalatable even for a Democratic American administration, let alone the Republican one that was in charge when the crisis hit. (Other countries, including Britain, were not so squeamish and may be able to clean up the mess better than America.) By refusing to nationalize, for ideological reasons, the American government set up a game of bluff with bank bosses about which assets were and were not toxic, much like the one that plagued Japan's efforts to rescue its banks in the 1990s.

Even though the U.S. government pumped billions of dollars into the banking system after the crisis, relatively little of this money was lent out by the banks. That made the government's efforts at monetary and fiscal stimulus much less effective, although by using the government funds for relatively low-risk activities, some banks were able to increase their profits dramatically and controversially. By declining to take ownership of failed banks in September 2008, the government ended up pumping money into the pockets of private shareholders, when it could have recouped some of the cost of the bailout by taking shares in the banks and selling them later. (Of course, for a policy of nationalization to be effective, it would need to be explicitly temporary from day one, and the government would have to resist the temptation to meddle too much in the day-to-day running of the banks.)

Again, this is a lesson for future crises, not this one. Politically, the only moment of opportunity to nationalize the banks, especially in an enthusiastically capitalist country like America, is at their moment of greatest crisis—on this occasion, during the few weeks starting with the bankruptcy of Lehman Brothers.

RIGHT TURNS AND BLIND ALLEYS

Once the worst of a crisis passes, the next danger is that governments try to revert too quickly to business as usual. When the whole financial system teetered on the brink and the global economy threatened to implode, governments and central banks had the political capital they needed to take decisive action by pumping money into the economy, even though this would impose a massive cost on future taxpayers. As soon as things start to get better, the danger is that political point-scoring about the impact of these measures on the public finances causes the government to bring them to a premature end.

This time, it was not long before the scaremongering about a fiscal crisis began. "While the short-term pain of a deepened recession is quite sharp, the long-term consequences of double-digit inflation are devastating," warned Ronald Reagan's favorite economist, Arthur Laffer, in the *Wall Street Journal* in June 2009. "For Fed chairman Ben Bernanke it's a Hobson's choice. For me the issue is how to protect assets for my grandchildren," he said. Laffer had a point. The public finances would have to be fixed, and there was a risk that if government kept its foot on the gas for too long, it could reignite inflation. Yet he failed to acknowledge the risk that if the government stopped the monetary and fiscal stimulus too early, the economy could quickly slide back into recession or even depression.

Getting the judgment right about when to turn off the taps is difficult enough when based on purely economic criteria, but it is even harder when the government is under pressure to reduce the deficit for short-term political reasons.

The failure in the financial markets in 2008 was spectacular. So no wonder the critics of financial capitalism were quick to call for aggressive government action to restructure and reregulate the financial system. Certainly, regulatory failures were revealed by the crisis that need to be put right, but there is a huge risk of regulating too far and too fast, and of addressing symptoms rather than causes.

Many people have reacted to the crisis by blaming it on financial innovation. Nobel Prize–winning economist Paul Krugman, for example, said that the financial innovations of recent years had simply "directed vast quantities of capital into the construction of unsellable houses and empty shopping malls. They increased risk rather than reducing it, and concentrated risk rather than spreading it. In effect, the industry was selling dangerous patent medicine to gullible consumers." Former Fed chairman Paul Volcker went even further when, early in 2009, he posed the question: "What is the most important innovation in finance in the past twenty-five years? The ATM, which is technology, not finance." He dismissed the supposed financial sophistication of recent years as largely a waste. So too the financier George Soros, who called for financial engineering to be constrained through regulation that tests the safety of any innovation: "New products must be registered and approved by the appropriate authorities before they can be used," much like in the pharmaceutical industry, he argued.

In fact, financial innovation was not the primary cause of the crisis of 2008. It would be a huge mistake to heavily regulate it. This was recognized even by the expert on financial irrationality and bubbles, Robert Shiller. In an article for the *New York Times* in July 2009, Shiller looked back to one of the great innovations of the Industrial Revolution, the steam engine. When James Watt came up with this invention in 1765, Shiller explained, he was so worried about the safety of using high-pressure steam that he opted for a less efficient, low-pressure engine that was, frankly, not much of an improvement on water or horsepower. The age of steam was only possible after Richard Trevithick finally took a risk with a high-pressure steam engine in 1799. This, explained Shiller, is the nature of innovation: "learning from errors and hazards and gradually conquering problems through devices of increasing complexity and sophistication." The same, he said, is true of financial innovation, unfashionably pointing out that subprime mortgages brought benefits as well as risks.

This does not mean that all innovation is good. Harnessing innovation for the benefit of society requires us to figure out the right balance of benefits and risks. That, as we have seen throughout history, is what bubbles are all about—the process of trial and error as we find out what does and does not work. The error is to see novelty or complexity as the problem and to try to block financial innovation that could help us deal with the problems we currently face.

What we need, Shiller argued, is "financial innovation that responds to central problems. The effectiveness of our free enterprise system depends on allowing business people to manage the myriad risks—including the risk of asset bubbles—that impinge on their operations in the long term. And this process needs constant change and improvement." High-pressure steam engines did bring new risks, which our ancestors had to learn how to manage with better design and new innovations. The same is true of finance—rather than trying in vain to uninvent financial innovations, we need to learn how to make them work better.

A crisis will always produce lots of false remedies. Often the more superficially attractive they are, the worse they look on closer scrutiny. For example, in response to the latest crisis, some economists have argued that the government should split the banking system in two. In its most extreme form, this would involve creating a risk-free "narrow banking" system that does only the boring things required by individuals and businesses, such as looking after their savings and making payments, and a separate investment-banking business that does risky things. Government would protect only those depositors who kept their money in the safe narrow banks. "We don't want risk-taking to bring down the essential financial infrastructure of the economy, such as the payment system," argued one champion of this idea, the British economist John Kay.

Narrow banking has an obvious appeal: protect the core of what we all need from a banking system and let the rest stand or fall on its own. Yet, as *Financial Times* columnist Martin Wolf has argued, this proposal is at once both "attractive and unpersuasive." The lesson from history is that it is incredibly hard to require financial institutions to refrain from taking risks. Customers will desert the uncompetitive narrow-banking system for the better returns offered by broader financial institutions, and, no matter how loudly government protests, when things go wrong they will expect their deposits to be protected just as in the narrow-banking system. Government will inevitably succumb to these demands, as happened with money market funds and other uninsured deposits in the latest crisis.

A common twist to this argument in the United States was to call for the restoration of the Glass-Steagall split between commercial and investment banking. This proposal had an obvious "turn-back-the-clock" appeal: there was no financial crisis of this scale in the sixty-five years Glass-Steagall was in force until its abolition in 1999. That is true. But there is no evidence whatsoever that the mixing of commercial and investment banking was a significant cause of the financial collapse of 2008. Both Bear Stearns and Lehman Brothers, the first casualties of the crisis, were classic investment banks with no commercial banking operations. And AIG was not a bank at all.

Another superficially attractive remedy is not to worry about what different institutions do but about how big they are. "Nothing should ever become too big to fail," pronounced Nassim Nicholas Taleb. He argued that government should prevent any single institution, whether it be a bank, an insurer (like AIG), or a hedge fund, from getting so large that its failure would cause a crisis for the entire financial system. Despite its obvious appeal, this proposal runs into the ancient problem of "how long is a piece of string?" Any judgment on whether an institution is too big to fail will, inevitably, be arbitrary. Moreover, the crisis of 2008 was caused by the risks that built up across the financial system as a whole. It is not clear that limiting the size of banks would offer much protection. Indeed, such a prohibition might make matters worse by creating a false sense of security.*

Another popular proposal to make financial institutions safer, which even has the support of Alan Greenspan, is to require them to keep a bigger capital cushion as a protection against losses. Again, this has intuitive appeal but also suffers from the problem that there is no "right" size for a capital cushion. In the short term, significantly higher capital requirements would accelerate the process of deleveraging, further sucking liquidity and credit out of the financial system. In the longer term, it could simply incentivize banks to come up with creative ways to wriggle out of the straitjacket. Moreover, it does not address the real problem with capital requirements that has been highlighted by the current crisis, which is that current risk-management models raise the level of systemic risk in the financial markets by increasing the synchronization of the buying and selling of assets. As a result, there is much less diversity than is desirable for the system as a whole. Part of the solution here may be to build in countercyclical capital requirements, which, although they may also increase the synchronization of the system and would be hard to implement effectively, if done right might help to stop bubbles from forming.

The crisis showed conclusively that the efficient market hypothesis is flawed. The danger now is that regulators will rush to fill the void, seeing bubbles everywhere they look. While some financiers, such as George Soros, and commentators, such as Taleb

---

* Size may matter, but not in the way that Taleb suggested. There has long been a problem of overconcentration in (parts of) the banking sector, which reduced competition and hurt efficiency. The mergers and takeovers of recent years made that problem worse. But that is primarily an antitrust problem rather than an issue of financial-system stability.

or Nouriel Roubini, can boast that they spotted the current bubble before it burst, how do we know if they, or anyone else, will be able to spot the next bubble forming? The risk is that anyone tasked with spotting bubbles will constantly overreact, seeing bubbles where none exist (so-called ghostbusting).

The new insights from behavioral economics need to be explored carefully to find ways to nudge the markets to restrain their irrational exuberance but not to stop the sort of risk taking that is the lifeblood of markets. Proposals like the one to get Fannie Mae and Freddie Mac to lean into the wind of real-estate bubbles by increasing the minimum down payments required on mortgages if home prices surge should be explored.

Regulators need to understand and monitor changes in the stability of the financial system as a whole, and they need to figure out how to warn participants when it is becoming dangerously unstable. As Andrew Haldane of the Bank of England has explained, the current crisis was the result of risks building up across a network (the financial system) that no individual "node" (bank) within the network understood.

A top priority should be to fix this information failure in the financial markets. Each financial institution needs to be able to see the big picture of the sorts of risk building up in the system as a result of the decisions made by individual banks. Greater awareness of what is really going on would probably be the best protection against blinkered decision-making. A regulatory system that created such information would be valuable to the banks and other financial institutions. It would also be less susceptible to cheating than one based on arbitrary rules.

To aggregate the data from individual financial institutions in order to describe the risk in the system would require a new sort of systemic-risk regulator to collect and share that information. Better global regulation through information sharing (rather than trying to get different countries to agree on what is a bank and how much capital a bank should have) may also be the most practical way to tackle the interconnectedness of the global financial system, in that it might actually get agreed on.

Yet it is hard to see how an effective systemic regulator could become a reality while U.S. financial regulation remains so fragmented. Even in the aftermath of the financial crisis, the idea of merging America's many financial regulators met fierce opposition in Congress, for the worst of political reasons—protecting turf. Equally, there have been complaints that the Fed has become a stealth superregulator by obtaining various new powers to intervene in the financial sector—growth that threatened to prompt action by Congress to rein it in.

While there are good reasons to retain an independent Fed with overall responsibility for monetary policy, its banking regulation functions need to be combined with those of other regulators, including the SEC, CFTC, and the treasury department, to create a separate, meaningful systemic regulator. Such a move would also demand a complete overhaul of regulatory practice in the United States, away from legalistic, compliance-based regulation to an approach based on clear principles and a consistent treatment of different sorts of financial activities and risks, regardless of which institution takes them. This promises to be a real test for the Obama administration and one that it must not fail.

THINKING LONG-TERM

The reaction of the financial industry and the business community as a whole to the crisis will be crucial to deciding which road from ruin we take. Continuing to focus on short-term performance regardless of its long-term consequences would likely mean that we end up on the road to stagnation or depression rather than to prosperity.

Performance incentives need to be based on long-term success, not quarterly profit figures, and business leaders need to recognize that it is in their enlightened self-interest to focus on doing well by doing long-term good, both for their shareholders and for society as a whole. To make this change corporate governance needs a fundamental overhaul to give shareholders a stronger say in how their firms are run. Institutional investors also need to rethink how they incentivize the companies they invest in. Before the crisis, fund managers could hide behind the efficient market hypothesis to argue that their only obligation was to track the market since, by definition, they were never going to be able to beat it. That excuse has been blown away, along with the savings of many of their customers. Institutional investors now need to do far more to ensure that their decisions actually serve the long-term interests of the public whose money they are investing.

Fortunately, changes were already starting to happen in the business world before the crisis, as new models of success based on longer-term visions of a more responsible capitalism started to enter the mainstream. Consumer power must take some of the credit for this change, along with the emergence of some business leaders whose vision stretched well beyond the next quarter's profits. It would be a terrible waste of this crisis if business leaders did not learn the lesson that they need to accelerate this change toward philanthrocapitalism.

Yet real change in the behavior of corporations and investment funds will not come unless we, the shareholders and investors, are willing to step up. Each year, the legendary stock picker Warren Buffett, who by consistently beating the market is a living refutation of the efficient market hypothesis, holds a three-day jamboree for the shareholders of his Berkshire Hath-away investment company. Known as "Woodstock for Capitalists," this event draws huge numbers of investors to Omaha, Nebraska, where the firm is headquartered. Part of the appeal, presumably, is that they have much to celebrate, but it is also because Buffett values the chance to interact with the "other people" who have entrusted him with their money.

This level of interest and engagement in the decisions of a financial institution is notable because it is so rare. One lesson of this latest crisis is that it needs to become the norm, especially for the institutional investors who manage the public's retirement savings. In a world of transparent, accountable institutions and a financially competent citizenry, surely every fund-management firm serving the public would hold its own annual capitalist Wood-stock. As at the Berkshire Hathaway meeting, investors would be given the chance to sample the products of some companies in which they have a stake and could pose questions to the invest-ment managers. The result would surely be a far more long-term approach to investing and better corporate governance.

Government, too, has a role to play in remaking capitalism, principally by strengthening shareholder control over managers (although it should not overreach by regulating pay and benefits, however tempting that may seem politically).

Fixing the financial system will not be enough on its own. The failure of the markets does not mean that government has sud-denly gotten smarter. The strain that the cost of the bailouts and stimulus packages will put on already stretched budgets for decades to come is going to demand a productivity revolution in government and a refusal of politicians to succumb to the ancient temptation of inflating the debt away.

An equally important challenge for government, however, is reducing the massive global economic and political imbalances that were the backdrop to the crisis. Unless world leaders take steps to reduce these imbalances, the global economy will remain inherently unstable and prone to crises. Indeed, "crises have always reflected some imbalances in the underlying economy," as Paul Volcker has explained. "This time, nobody did anything about well-known imbalances." Leaving the global financial system unreformed would not only risk future financial crises caused by monetary imbalances, it would also increase the risk of national governments or regional blocs taking the law into their own hands to "protect" their own economies—for example, by restricting trade. A world of barriers would be one that is less prosperous for everyone.

The crisis has prompted much talk of the need for a "new Bretton Woods." This is an important idea but one that will require the world's leaders to rise above their short-term national interests in a visionary way that has previously been achieved—as was the case with the original Bretton Woods—only in the aftermath of war. To be successful, this new Bretton Woods will have to rewrite the rules and redraw the architecture of global finance.

The first requirement is to ensure that the huge progress that has been made on freeing up trade over the past half century is not thrown into reverse. Despite the lessons of the 1930s, when the collapse of world trade deepened the Great Depression, the current crisis has encouraged protectionist attacks on the free flow of goods and services. In the United States, CNN pundit Lou Dobbs, for example, was quick to blame the crisis on "irresponsible so-called free-trade policies of Democratic and Republican administrations over the past three decades," misdiagnosing the cause of the massive U.S. trade deficit. Rather than retreat into protectionism, America and the world need to move decisively not just to make the case for the current trading system but also to push ahead with reductions in tariffs and subsidies, particularly in agriculture.

The free flow of capital around the world also needs to be protected. Despite the renewed enthusiasm among some economists for the restoration of capital controls, this would be a poor choice for most countries and the global economy as a whole. Equally, however, if capital is to continue to be allowed to move freely, the IMF must be equipped with the resources and political legitimacy it needs to act as a true lender of last resort to countries that get into financial difficulties.

There is also an urgent need for a new reserve currency to replace the dollar. For some this will be resisted as a sign of the decline of U.S. power. Even Nouriel Roubini, who acknowledges the dollar's role in causing the crisis in that it "allowed us to prolong reckless borrowing," has argued that the American government should implement reforms that "slow down the decline of the dollar, and sustain our influence in global affairs." Yet, in fact, the dollar's role as reserve currency contributed to America's current difficulties. America has as much to gain as any country from the stabler world economy that would result from using a more suitable reserve currency.

CHOOSING THE RIGHT ROAD FROM RUIN

Getting back on the road to prosperity will involve tough decisions. Vision and imagination will be required from our leaders. They will need to avoid easy populism and to reject entrenched orthodoxies. Yet, as Keynes would point out, the facts have changed, sir, and our thinking needs to change, too.

Fresh thinking and rejecting our existing toxic ideas will be a challenge for all of us: as business leaders, politicians, the economics profession, the media, and citizens. We have to rise to that challenge. If we do not, we could easily find ourselves on the road to stagnation or depression.

The fact that we have failed, by becoming irrationally exuberant only to see our hopes dashed by an almighty crash, should not discourage us from being willing to take a chance on new ideas for a better world. Unfortunately, that is what many critics of the events that led up to the crisis have advocated.

"Bubbles and fads are part of cultural life," says the leading Dr. Doom, Nassim Nicholas Taleb, who regards that as evidence of a fundamental human failing that we need to restrain. He believes that we have to act far more cautiously in a world where unpredictable dangers lurk around every corner. Taleb is right that we are prone to overconfidence but wrong to think that this is such a bad thing.

We would do better to look for guidance to those great defunct economists Adam Smith and John Maynard Keynes. Both of them recognized the human tendency to let our hopes triumph over rational caution. Smith believed that people are often driven by an "overweening conceit," which means that "the chance of gain is by every man more or less over-valued, and the chance of loss is by most men under-valued." For Keynes, this was even more fundamental. "Human decisions affecting the future, whether personal or political or economic, cannot depend on strict mathematical expectation," he warned, "since the basis for making such calculations does not exist." Instead, he argued, we often do things because of the "spontaneous optimism" created by the "animal spirits" inside us.

It is the continued existence of these animal spirits that means that the idea, so popular with politicians, that it is possible to "abolish" the business cycle of boom and bust must be consigned to the dustbin of history, along with all the other utopian twaddle that goes against human nature. Likewise the dystopian twaddle offered by Taleb when he says that "economic life should be definancialized" and that "only Ponzi schemes should depend on confidence." Confidence is at the root of capitalism: our word "credit" comes from the Latin *credo*, "I believe." Without confidence we would not have mortgages, or pensions, or insurance, or, for that matter, jobs, innovation, entrepreneurship, and prosperity.

Finance, although imperfect, is still our best tool for managing the risks of an uncertain world. Taleb wants us to shy away from risk, lest one of his dreaded, unpredictable black swans comes to gobble us up. By contrast, when Keynes talked about animal spirits and Smith talked about overweening conceit, they were each conscious of the positive power as well as the downsides of our irrational tendency to be optimistic. "Keynes, in my reading, had a radical thought here," says the Nobel Prize–winning economist Edmund Phelps. "Entrepreneurs' willingness to innovate or just to invest—and thus create new jobs—is driven by their 'animal spirits' as they decide whether to leap into the void."

The last time we faced a crisis of this magnitude, in the Great Depression, President Franklin Delano Roosevelt used his inauguration speech in 1933 to warn that "the only thing we have to fear is fear itself." He was right. If we succumb to fear, the road ahead will be long and miserable. More than anything, whether we are able to once again set free our animal spirits and believe in our ability to create a better world will determine how quickly, or indeed whether, we can get back on the road to prosperity.

ACKNOWLEDGMENTS

This book would not have been possible without the insights that market participants and observers have shared, on and off the record, with Matthew over the years he has been writing about finance and economics for *The Economist*. They include, in no particular order, Alan Greenspan, Myron Scholes, Hank Paulson, Paul Volcker, George Soros, John Paulson, Bill Sharpe, Gary Becker, Robert Merton, Jamie Dimon, John Meriwether, John Thain, Franklin Allen, Richard Thaler, Robert Shiller, Joseph Stiglitz, Jeffrey Sachs, Meredith Whitney, Mike Mayo, Abby Joseph Cohen, Henry Blodgett, Steve Schwarzman, David Rubenstein, Michael Jensen, Peter Bernstein, Richard Grasso, Mervyn King, John Kay, Edmund Phelps, Daniel Kahneman, Colin Camerer, Eugene Fama, Merton Miller, Christopher Flowers, Hank Greenberg, Sandy Weill, Bill McDonough, William White, Avinash Persaud, Richard Perry, Harvey Pitt, Arthur Levitt, Roger Altman, John Snow, Glenn Hubbard, Laura Tyson, Annette Nazareth, Roger Ferguson, Gemma Mortensen, Paul O'Neill, Dick Fuld, Bill Gates, Michael Bloomberg, Stanley O'Neal, Robert Pozen, Rodgin Cohen, Martin Lipton, Ira Millstein, Robert Monks, Stan Fisher, Amy Butte Liebowitz, Jed Emerson, Henry Kaufman, Nouriel Roubini, Scott Friedheim, Barry Gossin, David Swenson, Leo Tillman, John Studzinski, Ron Grzywinksi, Peter Blom, Muhammad Yunus, John Bogle, Joseph Ackerman, Gaurav Dalmia, Benn Steil, Mark Goyder, Colin Melvin, Nell Minow, Ngozi Okonjo-Iwaela, Andrew Cohen, Thor Bjorgolfsson, Len Blavatnik, Bill Ford, Glenn Hutchins, Robert Steel, Howard Davies, Lloyd Blankfein, William White, Jim O'Neill, Dan Loeb, Robert Rubin, and President Bill Clinton.

David Maude, Sylvia McLain, Tom Easton, Owen Barder,

Richard Springate, Amar Bhidé, Nick Lea, Diane Garnick, Will Goetzman, and Holly Finn all gave generously of their time to read and comment on all or parts of the manuscript. We are grateful for their kindness and wisdom in making this a much better book—though all errors are, of course, our own.

Our agent, Dan Mandel, was, as always, a source of calm and sage advice. John Mahaney, our editor at Crown, inspired us with his enthusiasm for the project and edited the manuscript with the perfect balance of support and challenge. We are grateful to Nancy Stabile, our deft and sympathetic copyeditor.

John Micklethwait, the editor in chief of *The Economist*, generously allowed Matthew time off from his day job, and has been a constant source of support and encouragement. Matthew would especially like to thank all his colleagues for putting up with the extra work caused by his absence during one of the busiest times in decades for economic and financial reporting. Special thanks to Justin Hendrix of *The Economist*, who suggested that we should have something to say on this topic. Barbara Beck, the special reports editor of *The Economist*, played an invaluable role in shaping several reports by Matthew on topics covered in this book.

Thanks also to Shifu Shi Heng Sheng for teaching Michael to stand like a tree, Sushiya restaurant on West 56th Street for the most abundant sushi in Manhattan, Jonathan Norris's fish stall at Tachbrook Street Market for the best kippers in Britain, Henry Timms and his colleagues at the 92nd Street Y for generously providing a base and a platform in Manhattan, Alex Poppleton for coaching Michael to freedom, John Turner for orthogonal inspiration, Sina Odugbemi for showing the importance of deliberation, Catherine Howarth for challenging us on the message of the book, Martin Dinham for seeing the win-win, and Michelle Savage for encouragement beyond the call of duty.

Most of all, thanks to our families and friends for putting up with us during the ups and downs.

A NOTE ON SOURCES

The story of the economic crisis has moved so fast since the meltdown of September 2008 that we have had to rely heavily on news and analysis from the media—some of which, happily, have been excellent. As well as reporting in *The Economist*, by Matthew and his colleagues (especially Matthew Valencia, Zanny Minton Beddoes, Edward Carr, Tom Easton, Patrick Lane, Philip Coggan, Pam Woodall, Simon Cox, Greg Ip, Patrick Fowles, and Andrew Palmer), we have found *The Financial Times, Wall Street Journal, New York Times, Harvard Business Review, Breaking Views, Fortune, Time, Forbes, The New Yorker* (and its sadly departed sister, *Portfolio*), *The Atlantic,* and *Barron's,* as well as the Bloomberg and Reuters newswires, invaluable as sources of information and comment.

One industry that has grown as a result of the crisis is economics blogging. Indeed, the level of interest in economic issues and the richness of the debate about them are unparalleled in our adult lifetimes. Paul Krugman's *New York Times* blog and column provide useful updates on the Nobel Prize winner's ideas in response to new data, including technical (what he calls "wonkish") material for professional economists. Michael Lewis is consistently interesting and entertaining. Martin Wolf's "Economists' Forum" on the *Financial Times* website is a rich source of debate among a range of more and less well-known thinkers, although the most challenging and provocative commentary from the *FT* stable has come from Willem Buiter's aptly named Maverecon blog. Clive Crook, John Gapper, John Cassidy, James Surowiecki, and Megan McArdle are always insightful, as are the blogs by Tyler Cowen (Marginal Revolution), Brad de Long, Gary Becker, and Richard Posner, and *The Economist* (Free Exchange). Felix

Salmon, who blogs at Reuters, and Justin Fox and Barbara Kiviat at *Time*'s Curious Capitalist blog, have been a constant source of contrarian thinking, as has the ever-irreverent John Carney at Clusterstock. We have also drawn on television interviews, particularly from CNBC, the BBC, Charlie Rose, and *The Daily Show*.

The full bibliography below includes many books about the current crisis, which vary widely in quality. Taking a broader look at financial crises throughout history, the late Charles Kindleberger's *Manias, Panics and Crashes: A History of Financial Crashes*, now being updated by Robert Aliber, is still essential, if flawed, reading. John Maynard Keynes's *General Theory of Employment, Interest and Money* still dazzles, as does Robert Skidelsky's magnificent three-volume biography of the great British economist. We also owe a particular debt to four works of economic history, one general—Niall Ferguson's *Ascent of Money*—and three specific: Liaquat Ahamed's *Lords of Finance*, a terrific account of the last great economic crisis of the 1930s; Justin Fox's history of the rise and fall of the efficient market hypothesis, *The Myth of the Rational Market*; and J. K. Galbraith's *Great Crash of 1929*, which has been overtaken in terms of the analysis of the crash but remains a lively and provocative account of those dramatic months. Allan Sloan's award-winning article in *Fortune*, "House of Junk," was particularly helpful in illuminating the nuances of sub-prime mortgage securitization, and David Colander's fascinating article "Edgeworth's Hedonimeter and the Quest to Measure Utility" was useful in explaining early economic ideas about human psychology.

We have also benefited from the insights of many people who were working in the financial markets during the crisis, as well as some brilliant analysts and commentators. Those who are happy to be named are mentioned in the Acknowledgments. We also owe particular thanks to the organizers and participants at the Emerging from the Financial Crisis conference at Columbia University's Center for Capitalism and Society in February 2009, which contributed greatly to our thinking. Discussions at the World Economic Forum have been invaluable, especially with members of the Forum of Young Global Leaders.

SELECT BIBLIOGRAPHY

Ahamed, L. *Lords of Finance: The Bankers Who Broke the World.* New York: Penguin, 2009.

Akerlof, G. A., and R. J. Shiller. *Animal Spirits: How Human Psychology Drives the Economy, and Why It Matters for Global Capitalism.* Princeton, N.J.: Princeton University Press, 2009.

Allen, F., and D. Gale. *Financial Innovation and Risk Sharing,* 1994.

Ashraf, N., C. F. Camerer, G. Loewenstein. "Adam Smith, Behavioral Economist," *Journal of Economic Perspectives,* Vol. 19, No. 3, Summer 2005.

Augar, P. *The Greed Merchants.* London: Penguin, 2005.

Bagehot, W. *Lombard Street: A Description of the Money Market,* 1910.

Berle, A., and G. Means. *The Modern Corporation and Private Property,* 1932.

Bernanke, B. S. (ed.). *Essays on the Great Depression.* Princeton, N.J.: Princeton University Press, 2000.

Bernstein, P. *Capital Ideas: The Improbable Origins of Modern Wall Street.* New York: Free Press, 1992.

Bogle, J. *The Battle for the Soul of Capitalism,* 2005.

Borchard, E. *State Insolvency and Foreign Bondholders: General Principles.* New York: Garland, 1951.

Bordo, M. D. *The Gold Standard and Related Regimes: Collected Essays.* Cambridge: Cambridge University Press, 1999.

Brandeis, L. *Business—A Profession,* 1914.

————. *Other People's Money and How the Bankers Use It,* 1914.

Bruner, R. F., and S. D. Carr. *The Panic of 1907: Lessons Learned from the Market's Perfect Storm.* Hoboken, N.J.: John Wiley & Sons, 2007.

Calomiris, C. W., and J. R. Mason. *Contagion and Bank Failures During the Great Depression: The June 1932 Chicago Banking Panic.* Cambridge, Mass.: NBER Working Paper 4934, 1994.

Carswell, J. *The South Sea Bubble.* Stroud: Alan Sutton, 1993.

Colander, D. "Edgeworth's Hedonimeter and the Quest to Measure Utility," *Journal of Economic Perspectives,* Winter 2007.

Cooper, G. *The Origin of Financial Crises: Central Banks, Credit Bubbles and the Efficient Market Fallacy.* New York: Random House, 2008.

Crane, D. B., et al. *The Global Financial System: A Functional Perspective,* 1995.

Dale, R. *The First Crash: Lessons from the South Sea Bubble.* Princeton, N.J.: Princeton University Press, 2004.

Davies, N. *Europe: A History.* London: Pimlico, 1997.

Dawson, F. G. *The First Latin American Debt Crisis.* New Haven, Conn.: Yale University Press, 1990.

De Cecco, M. *Money and Empire: The International Gold Standard, 1890–1914.* Oxford: Blackwell, 1974.

Dimson, E., P. Marsh, and M. Staunton. *Triumph of the Optimists: 101 Years of Global Investment Returns.* Princeton, N.J.: Princeton University Press, 2002.

Dunbar, N. *Inventing Money.* New York: John Wiley & Sons, 2000.

Eichengreen, B. *Globalizing Capital: A History of the International Monetary System.* Princeton, N.J.: Princeton University Press, 2008.

Eichengreen, B., and M. Flandreau (eds.). *The Gold Standard in Theory and History.* London: Routledge, 1997.

Elkind, P., and B. McLean. *The Smartest Guys in the Room: The Amazing Rise and Scandalous Fall of Enron.* London: Viking, 2003.

Engels, F., and K. Marx. *The Communist Manifesto*, 1848.

Faber, D. *And Then the Roof Caved In: How Wall Street's Greed and Stupidity Brought Capitalism to Its Knees.* Hoboken, N.J: John Wiley & Sons, 2009.

Fama, E. "Efficient Capital Markets: A Review of Theory and Empirical Work," *The Journal of Finance*, 1970.

————. "Efficient Capital Markets II," *The Journal of Finance*, 1991.

Ferguson, N. *The Ascent of Money.* New York: Penguin, 2008.

————. *The Cash Nexus: Money and Power in the Modern World, 1700–2000.* London: Penguin, 2001.

————. "Wars, Revolutions and the International Bond Market from the Napoleonic Wars to the First World War," paper to Yale International Center for Finance, 1999.

Flandreau, M., "An Essay on the Emergence of the International Gold Standard, 1870–80." CEPR, 1995.

Fox, J. *The Myth of the Rational Market: A History of Risk, Reward, and Delusion on Wall Street.* New York: Harper Business, 2009.

Friedman, M., and A. J. Schwartz. *A Monetary History of the United States, 1867–1960.* Princeton, N.J.: Princeton University Press, 1963.

Galbraith, J. K. *The Great Crash.* New York: Houghton Mifflin, 1997.

————. *A Short History of Financial Euphoria.* New York: Whittle, 1994.

Garber, P. M. *Famous First Bubbles: The Fundamentals of Early Manias.* Cambridge, Mass.: MIT Press, 2000.

Goetzmann, W. N., and K. G. Rouwenhorst (eds.). *The Origins of Value: The Financial Innovations That Created Modern Capital Markets.* Oxford: Oxford University Press, 2005.

Goldgar, A. *Tulipmania: Money, Honor, and Knowledge in the Dutch Golden Age.* Chicago: University of Chicago, 2007.

Greenspan, A. *The Age of Turbulence.* London: Penguin, 2008.

Gross, D. *Dumb Money: How Our Greatest Financial Minds Bankrupted the Nation*. New York: Free Press, 2009.

Grossman, S., and J. Stiglitz. "On the Impossibility of Informationally Efficient Markets," *American Economic Review*, 1980.

Haldane, A. G. "Rethinking the Financial Network," speech at Financial Student Association, Amsterdam, April 2009.

Harris, E. S. *Ben Bernanke's Fed: The Federal Reserve After Greenspan*. Boston, Mass.: Harvard Business Press, 2008.

Harrison, S. G., and M. Weder. *Did Sunspot Forces Cause the Great Depression?* CEPR, 2002.

Hayek, F. *The Road to Serfdom*, 1944.

Homer, S., and R. Sylla. *A History of Interest Rates*. Hoboken, N.J.: John Wiley & Sons, 2005.

James, H. *The End of Globalization: Lessons from the Great Depression*. Cambridge, Mass.: Harvard University Press, 2001.

Jensen, M. "Eclipse of the Public Corporation," *Harvard Business Review*, 1989.

Jensen, M., and W. Meckling. "Theory of the Firm: Managerial Behavior, Agency Costs and Ownership Structure," *Journal of Financial Economics*, 1976.

Kamensky, J. *The Exchange Artist*. New York: Penguin, 2008.

Kaplan, E., and D. Rodrik. "Did the Malaysian Capital Controls Work?" NBER Working Paper 8142, 2001.

Kennedy, P. M. *The Rise and Fall of the Great Powers: Economic Change and Military Conflict from 1500–2000*. London: Random House, 1987.

Keynes, J. M. *The General Theory of Employment, Interest and Money*, 1936.

Kindleberger, C. P., and R. Z. Aliber. *Manias, Panics and Crashes: A History of Financial Crises*. Basingstoke: Palgrave Macmillan, 2005.

Knight, F. *Risk, Uncertainty and Profit*, 1921.

Kroszner, R. "Rethinking Bank Regulation: A Review of the Historical Evidence," *The Bank of America Journal of Applied Corporate Finance,* 1998.

Krugman, P. *The Return of Depression Economics and the Crisis of 2008.* London: Penguin, 2008.

Landes, D. S. *Dynasties.* New York: Viking, 2006.

———. *The Wealth and Poverty of Nations: Why Some Are So Rich and Some So Poor.* New York: W. W. Norton, 1998.

Law, J. *Money and Trade Consider'd: With a Proposal for Supplying the Nation with Money.* London: W. Lewis, 1720.

Lewis, M. (ed.). *Panic: The Story of Modern Financial Insanity.* London: Penguin, 2008.

Lowenstein, R. *When Genius Failed: The Rise and Fall of Long-Term Capital Management.* London: Fourth Estate, 2001.

Mackay, C. *Extraordinary Popular Delusions and the Madness of Crowds.* Ware: Wordsworth, 1995.

McDonald, L. G., and P. Robinson. *A Colossal Failure of Common Sense: The Inside Story of the Collapse of Lehman Brothers.* New York: Crown Business, 2009.

McKinnon, R. I. *The Rules of the Game: International Money in Historical Perspective,* JEL, 1993.

Mitchener, K. J., and M. D. Weidenmier. "Supersanctions and Sovereign Debt Repayment," NBER Working Paper 11472, 2005.

Mixon, S. "The Crisis of 1873: Perspectives from Multiple Asset Classes," *Journal of Economic History,* Vol. 68, No. 3, September 2008.

Morris, C. R. *The Trillion Dollar Meltdown: Easy Money, High Rollers, and the Great Credit Crash.* Philadelphia: PublicAffairs, 2008.

Neal, L. *The Rise of Financial Capitalism: International Capital Markets in the Age of Reason.* Cambridge: Cambridge University Press, 1990.

Perez, C. *Technological Revolutions and Financial Capital.* Cheltenham: Edward Elgar, 2002.

Posner, R. A. *A Failure of Capitalism: The Crisis of '08 and the Descent into Depression.* Cambridge, Mass.: Harvard University Press, 2009.

Rajan, R. G., and L. Zingales. *Saving Capitalism from the Capitalists.* New York: Crown Business, 2003.

Rand, A. *Atlas Shrugged,* 1957.

Reinhart, C. M., and K. S. Rogoff. "The Aftermath of Financial Crises," NBER Working Paper 14656, 2009.

———. "Banking Crises: An Equal Opportunity Menace," NBER Working Paper 14587, 2008.

———. "This Time Is Different: A Panoramic View of Eight Centuries of Financial Crises," NBER Working Paper 13882, 2008.

Ritholtz, B. *Bailout Nation: How Greed and Easy Money Corrupted Wall Street and Shook the World Economy.* Hoboken, N.J.: John Wiley & Sons, rev. ed., 2009.

Scott, W. R. *The Constitution and Finance of English, Scottish and Irish Joint-Stock Companies to 1720.* Cambridge: Cambridge University Press, 1912.

Shiller, R. J. *Irrational Exuberance.* Princeton, N.J.: Princeton University Press, 2000.

Sinclair, D. *The Pound: A Biography.* London: Century, 2000.

Skidelsky, R. *John Maynard Keynes: The Economist as Saviour, 1920–1937.* London: Macmillan and Co., 1992.

———. *John Maynard Keynes: Fighting for Britain, 1937–1946.* London: Macmillan and Co., 2000.

Sloan, A. "House of Junk," *Fortune,* October 2007.

Smith, A., *The Theory of Moral Sentiments.* Cambridge: Cambridge University Press, 2002.

———. *An Inquiry into the Nature and Causes of the Wealth of Nations.* London: W. Pickering, 1995.

Sornette, D. *Why Stock Markets Crash: Critical Events in Complex Financial Systems.* Princeton, N.J.: Princeton University Press, 2004.

Soros, G. *The Crash of 2008 and What It Means: The New Paradigm for Financial Markets.* New York: PublicAffairs, 2009.

Steil, B., and M. Hinds. *Money, Markets, and Sovereignty.* New Haven, Conn.: Yale University Press, 2009.

Stiglitz, J. (chair). "Recommendations by the Commission of Experts of the President of the General Assembly on Reforms of the International Monetary and Financial System," 2009.

Swagel, P. "The Financial Crisis: An Inside View," Brookings Papers on Economic Activity, Spring 2009.

Taleb, N. N. *The Black Swan: The Impact of the Highly Improbable.* London: Penguin, 2008.

Tett, G. *Fool's Gold: How Unrestrained Greed Corrupted a Dream, Shattered Global Markets and Unleashed a Catastrophe.* New York: Free Press, 2009.

———. *Saving the Sun: A Wall Street Gamble to Rescue Japan from Its Trillion-Dollar Meltdown.* London: Random House, 2003.

Tomz, M. *Reputation and International Cooperation: Sovereign Debt Across Three Centuries.* Princeton, N.J.: Princeton University Press, 2007.

Ubel, P. A. *Free Market Madness: Why Human Nature Is at Odds with Economics—And Why It Matters.* Boston, Mass.: Harvard Business Press, 2009.

Vines, S. *Market Panic: Wild Gyrations, Risks and Opportunities in Stock Markets.* Singapore: John Wiley & Sons, 2003.

Wessel, D. *In Fed We Trust: Ben Bernanke's War on the Great Panic.* New York: Crown Business, 2009.

Wicker, E. *The Banking Panics of the Great Depression.* Cambridge: Cambridge University Press, 1996.

Wilmarth, A. E. "Did Universal Banks Play a Significant Role in the U.S. Economy's Boom-and-Bust Cycle of 1921–33? A Preliminary Assessment," George Washington Law School Working Paper 171.

Winkler, M., and T. H. Healy. *Foreign Bonds: An Autopsy*. Philadelphia: R. Swain, 1933.

Wolf, M. *Fixing Global Finance*. Baltimore, Md.: Johns Hopkins University Press, 2008.

Zak, P. J. *Moral Markets: The Critical Role of Values in the Economy*. Princeton, N.J.: Princeton University Press, 2008.

Zakaria, F. *The Post-American World: And the Rise of the Rest*. London: Allen Lane, 2008.

INDEX

ABOUT THE AUTHORS

MATTHEW BISHOP is the U.S. business editor of *The Economist* and a former faculty member of the London Business School. MICHAEL GREEN is a London-based writer who previously taught economics at Warsaw University and was a senior official in the British government. They are also the authors of *Philanthrocapitalism.*